The Ringing in History Companion

Also by Steve Coleman

The Bellringer's
Early Companion

The Bellringer's
Bedside Companion

The
Method Ringer's
Companion

The Bob Caller's
Companion

For more details of all four
see pages 437-440

The Ringing in History Companion

Steve Coleman

SUE COLEMAN PUBLISHING

Some of this book was first published
as articles in The Ringing World

Published August 2013
by Sue Coleman
46 Byfords Road, Huntley
Glos. GL19 3EL

ISBN 978-0-9523896-5-1

British Library Cataloguing in Publication Data. A catalogue
record for this book is available from the British Library.

Printed and bound in Great Britain by
CPI Antony Rowe, Bumper's Farm, Chippenham. SN14 6LH

To

GEOFFREY AND NANCY BOOTH

My good friends

and

Parents-in-law

Who produced the publisher of this book

Contents

The Sight of Gentle Maiden Deftly Handling of a Rope

Going Way Back

A Word Before We Start

If you're sitting comfortably, I'll begin.

This is a ringing history book. Or, at least, it *sort of* is. It's accurate, certainly – and in places it's even a tad scholarly – but it's only the interesting, fun and exciting bits of our history, with the boring bits missed out.

So it's not a history book for peal-bores and bell-bores, but a history book for ordinary ringers like you and me. It's *about* ordinary ringers too. It's about ordinary ringers caught up in extraordinary times and events; and it's about the way ringing meshed in with the great sweep of history.

If you want to read about something particular, there's an index at the back. But if you just want to amble gently through some fascinating bits of our rich ringing past, just turn the page.

And we'll amble there together.

When the Ringing Had to Stop (but sometimes didn’t)

1. When the Balloon Went Up

Every time I saw my Grandmother at Christmas she'd say, "*There wasn't any ringing in The War, you know*;" and then she'd tell me all over again about putting grated carrot in her Christmas puddings. In fact Christmas puddings really *are* better with grated carrot in, but I'm not so sure about her *ringing* recollections.

So what exactly *did* happen in the War?

Alison
Lincolnshire

Let's start at the very beginning – or rather, let's start two days earlier. The War officially began on 3rd September 1939 but everyone knew it was coming, and the whole country was already on a war footing. Most people still *hoped* that some last minute action would prevent it, but only the very optimistic thought it conceivably could.

So even the editor of *The Ringing World* had to face up to the fact that this was one of those rare occasions when national matters outweighed ringing matters, and in his editorial of 1st September, he addressed his readers in a suitably grave and pompous tone.

"This article is written at a moment when

> **the international crisis is such that no one can forecast what the next few hours may bring forth. ... Not unnaturally, the thoughts of many of our readers will turn to what may happen in regard to ringing should war break out. ... What is almost certain to be imposed – it was necessary last time, and it is likely to be immensely more necessary if there is another conflict – is the complete silencing of church bells during hours of darkness."**

And with the inherent sexism of the time, he added:

> **"The ladies proved their worth in the belfry in the last war and would do so again."**

The First Ban

So the Editor's clear message was *ringing as usual*, and that was the clear intention of most ringers too. They saw bells as important to maintaining national morale and they were probably right. But what *actually* happened was that ringing stopped virtually completely. It only stopped for a short time, but stop it did – and it was the first of many instances of Wartime ringing confusion.

But this particular confusion wasn't the result of muddle, it was the result of a very real problem that affected ringers and non-ringers alike. Essentially, wars move fast and parliamentary procedures move slowly, so in a time of war it simply isn't practicable for new, but entirely necessary, laws to go through the normal process. So under the *Defence Regulations, 1939* the Government – or more technically, the *Minister of Home Security* – had the power to issue things called *Orders*, which had the same force of law as Acts of Parliament but which didn't need Parliamentary approval.

They were intended to control public and private actions that might either jeopardise the war effort or make the country more vulnerable to attack; and one of these Orders was *The Control of Noise (Defence) Order, 1939.*

Of course, the Order's very title was worrying to ringers; but in fact, at the start of the War, the Government weren't bothered about church bells at all. They *were* bothered, though, about air raids and – much more serious still – they were bothered about gas attacks.

Air raids – and very probably, gas attacks – were expected to start immediately, and the Order was designed to ensure that warning sirens – and for gas attacks, warning *rattles* – could be clearly heard and understood. There had to be no extraneous noises that could drown them or be confused with them, so the Order prevented ...

> **"... the sounding of sirens, hooters, whistles, rattles, bells, horns, gongs or similar instruments, unless used for the purpose of air-raid or gas warnings."**

Bells Included

So since bells were included in the Order, it wasn't just the title that sounded bad, it was the content too. And since the full text wasn't available immediately, ringers had to rely on hearsay. And although air raids got mentioned first – and although in due course the bombing became one of the major features of the War – the really *big* fear in September 1939 was gas attacks. The Germans had the gas – as, indeed, did the British – and they had the means of delivering it too; and although in theory it was banned under the Geneva Protocol, there was no reason to suppose that the Germans wouldn't use it.

Indeed, the Post Office agreed with the Home Office that Local Authorities could paint the tops of pillar boxes with gas detector paint – coloured yellowish green rather than red – so that Air Raid Wardens could recognise when gas had been dropped. And since, if it *had* been dropped, the *All Clear* signal was to be a handbell, *tower* bells could have caused confusion.

Church Bells

What was more, the Order made a lot of sense in 1939 because loud noises weren't just a background nuisance, they were a common and ubiquitous form of communication. Factories, collieries, shipyards, docks and many other undertakings had hooters, buzzers, whistles, gongs and bells that blasted across towns and villages. They not only marked the beginnings and ends of shifts, they also gave five minute *warnings* of the beginnings and ends of shifts; and in industrial towns, they even acted as alarm clocks by providing early morning wake-up signals.

Schools, of course, called pupils in with strident handbells; and public and industrial railways used seriously loud whistles to communicate truck and train movements. Loud gongs were used in many places as warnings of danger – and essential warnings they were too – ***but*** the Order specifically exempted church bells; and in its usual dry but completely clear style, *The Times* newspaper explained.

> **"The Order does not affect the use of instruments of the kind mentioned, by railwaymen and by members of a ship's crew, nor does it prevent police officers from sounding whistles ... It does not apply, also, to church bells or to the normal use of bicycle bells and motor horns."**

Customary Ringing

In fact, *The Times* wasn't telling its readers the *full* story, because what the Order *actually* exempted was church and chapel bells rung "**... in such a manner as has been customary**" – which begged the intriguing question: what was a *customary manner*? The Home Office officials weren't sure either. They'd put the phrase in to prevent unusual ringing confusing people, but they realised later that it appeared to prevent new bands being taught in silent towers, or tunes being played on Ellacombes in parishes without ringers.

But of most interest to us is that the Order created the only period in history when not calling stand during a fire-up constituted a criminal offence liable to a fine of £100, three months in prison, or both.

The Effect

But whatever the wording and whatever the intention, the immediate effect was the virtual cessation of ringing. Vicars and churchwardens feared that bells would prevent people hearing air raid warnings, and ringers still remembered the restrictions of the First World War. In *that* war, *all* bells – even clock bells – had to stop sounding by *the end of evening civil twilight* – i.e. by the time the sun was exactly six degrees below the horizon. So in September 1939, practices stopped, most service ringing stopped, and a great many Association meetings were immediately cancelled.

Within a couple of weeks, though, things changed. The anticipated air raids and gas attacks didn't materialise and, human nature being what it is, the fear of them quickly evaporated too. Ringing for services resumed and some practice night ringing resumed as well. In general, though, it didn't continue after dark, especially as in some villages, church bells were to be the air raid warning. And much to everyone's surprise, it wasn't just ringers who wanted ringing to restart, it was the general public too. Church bells quickly became seen as an essential feature of *business-as-usual*, and that made ringing an important part of the War Effort. This letter from *P. Spice (Secretary)* of Bromley was typical.

> **"Our leader, Mr. Emery, suggests that I write you to say that we at the Parish Church, Bromley, are doing everything possible to keep the ringing fraternity together during these times."**

Or as the Editor succinctly expressed it, the ringers were, "**... carrying on at Bromley**."

The Black-Out

But although the intention to ring was there, the practical problems were considerable. For a start, there was an immediate shortage of ringers – particularly young ringers – not just because they'd joined the Services but because they were involved in war work generally. In country areas, looking after evacuees took up considerable time too; yet the biggest problem of all was the black-out.

Being September, the nights were already drawing in, and even when ringing after dark became acceptable again, lighting was a real issue. Some ringers were able to black-out their ringing chamber completely, but others found it simply wasn't possible, especially if the bells were rung from the chancel crossing or a ringing balcony.

Some bands solved this by holding practices on Saturday afternoons – often combining with other towers to overcome the ringer shortage – but since Association meetings normally went on into the evening, something had to be done about the ringing then. The Leatherhead District of the Guildford Guild thought they'd found the answer.

> **"It is hoped ... to hold a series of Saturday meetings at the periods of the full moon."**

Road Accidents

And although the thought of dozens of Leatherhead ringers ringing happily by moonlight is engaging, it almost certainly wasn't the light in the ringing chamber they were bothered about. It was the travelling.

As we shall see in Chapter 11, even before the War started there were more than twice as many road deaths in the 1930s than now, and that was despite there being only a fraction of the number of vehicles on the roads. Each vehicle travelled far fewer miles too. But bad as road accidents had been before the War, once it started, they immediately became a very great deal worse.

Under the black-out regulations, all the small lights on cars – such as the side lamps, the brake lights and the little indicator arms that popped out of each side – had to be dimmed. But more serious, only one headlight per vehicle was permitted, and that headlight had to be fitted with a mask that allowed no more than a narrow strip of light to pass through. Not surprisingly, motorists couldn't see pedestrians and cyclists, and pedestrians and cyclists couldn't see cars. For that matter, cars couldn't see each other. And although a 20 mph speed limit and white lines were immediately introduced, they didn't help much.

The result was a truly dreadful number of road deaths and serious injuries, particularly as the general standard of driving was much poorer than today. Most drivers had never received any proper lessons or taken a test, and there was considerable drunken driving too. There was also a curious class prejudice whereby car owners – who were generally upper and upper-middle class – thought it was the responsibility of pedestrians – seen as working class – to get out of their way.

Exact figures of deaths aren't available because the compilation of road accident statistics ceased at the outbreak of war; but everyone recognised that accidents had gone up by a colossal amount. Indeed, in the first months of the War far more people were killed in road accidents as a result of the black-out than by enemy action. And it wasn't just cars that pedestrians had to be careful of. Being hit, and even killed, by bicycles was common too – especially as most people wore dark clothing and there was no adequate street lighting even in towns.

And there were other travel dangers of the black-out too. Many people were drowned by walking into lakes and ponds, and many more were severely injured by stepping into holes or tripping over things. There were no lights at railway stations, so passengers couldn't be sure whether they'd stopped next to the platform or not, and there were many instances of people falling onto the line. One man even stepped off the edge of a viaduct and fell eighty feet; and in the first months of the War even small torches were banned, no matter how dim their light.

Being Shot

And on top of all that, from May 1940 there was an even more remarkable danger – being shot. The Home Guard were required to mount check points on public roads and challenge all cars, cycles and motor-cycles that came along. But to begin with, there was no consistent method for doing that, and many sentries simply shouted a challenge. Not surprisingly, even people with normal hearing couldn't hear the challenge with their car windows closed, and nothing was placed in, or across, the road to give a hint. The darkness was virtually absolute too, so motorists were completely unaware that the check point even existed, and they *certainly* weren't aware that a trigger-happy sentry with a rifle was stationed next to it.

Or more accurately, they weren't aware until the sentry started shooting. There are no published records of how many people were shot at altogether, but a quick trawl through June 1940 reveals a good handful of fatalities in that month alone – all of which received a verdict of *justifiable homicide* from the coroner. Even the Bishop of Coventry had a narrow escape when his chauffeur was taken by surprise. Some sentries apparently showed a torch before shooting, but since it was only faint and no one knew what it meant, it didn't help. Eventually, instructions were given that sentries should swing a red light.

Until Dark

But all that meant that travelling to and from ringing was a serious hazard no matter how you did it, and with the black-out causing two distinct problems at the same time, most Associations addressed them together. This advert from the Hinckley District of the Midland Counties Association was typical.

> **"The next meeting is at Kirby Mallory on Saturday, Sept. 30th. Ringing from 3.30 p.m. until dark."**

And *until dark* was exactly how the Hinckley District organised it. Sadly, only fourteen members turned up, but they nonetheless rang "**... until darkness compelled**

members to proceed homewards," – although even then, they stopped for a drinking session outside as a number of members had "**brought jugs in their gas mask cases**." But looking to the future, they decided that:

> **"... meetings should be held as frequently as possible, preferably in weeks when use could be made of moonlight ..."**

Ringing Teas

But serious though the black-out was, it wasn't the only problem for Associations. Rationing wasn't introduced until the middle of January 1940, but even in 1939 food was already a difficulty in many villages because of the strains of coping with evacuees. The ringing tea was now firmly established and no one wanted it to stop, but changes had to be made. The Leatherhead District was quick off the mark on this issue too.

> **"Owing to the approach of rationing it was agreed that everyone should make their own arrangements for tea."**

And if tea was to be provided, it was absolutely essential that the hosts knew how many members would be partaking. Adverts contained strong words about proper notification but quite clearly, they weren't always meeting with success. By November 1939, the East Grinstead and District Guild were getting desperate.

> **"Mr. R. D. Divall has made arrangements for tea, so play the game, chaps, and send him a postcard before November 30th."**

But if there were to be no tea, there would be no church hall use either, and that meant no toilet facilities. And since that was a bigger problem for the women than the men, the Ladies Guild addressed the issue in a splendidly euphemistic way.

> **"There will be no tea. But refreshments will be provided for lady visitors at the home of the Hon. Sec."**

Rationing

And once rationing started, teas became a bigger problem still, and the remarkable thing was that so many Branches continued to provide them nonetheless. Sadly, there are almost no records of what was provided, so we simply don't know what was cut back on; but a little evidence comes from reports. Here's the Chester Diocesan Guild.

> **"From the appearance of things it seemed that no such thing as rationing had been heard of!"**

But although there are a few similar reports, they seem to have sprung more from gratitude than accuracy. In 1940, tea eulogies simply disappear from *The Ringing World's* pages; and from the increasingly strident calls for names in advance, we know that what *was* provided was only provided with a struggle.

> **"Owing to the prevailing conditions, it is essential that notice should be sent to the undersigned not later than February 1st,"**

wrote the Middlesex County Association; and the Lincoln Diocesan Guild were more authoritarian still.

> **"Arrangements for tea, but those who fail to send their names to me by Wednesday previous must accept the consequences."**

We're not told what the *consequences* were, but the Frome and Midsomer Norton Branch certainly resorted to harsh treatment of offenders.

> **"Tea and meeting 5 p.m. Butter for those who advise for tea, margarine for others."**

And a lot of Associations simply insisted that no name literally meant no tea. The Northern Division of the Essex Association stated quite baldly.

> **"Tea will only be provided for those who send their names."**

And other Associations issued tea tickets. The Sussex County Association – who were one of the few Associations to arrange special train fares for members – put it this way.

> **"Cost of tea 2s. 6d. (1s. to members), payable at the table, but supplied by ticket only on receipt of ½d. stamp by May 1st. Half rail fare (maximum 2s. 6d.) allowed to resident members."**

Cancellations

Several Branches of the Lancashire Association also stated, "**No card, no tea!**" but even *that* approach had to be abandoned when postal rates rose sharply. Many Associations took the simple approach of not providing tea at all.

> **"Please note that the tea arrangements advertised previously have been cancelled. Will ringers please make their own tea arrangements?"**

wrote the Lincoln Guild; and the Cary Deanery Branch of the Bath and Wells advised members to "**... bring your own**

nosebag." The Northern Branch of the Lincoln Guild suggested that ringers attending their seven hour meeting at Caythorpe should, "**Bring your own tea and picnic in the fields**."

Some Associations cancelled part of the tea but not all of it. For example,

> **"Visitors *must* bring their own food, tea (beverage) will be provided at small charge in the Parish Room."**

And in an era when working men put substantial sugar into every cup of their very strong tea, the worry of free-loaders demolishing the home tower's tiny sugar ration was a problem in itself. Like other Guilds, the Southern District of the Ladies Guild at their joint meeting with the Guildford Guild, told everyone:

> **"Owing to catering difficulties, please bring your own sugar if you require it."**

Eating Elsewhere

But another possibility was to opt out of the rationing problem completely. Before the War, teas were occasionally organised in pubs and cafes, but that now became quite common. The London County Association had a tea in *Perdy's Restaurant*, the Guildford Guild went to *The Duke's Head*, and the Peterborough Association used the services of *The Co-operative Hall*.

The Warwickshire Guild's tea was provided at *The Rainbow Inn*, the Hereford Guild went to *The Royal Oak Cafe*, and The Midland Counties Association had a hot supper at *The Queen's Head*. The hotel lounge of *The Lion Hotel* served the Bedfordshire Association well, but *The*

Babington Cafe had a real problem at the Midland Counties AGM in April 1940.

> **"Tea was served at 5 p.m. at the Babington Cafe, Babington Lane. This was, perhaps, somewhat awkwardly arranged, but the fault lay, not with the caterers, but with those members who failed to notify their intention of being present. Some 60 *did* notify, but 90 turned up and it was noticed that, as usual, the erring ones were those who complained the most."**

Air Raids

But both before and after rationing was introduced, the possibility of air raids and gas attacks during meetings had to be considered. In some places a watcher or watchers were left outside, and in others, only short touches were rung so that air raid sirens could be heard. Even then, some churchwardens and tower captains thought extra precautions were called for, and *The Ringing World* carried this splendid piece by a District Secretary attempting to arrange a quarterly meeting.

> **"Bill said, against emergencies, the stokehole just outside the belfry door should be made into a bomb-proof shelter; in accordance with his A.R.P. instructions, he will have to wear his 'tin hat,' everyone must put on their gas masks while they are ringing."**

There were other problems too. Some ARP wardens issued orders that Association meetings couldn't take place – even though they had no authority to do that – so the Winchester and Portsmouth Guild meeting at Upham was forbidden at the last minute even though it was to finish before sunset. In other places – such as the Chilvers Coton meeting of the Warwickshire Guild – a Police Superintendent stopped the ringing, once again late on and without any real reason.

Of course, the Blitz hadn't yet started, so the various dangers of air raids were still only theoretical, but the question of what to do if the sirens went off during ringing troubled everyone. E. Alexr. Young – adding the letters A.R.I.B.A. F.S.I. (retired) after his name – wrote with the answer.

> **"... May I take the opportunity of pointing out to ringers that ordinary spiral stone stairs have a remarkable natural strength, and that the lower portion affords excellent air raid shelter. I observed evidence of this on visiting France immediately after the last war."**

And as advice for ringers in their homes he added.

> **"As one of the district surveyors for London, I also noticed, in surveying many bombed buildings, how safe a place was the cupboard under the kitchen stairs."**

And indeed, this was sound advice which many people – ringers and non-ringers alike – were to find extremely valuable.

Keeping Chickens

But no matter how bad the times, *someone* is always ready to make a profit from them, and in October 1939 P. Amos of Northampton became the first person to advertise chickens in *The Ringing World.*

"IF YOU CAN'T RING BELLS, GO IN FOR POULTRY, Buy from a practical breeder. Profitable 1938 Pullets, Rhodes, Rhode Island cross Sussex, Leghorns, etc. £1, 22s. 6d. and 25s. five. – P. Amos, Breeder and Exhibitor, 47, West St., Northampton."

And in the same way, the Press are always looking for angles by which to profit from disaster too. So G. W. Steere recorded this incident on the last day of 1939.

"While ringing was in progress for morning service at St Martin's-in-the-Fields, on December 31st, a Press photographer entered the belfry accompanied by two soldiers.

When the ringing was finished and the bells lowered the camera-man proceeded to pose the soldiers as ringers and took their photograph holding ropes.

On being asked for what purpose the pictures were required, he said it was to illustrate New Year celebrations in the Press – the London dailies.

Neither of the soldiers had ever been in a belfry before and the ringers present had considerable difficulty in persuading them to remove their hats, which the pressman wanted retained 'for added effect.'

It was stated that the name of the church would not be published but if any ringer should see such a picture in any paper he

will know just how much truth there is in whatever caption may be underneath it."

Dunkirk

But inconvenient though the first eight months of the War were, for most people in the UK they were at least safe. The bombs hadn't started falling and the expected gas attacks hadn't materialised. But in May 1940 came Dunkirk, and with Dunkirk came the promise of far worse to come. The Whitsun bank holiday was cancelled and a good many Association meetings and AGMs were cancelled with it. The country, the World and ringing were entering a dark time.

And *that* is what we'll be looking at next.

Of course, all wars are utterly appalling, and the Second World War was no less appalling than any of the others. A huge number of people died, and a huge number of others had their lives completely devastated. Every death and every devastated life is a tragedy in itself, and the fact that the UK lost under 1% of it's population while Russia, Poland and Germany, lost over 10% of theirs, doesn't alter the enormous personal loss of each individual and each person who loved them.

Nothing in these chapters says anything else, but the reality of being human is that much of normal life carries on no matter how awful the surrounding circumstances. So in the Second World War, as in all wars, great tragedy and everyday banality continued side by side; and while some people were being killed or experiencing overwhelming grief, others were smiling at their baby's first steps, or getting irritated that the bus was late.

And that banality was typified in ***The Ringing World*** *of 1st September 1939. The country was only a couple of days* *from the outbreak of a horrendous war, and yet most of the pages were taken up with matters that spoke of nothing but endless peace and contentment. Peals, outing reports and notices of forthcoming meetings all appeared as if nothing out of the ordinary had happened or was ever likely to happen.*

Indeed, apart from the editorial, only a couple of pieces in ***Belfry Gossip*** *suggested any national difficulties at all; and even* those *pieces were soundly ringing-based. The feeling was not so much that war would disrupt the entire nation, but rather that ringing would experience a mild but temporary inconvenience. A few peals, for example, would be cancelled.*

> **"The peal-ringing tour in Bedfordshire and Northants, which was to have begun tomorrow, has been abandoned, most of those who were to have taken part having had their holiday leave cancelled."**

And a splendidly old-world traffic accident was reported too.

> **"We regret to say that last Saturday Mr. Tom Groombridge, sen., of Chislehurst, met with an accident. He was knocked down by a pedal cyclist and rather badly hurt. He was taken to Farnborough (Kent) Hospital and detained. He had just left home for a peal attempt at Lewisham when the accident happened."**

And in a normal week that would have been the end of the report; but since this week wasn't ***quite*** *normal, a short note was added.*

> **"Subject to the results ascertained by an X-ray examination, it is possible he may be returned home before the end of this week, as the hospital is being cleared as rapidly as possible owing to the crisis."**

Even a fortnight later it was clear that, for some, the enormity of the situation still hadn't sunk in. So the editor was asked to pass on this message to his readers.

> **"We are officially informed that the peal ringing tour, which was arranged for this week in Yorkshire, has not been cancelled, as stated in our last issue, but has been postponed until the end of the war."**

And that rather curious view of the War as an unscheduled interruption to normal ringing, surfaces quite strongly in these chapters. They are, after all, the history of the War looked at from a ringing standpoint, so they're about ordinary people trying to carry on their chief leisure activity while terrible things are going on around them.

And splendidly, that makes for a fair deal of unexpected humour. But it isn't the fabricated, propaganda-style humour that featured so strongly in Wartime and post-War films; and nor is it the humour that was purposely created to bolster the nation's morale and make people feel proud in hindsight. It's the spontaneous humour that arose from the ringing aspects of the War as they actually happened, and it's a humour that the ringers of the time undoubtedly understood and shared in.

And that humour was never more to the fore than when suddenly and completely unexpectedly, ringing actually stopped ...

2. The Silence

Ever since I was in primary school I've been interested in how everyone coped during the War. I'm interested in the queuing, the rationing, the shortages, the air raids, the black-outs, the fire watching, the recipes, and all the ways in which ordinary people kept things going. But although I've read repeatedly about the ban on ringing except if there was an invasion, nothing is ever said about the details. Please tell all.

Matt
London

On Sunday 26th May 1940, the ringers of Hatherop in Gloucestershire rang for service as normal. There were only three of them now as the rest were in the forces, and even those three couldn't always get there. But they nonetheless carefully marked up the attendance book, rang the bells down, left the attendance book open on the ringing room table, and departed, fully expecting to be back again in a couple of weeks' time.

But they *weren't* back in a couple of weeks' time. Indeed, they weren't back for more than five years. To their complete surprise, before their next service ring, all ringing was banned with immediate and indefinite effect, and for five years the Hatherop ringing chamber remained unvisited. The Hatherop bells remained unrung too, and the Hatherop attendance book remained forlornly open at the page for 1940, gathering dust, damp and spider droppings as the weeks, months and years went by.

And that forlorn period still shows in exactly that way in the Hatherop attendance book today. The 1940 page is pock-marked by dust and damp while the pages before and after are neat, clean and meticulously cared for. Nothing about the war is actually *written* in the book; no one recorded that ringing stopped, and no one recorded that it started again, but the condition of the page is itself the most telling testimony possible. And a similar story can be told for almost every tower in the country. The suddenness was as shocking as the decision itself.

The Announcement

So how exactly did it happen?

In Chapter 1 we looked at the *Control of Noise* Order issued at the very beginning of the War, and in Chapter 6 we'll be looking at a similar Order issued two months later. But on 13th June 1940 the Government promised a third and far more draconian Order. It was to be called *The Control of Noise (Defence) Order, 1940*, and it said – quite simply:

> **"No person shall, in any area in Great Britain, sound any church bell or cause or permit any church bell to be sounded except for the purpose of making a signal, in accordance with directions given by a commissioned officer of His Majesty's forces or the chief officer of police for the area, to indicate that members of an enemy force are landing or attempting to land or have landed from the air."**

And the astonishing effect was that – as detailed in countless histories and novels of the War – church bell ringing became illegal from the following weekend, thus making Sunday 16th June 1940 the first completely bell-free Sunday in the UK for more than a thousand years.

The Truth

Except that it didn't!

Although that is indeed what you can read in countless histories and novels of the War, it's not actually true. For a start, not everyone had heard the news. Bishops had written to all their clergy on the previous Thursday, but the post had become less reliable, and some vicars didn't receive their letter until the following Monday. Most *ringers* knew of the ban, of course, but in churches without ringers – or in churches with only one or two bells – preoccupied vicars, vergers with Alzheimer's and small boys without newspapers, chimed as they always had done.

And more bizarre still, ***there wasn't actually any reason why they shouldn't have***. Although everyone *believed* that ringing was illegal on 16th June, it wasn't illegal at all. Contrary to popular belief, the Government *hadn't* issued the *Control of Noise Order* on 13th June, and nor had they ever intended to. What they *had* done was let the Archbishop of Canterbury know that an Order was coming up.

Or to be more accurate, it wasn't the *Government* itself who'd told the Archbishop, it was the Home Office. They'd done it in advance of the full letter being drafted by the War Office and they'd done it in confidence. The Church Assembly was taking place in London that week, and it seems they wanted the Archbishop to tell the other bishops – also in confidence – before they left. Some confusion arose, though – probably involving the Archbishop's chaplain – and so not realising he shouldn't, the Archbishop became the first person to announce the ban publicly. At the end of his address to the Church Assembly on 12th June, he just popped it in.

Of course, being the Archbishop, he had to express it in a suitably self-important way, so he said that he had "**received a communication**" from the Home Secretary that directions to prohibit church bell ringing would "**become operative before next Sunday**." And although this might have seemed a fairly small thing to the Archbishop, the Press received it as major news, and all the newspapers reported it, some of them on the same day.

The Home Office was now in a quandary. With the whole country believing that an Order had been issued which took effect immediately, they didn't want to make either the Archbishop or themselves look silly. So having been bounced into it early by the Archbishop's gaff, they made their own announcement on the evening of 13th June. *Their* announcement was certainly truthful in that it said that an Order was *going* to be made – but it nonetheless very cleverly suggested otherwise. *The Times* reported it this way.

> **"The military authorities having decided that it is essential to make use of church bells for the purpose of giving warning of the approach of parachutists or other airborne troops, their use for any other purpose must now be prohibited. An Order to this effect will be made by the Minister of Home Security. In future, therefore, neither church nor chapel bells may be rung at any time except by the Military or Local Defence Volunteers to indicate that a raid by parachutists or airborne troops is imminent."**

So having read this statement and the reports of the Archbishop's address, it's not surprising that ringers and church authorities everywhere thought that ringing on 16th June would be a criminal offence; and they didn't ring. In fact, though, the Order wasn't issued until 19th June which meant that ringing on the 16th was still perfectly legal. But whatever *should* have happened, the reality was that from 16th June onwards, the overwhelming feature of Sundays was the silence.

The Background

But to get an idea of the background to the ban, it helps to put the week of 13th June in its War context. In short, things were going badly. At the beginning of the week, Italy had entered the war on the side of Germany, and at the end of the week, Paris fell – with France falling a few days later. *Dunkirk* had been only a few weeks earlier, and an invasion attempt was now seen as a certainty. And on top of all that, there lurked a potential setback every bit as serious as an invasion attempt. The fall of France was likely to reveal the British knowledge of the *Enigma Machine*.

And by way of further background, the Enigma Machine was a coding device used by the German Military. It had originally been invented for commercial purposes just after the First World War but it had swiftly been commandeered by the German Military who saw its enormous military potential. The British weren't much interested in it back then, but the Poles – who shared a common border with Germany – definitely were. So they set about breaking the code, and in 1928 they succeeded.

Unfortunately their success was short-lived because the Germans then increased Enigma's complexity. In 1932 the Poles broke it again, but when in 1938 the Germans improved it yet again, the Poles knew they no longer had the resources to tackle it, so they held a secret meeting with British and French cryptographers in July 1939.

At that meeting they shared all their knowledge and ideas, and the British then cracked the updated Enigma in January 1940. The military benefits of this were absolutely colossal, and expert opinion has it that it shortened the War by at least two years.

But the British Government very reasonably supposed that once France fell and a quisling government was installed, the French cryptographers would be compelled to hand over all their Enigma information to their new government who would, in turn, pass it on to the Germans. We *now* know that the French cryptographers performed an outstanding service to both *their* country and ours by not passing on any information whatever, but in June 1940 the outlook appeared very different.

The Practicalities

Of course, the general public knew nothing about Enigma, but they *did* know that the Germans were now only a few miles away, and that was serious enough. Ringers could certainly see an immediate justification to the ban, but they nonetheless had to cope with it, and they repeatedly asked themselves three questions. How should they sound the warning? What should they do if the warning was sounded? And most important, what should they do instead of ringing?

The first question wasn't an easy one. Since the Order came into effect before it was even issued, no official guidance was forthcoming, so each band had to make up it's own system. Some of those systems teetered on the bizarre, as many ringers didn't seem to realise that a nice touch of Grandsire wasn't what was required. Indeed, they didn't even realise that they needn't ring *all* their bells at all, and that a single bell clanging away would be warning enough. The ringers of Pudsey in Yorkshire, for example, not only immediately organised a complex system but they set it out carefully in writing.

> **"In the event of air invasion alarm at Pudsey.**
>
> **First, the verger will be notified by the Home Guard that an air invasion has taken place, or is imminent, and he will accordingly proceed to the church and await orders to ring.**
>
> **Second, if the invasion has taken place or is imminent, he will in due course receive orders to ring the treble bell.**
>
> **Third, the local commander of the Home Guard ... on hearing the bell which he has instructed the verger to ring, will issue instructions for a motor-car to collect the ringers from their homes or their work.**
>
> **Fourth, the ringers having first been found, will then be conveyed to the church."**

In retrospect, the unreality of this is breathtaking. The ringers actually expected – while the area was being invaded – that cars and manpower could be spared to ferry them around the town. And besides, the verger had already alerted everyone by ringing the treble. All the same, it showed that ringers took their responsibility seriously, and in many places they manned their tower in shifts so that someone was always ready if called on – and they kept up that vigil for several months.

The Military

But if ringers were unrealistic, so too were some of the Military. In Lincolnshire, for example, the General Officer Commanding issued his own instructions which he then released to the Press.

> **"In the event of an attempted invasion a general alarm will be rung by the sounding of every church bell throughout the county – perhaps throughout England – as a tocsin. The bells will be rung loudly and confidently as a call to battle, the peals continuing for five minutes."**

Clearly, he knew nothing at all about bellringing – and especially, he knew nothing about whether bells could be rung ***loudly and confidently*** – yet he made his announcement without making any attempt to find out.

A Ministry of Information Film

But even if ringers and General Officers Commanding were confused, the *Ministry of Information* wanted to make sure the general public wasn't. So they made a film to be shown at all cinemas telling people what to do. No copy seems to have survived, but William Stote of Coventry wrote this letter after seeing it.

> **"In a local cinema last Saturday evening I saw a ten-minute film, shown under the auspices of the Ministry of Information. ... The scene is set in the country home of two ladies, who are awakened at night by a local Air Raid Warden and told to get to the cellar as a raid is on. On their way they hear a knock at the front door, which they open to find a dying parachutist outside. At the**

same time they hear the local ring of eight going to rounds and call changes, which informs them that an air invasion is on.

A man in the uniform of a military officer then knocks, is admitted, and gives himself away as a German spy by asking for the use of an Ordnance Survey Map. He is held up by one lady with a revolver – taken from the dead parachutist – while the other rides to the Wardens' post to ask him to inform the Home Guard."

So astonishingly, even the Ministry of Information thought that in the midst of an invasion, eight men could be spared to ring call changes.

The Effect

And not surprisingly, to most ringers the whole system quickly seemed fairly barmy. Who would ring, what would they ring, and who would hear the bells anyway? But barmy as they thought it, would it have worked? And as far as giving a warning was concerned, we have abundant evidence that it would – although we also have abundant evidence that no one would know what to do when they heard it. First, here's a report from *The Daily Herald.*

"It is stated that many people ran into the street in the Lower Sydenham District of Greater London early on Thursday of last week when they heard what they believed to be the sound of bells rung as an invasion alarm. Police investigated the matter. At first the noise was thought to have come from the direction of St. Michael's Church, but it was found that the building was

locked and that the bells had been dismantled for many weeks. Then it was believed that a handbell had been rung in the street. Eventually the police traced the noise to the Sydenham Gas Works. Employees there had been engaged on work with steel tubes, and the hammering of the pipes caused a sound similar to the ringing of church bells."

And similarly, Phyllis Giblett recalled the day when the church tower at Cattistock in Dorset burnt down – albeit not as a result of enemy action. The bells had been left up since early June and once the stays had burnt through, the bells rang themselves down.

"It was September 15th 1940, the same day as the Battle of Britain, and I was a 17 year old working in Cattistock. We were eating lunch when we heard the Church bells ringing. We weren't expecting to hear this as this was the sign of an invasion. We all rushed outside to see the church tower in flames and the hands of the clock falling to point towards the ground. At this point we realised that there was no invasion and that it was the flames which were making the church bells ring."

The BBC

And the BBC certainly thought the system would work, and it took immediate action. It was an organisation that spoke with truth and authority, and the bulk of the population listened to it avidly for War news. So it had to make quite sure it never broadcast any bells; and that was a problem because in those days there were no *continuity announcers*, so its engineers had to use short bursts of sound to fill the gaps between programmes.

Those short bursts were known as *interval signals* and there were two of them stored on 78 rpm discs. One burst was on one side of the disc and the other was on the other, and each burst took care of a thirty second gap. If the engineer needed to fill a longer gap, he simply left the needle on the disc and the same burst was replayed after a short silence.

The signal on one side of the disc was the first chunk of *Lillibullero* played by the Coldstream Guards, but the signal on the other was Bow bells ringing a few simple call changes. So the Bow bells interval signal was suspended immediately, leaving nothing but *Lillibullero* for the next three years. With true BBC efficiency, though, the ban eventually went further. By 1941 the Light Entertainment Department had been evacuated to Bangor, and on 17th October 1941 this memo was issued by the Director.

> ***Memo from John Watt, Director of Variety, Bangor to all producers:***
>
> **BANNED SONGS**
>
> **Will you please note that recordings and live performances of Tchaikovsky's '1812' Overture in its original scoring (i.e. with the bells) are banned for security reasons.**
>
> **This restriction also applies to any work in which the realistic representation of a peal of Church bells takes place (as distinct from the use of tubular bells as an integral part of an orchestral texture).**

Certainly, it's hard to imagine anyone getting the wind up as a result of listening to the 1812 Overture, but banning songs inappropriate to the War effort was an essential part of the Director of Variety's duties. He was very concerned, for example, about ***Coming in on a Wing and a Prayer*** – which he referred to the RAF for guidance – and he completely banned ***Praise the Lord and Pass the Ammunition*** unless sung by a man rather than a woman.

Ringing by Mistake

But with tens of thousands of bells in tens of thousands of churches and chapels – not to mention all the bells in cemeteries, schools, great houses, stables and all manner of other places – some of them were bound to get rung from time to time by mistake or even for a lark. The official instruction was that bells were only to be rung if more than five parachutists were seen coming down together – the idea being that five or less were probably the crew of one of our own planes bailing out – but not everyone understood that.

Indeed, as this secret memo from Southern Command made clear, it wasn't just *ringing* that wasn't supposed to happen unless more than five parachutists were seen.

Subject:- Defence against Parachute Attack and Troop Carrying Aircraft

SECRET

3 September, 1940

From: Sn. Comd.

Reference the attached letter C.R.H.F. 1/2859/G dated 18th June, 1940.

Several cases have been reported recently in which injury has resulted to our own pilots descending by parachute. All ranks of Army

and Home Guard will be immediately informed that parachutists less than 6 in number will not be fired at.

Your attention is directed to this H.Q. letter S.C. No. Z/6274/G(0) dated 30th July, 1940.

But although the Home Guard could – and did – shoot at parachutists at will, *ringing* was only supposed to take place on the instruction of a senior police officer or military commander. Most people, though, mistakenly believed that anyone could – indeed, *should* – ring whatever bell was available when they thought it was appropriate, so there were many false alarms.

All the same, in many places a dedicated warning-ringer was officially appointed; so when George Grover of West Clandon in Surrey was in the Home Guard he failed an important examination question on the arrangements in the case of invasion. "Who is your nearest bellringer?" he was asked. "Me!" he replied. "Wrong!" said the examiner, "It's the Sexton."

A Grand Mistake

But on Saturday September 7th 1940 there was mistaken ringing on a truly exceptional scale. On that evening, bells were rung across the entire country, and *The Ringing World* reported it like this.

"Last Saturday night, while London was under the biggest air attack launched against it since the war began, there was an alarm sounded on the church bells in Surrey, Devon and Cornwall. No one seems to know why the alarm was given or by whom, and many have been the surmises. In

parts of West Surrey, bells of a number of churches were violently rung, calling out the Home Guard. It appears to have been a false alarm and it is reported that the authorities are trying to find out who was responsible for it being given.

Enquiries by *The Ringing World* have elicited the fact that messages were sent out soon after 10 p.m. to the incumbents of various churches to have the bells rung owing to 'a state of emergency,' and the instruction was complied with. In some cases only one bell was chimed, in others two. At one church with only one bell, the Vicar's wife undertook the task.

In the West of England, warnings are said to have been sounded from Cornwall to the outskirts of Bristol. That, too, was a false alarm and it is suggested that it may have been due to a fishing fleet returning to a Cornish harbour through the mist earlier than expected after making a lucky catch.

... The whole position is chaotic and will lead to unending confusion if unauthorised people, with nerves ajump, rush about giving orders to ring the church bells."

And of interest is that *The Ringing World* reported it at all. *The Times* didn't, the other national newspapers didn't, and the great bulk of local newspapers didn't either. It's just possible that a specific order preventing publication was issued – which didn't get to *The Ringing World* – but more likely, newspapers refrained on the basis of the general prohibition. The only newspaper report I can find, appeared in the following Monday's *Western Daily Press* under the headline **Church Bells' S.W. Alarm**.

> **"All Home Guard members in a South-West town were called out about midnight on Saturday night. Some were called by loud speakers in the streets and others by messengers. In a residential suburb church bells were rung.**
>
> **Roads were cleared of all civilian traffic and all people travelling through the night were stopped and questioned.**
>
> **There is mystery also over the ringing for a considerable time of the church bells in a Welsh coast parish on Saturday night. Police and other authorities say they cannot account for it, but there was much activity on the part of the A.R.P. and other home defence services.**
>
> **In the minds of many people it was feared that the ringing of the church bells had some relation to an invasion. This was absolutely groundless. During the air raid on Saturday night in the North-East area the church bells were also rung. Nothing transpired."**

And Other Places

In fact the bells appear to have been rung in a great many more places than *The Ringing World* and the *Western Daily Press* reported. Indeed, they were probably rung over much of Great Britain. Official sources don't much help because everyone involved wanted to hush up their bloomer. A few extraordinarily detailed official *confessions* came in, but this memo from Southern Command to H.Q. Home Forces was more typical.

> **"The danger of the existing system of giving warning of parachute landings by the ringing of church bells was made abundantly clear last night when at about 23.30 hrs, reports were received that church bells had been heard in BRISTOL, LONG ASHTON and CLEVEDON. This later proved to have been done by mistake.**
>
> **At about midnight, the Civil Police at ANDOVER rang up to enquire whether Southern Command had ordered the ringing of church bells, as bells at that place had been rung. The local H.G. there, when taxed with this, had told the police that bells were being rung by the order of this Headquarters. Needless to say, no such order had ever been issued."**

Probably far more reports were made on the grapevine than in writing because a hand written slip of paper in a Home Office file reads:

> **"There was a night early in the month on which bells rang in a great many places, owing to a 'stand-by' order given to the Home Guard in the middle of the night, and misinterpreted locally in many cases, but this night's entertainment is well known to G.H.Q. Home Forces!**
>
> **No action, I think."**

Personal Reports

There are also many personal recollections of the night by both ringers and non-ringers, although most only surfaced long afterwards. Bill Gibbons of Cheshire was in Oxford, and he had absolutely no idea he was hearing anything other than a local aberration.

> **"Early in September I moved into new 'digs.' I moved on a Saturday and I remember seeing a church tower from my bedroom window, brilliantly lit by moonlight as I retired for the night. Some time later, I heard the tenor start to ring so I counted the strokes in order to ascertain the time. At the 14th stroke, however, the significance of it all sank in! I leapt out of bed and dashed round to a friend's room down the corridor, calling that the Germans were invading. The muffled reply from under the bed clothes indicated, amid expletives, that there was little that we could blank, blank do about it! Undoubtedly he was right ...**
>
> **... so I went back to bed."**

What Really Happened

Even today, most people still believe that it was just an extraordinary, and very local, mix up. But that wasn't so at all. As we'll see later, Hitler had been preparing to invade, and the troops and boats were ready and waiting on the French and Belgian coasts. The sole purpose of the Battle of Britain was to destroy the UK air capability so that those troops could land safely.

In September there was a period when the tides and moon

were especially favourable to an invasion attempt, and the British Military were largely expecting one. They'd prepared a signal intended to raise the level of preparedness but they hadn't explained it very well. Many – perhaps most – recipients thought it meant *Invasion Imminent*; and that signal was **Cromwell**.

Exactly why the Blitz started when it did isn't completely clear, but the general belief is that it resulted from a lone German bomber losing its way in the Battle of Britain and dropping its bombs on the edge of London by mistake. The British retaliated with a bombing raid on Germany, and Hitler retaliated by starting the Blitz. At the time, though, the Military didn't perceive it that way at all.

In the UK, the minds of the Government and the Military were focused primarily on the Battle of Britain. Rightly, they saw it as a decisive battle since no invasion attempt by sea was likely to be successful unless the RAF was destroyed first. But on 7th September while the Battle of Britain was still in progress, the Germans turned aside from bombing the fighter bases in the South East and went on to bomb London. The Blitz had begun. But the British High Command thought the bombing might be a prelude to invasion – especially as the final preparations for invasion appeared to be being made – and the signal **Cromwell** was issued at 8.07 that evening.

It went to all commanding officers throughout the country, but it was a Saturday and most of them were having the night off. So the officers who received the signal were only junior, and they hadn't been fully briefed on invasion procedures. They weren't sure what the signal meant or what they were supposed to do, and many of them took it to mean that the invasion fleet had been launched or that an invasion was actually in progress; and they gave orders accordingly.

All sorts of extraordinary things happened. Bombs were loaded onto flimsy training planes, bridges were blown up, and soldiers were blown up by land mines. In addition, many military officers gave the order to ring. So contrary to the *Ringing World* report, there was no unauthorised ringing and no *nerves ajump*. The ringers simply did what they had been told to in accordance with their agreed instructions.

And significantly, the Home Guard – who had been renamed from *The Local Defence Volunteers* six weeks earlier – turned out at mustering points, ready and expecting to fight. Many of them had fought in the First World War and were experienced soldiers, but they were nonetheless virtually unarmed and completely ill-equipped to confront a formidable fighting force. In retrospect, the bravery of these men is breathtaking.

But brave though they were, at that time the Military had no real plan of how or *whether* to organise them, and they had no knowledge of who they were or where they were mustering. If nothing else, the mistake brought home to the Government that calling out the Home Guard in the event of an invasion – and particularly a general invasion by air – would create far more problems than it would solve; and within a week they had secretly changed their plans.

Why?

But before we get to that, we'll tidy up the remaining September dates. The Battle of Britain officially ended on 15th September, eight days after the mass ringing. On that day, the last great German push failed; and two days later on 17th September, Hitler issued a command postponing invasion "**... until further notice**" – although, naturally, that wasn't public information at the time. But we're still left with two questions. Who rang? And why was the order given?

As to the first, some years ago I tried to track down ringers who rang then, but I couldn't find a single one. Indeed, I couldn't even find anyone who knew of one. It seems the bulk of the bells were just chimed by vicars, sextons and members of their families.

But the second question is far more intriguing. Despite popular belief, the bells *weren't* supposed to be rung if an invasion was only in the offing. Indeed, they weren't supposed to be rung even if an invasion was actually taking place, as long as it was only an invasion *by sea*. They were *only* supposed to be rung to give warning that enemy forces were landing *by air* – and quite clearly, in Cornwall, Oxford and South Wales, they weren't.

But the misunderstanding of the ban – by both the general public *and* the Military – is one of the many puzzles surrounding it. And getting to the bottom of some of those puzzles is where our story will be going next.

Not surprisingly, a vast number of histories have been written about The Second World War. They've dealt in the minutest detail with almost every possible aspect – the causes, the battles, the economics, the espionage, the personalities, the logistics, the social conditions, and just about everything else you can think of. Histories are still being written too, because even all these years later, fascinating new information is still coming to light. Indeed, these very chapters contain many Government papers that have never been made public before.

But although that's good, it's also a real problem because it's always hard to accept that facts we learnt long ago, aren't really facts at all. Some of them are only partially true whilst others are completely false, yet putting them aside is desperately hard no matter how overwhelming the evidence. Somehow, accepting that a long believed War fact is false, is like challenging an essential part of our being.

*And when it comes to incorrect facts, although films, books and children's comics, have a lot to answer for, a great deal of **official** Wartime information was very inaccurate too. In wartime, lying is a practical necessity; so although it's inconvenient for historians, in the Second World War it was essential that our military plans and espionage capability were kept secret from the enemy, and if that meant the public being deceived at the same time, then that was how it had to be.*

*Equally, since success depended on the extraordinary effort and support of ordinary people everywhere, it was essential to maintain morale. And if that meant jollying the public along with a mass of inaccurate morale-boosting propaganda, then **that** was how it had to be too. There was nothing cynical about this; it was simply the proper exercise of Government in the people's interest.*

*But the problem is that once you start misleading people, you can't just stop. You can't suddenly tell everyone the whole truth about something simply because it's past. You can't even do it once the War's over. You can't destroy people's trust, and you can't jeopardise future dissimulations. You might reveal **favourable** military truths, but you don't want to reveal **un**favourable ones, and besides, you have to keep military and espionage capability secret from **future** enemies.*

In 1945 the international situation had certainly changed for the better, but it was still extremely difficult; and on top of that, the Government knew that the general public would be facing enormous privation and hardship for years to come; so their previous morale-boosting distortions had to be kept secret too.

Yet despite all that, as soon as the War finished, historians immediately started writing history books. Winston Churchill, for example, wrote a stack of them. He was a talented writer – and desperately short of money – and at one time he had seven secretaries working simultaneously so he could publish as quickly as possible. But he had to conceal great quantities of the truth – indeed, he never mentioned the ringing ban at all – and other writers were even more hampered. At least Churchill ***knew*** *the truth even if he couldn't reveal it.*

So if, while you're reading these chapters, you come across something that makes you say, "I ***know*** *that's not true," at least consider whether just* ***perhaps*** *– notwithstanding what your mother or primary school teacher told you years ago – it might be true after all.*

For example, ringers have always believed the Government virtually ignored them during the War, whereas nothing could be further from the truth. The Civil Service, the War Cabinet, Winston Churchill and even the King, were very concerned indeed about ringers; and they were all having the most remarkable discussions **In the Corridors of Power**.

3. In The Corridors of Power

Some years ago someone wrote an article in *The Ringing World* saying that the Second World War ban was the most bizarre period in the whole history of ringing. He said it must have been ordered in a panic by some *petty bureaucrat* who then couldn't admit he'd made a mistake, and the whole idea was ridiculous from start to finish. But I've always been doubtful about assuming everyone in history was an idiot, and I'd like to know how the decision *really* came to be made.

M.R.
Warwickshire

Last time we looked at how the ban began, and how the use of bells for signalling an invasion attempt was designed to work. And we saw that in a rough and ready way it certainly *did* work – at least as far as making people *think* an invasion was happening even though it wasn't. But we also saw that the public was left in the dark about how the decision came to be made.

Muddling Through

But before we delve into this extremely fascinating story, let's hit the War's one great and enduring myth firmly on its head. The British War effort was most definitely *not* inefficient and muddly – at least, not for the most part. The great bulk of it was highly organised and highly efficient, and there's abundant evidence for that. Certainly, the Government liked to create an image of *the British muddling through* because that was good for morale and confusing to the enemy, but the reality was very different.

Of course, all wars, by their very nature, involve a great deal of confusion and mistakes. Situations change fast and information is always inadequate, and in that respect the Second World War was no different. Indeed, a good many of Hitler's quite extraordinary decisions couldn't possibly have been anticipated. But that doesn't of itself imply incompetence. So dismissing the ban as a muddle instigated by a *petty bureaucrat* won't get us anywhere.

Equally, dismissing it as a silly mistake that no one had the courage to admit to, won't get us anywhere either – although you can certainly read that in lots of places. Throughout the War, the Government was extremely good at admitting mistakes and correcting them – and it was extremely good at rapidly amending instructions and procedures in the light of changing circumstances too. Success depended on it, and the Government and the Civil Service both understood that.

Organisation

But all the same, conducting any war is fantastically complicated, and the Second World War was the most complicated war ever. Feeding and equipping the Military whilst at the same time, feeding, equipping and defending the civilian population, required detailed Government intervention on a completely unprecedented scale; and the uncomfortable truth was that the War not only needed soldiers, it also needed an army of managers and office workers. Indeed, one of Churchill's great strengths was his supreme management ability. The Government had to make huge and multiple changes to every detail of normal peace-time organisation, and an army of pen-pushers had to think out each one of them and then implement and monitor it.

What was more, those pen-pushers knew full well that every single one of the changes had significant downsides as well as significant upsides. Security always creates inconvenience, and great security creates great inconvenience. Worse, all the changes interacted with each other in ways that couldn't possibly be anticipated because no one knew everything.

So although the *Control of Noise* Orders were a big deal to ringers, they were only a tiny fraction of the total Orders issued. The full compliment covered everything from the black-out regulations to the control of wool; and to put the *Control of Noise* Orders in context, the first was issued on 1st September 1939 but was nonetheless the 1,169th Order of the year. Even more astonishing, the 1,000th Order had only been issued *earlier that day*; and by the end of October, the Orders were well past 1,500.

Yet every one of those Orders was carefully considered in advance, and every one of them was carefully – and rapidly – reviewed and amended as circumstances and further information suggested. There was no complacency with those Orders and there was no reluctance to stand earlier decisions completely on their heads; and the *Control of Noise* Orders were no exception. So if we're looking to find out why the ban came about and why it lasted so long, the one thing we *can't* do is assume it was a silly mistake that no one was prepared to admit to. *Nothing* in the War was that simple.

Official Papers

All the same, you'd suppose that somewhere there'd be a handful of Government papers that tell us exactly what we want to know. But regrettably there isn't. Instead, there's a truly massive quantity of documents held in a positively huge number of files. Some are stuffed with hundreds of sheets of paper and some have only a few. Some were created by the Home Office and some under their alter ego, the Department of Home Security. Others were created by the War Office, the Ministry of Information and the Prime Minister's Office. Some have been accidentally or deliberately destroyed in part, and some have been accidentally or deliberately destroyed in total.

And there aren't just files dealing with the *Control of Noise Orders* generally, there are also files dealing with church bell ringing specifically. There are also references to ringing in the myriad of files on invasion, parachutists, the Home Guard, the police, air-raids, public information, and all sorts of other things. And confusingly, the Home Secretary and the Minister of Home Security were the same person with two legal statuses, so in these chapters I'm referring to both sets of his civil servants as "The Home Office."

Decision Making

We'll come back to what those official papers tell us in a moment, but before that, we must look at how Wartime decisions of this sort were taken. First, someone had to believe that a particular restriction was necessary. That person could be a military officer, a civil servant or a politician. Ordinary members of the public made suggestions too, as did influential men who *dined* with Ministers. If an idea appeared to have merit, a file was opened and it was passed rapidly round all the relevant people for them to have their say. Memos were sent from one Government

Department to another – so more files were opened – and the process was then repeated over and over again to enable everyone to amend their views in the light of everyone else's. ***But***, at the end of the day, any matter of significance was decided by Churchill himself, and whatever anyone else had thought in the meantime made no difference except as advice. *His* decision was final.

So for many of his decisions, the papers leading up to them only tell us part of the story because the people who wrote them didn't have the full information. Much information had to be kept so secret, it was known only to Churchill and a few others. So the *real* reason for any decision isn't necessarily easy to establish.

Using Churches

All the same, the papers tell a good story, and in May 1940 two threads were coming together. First, several local commanders had hit upon the idea of using church towers for military purposes; and it was certainly a *good* idea. Towers would have made good observation posts, but more than that, they were excellent sites for machine guns. They could control a wide area, they required almost no building work and they could easily be fortified; and since the Church of England was preaching that the War was a fight against evil, the commanders supposed that vicars wouldn't object.

But of course, they *did* object, and the Bishop of London led the way. He didn't even want searchlights on church towers, and the Bishop of Winchester even objected to a gun in a corner of his private grounds. There was a whiff of selfishness and hypocrisy in all this – although the moral issues were certainly complex – but there was also a quite remarkable belief that the Germans wouldn't damage churches if they weren't used for military purposes.

The Government were in a quandary. Back in September 1939 when an invasion had seemed an impossibility, they'd given an undertaking not to use churches in any way. Now, though, they naturally wished to backtrack, so civil servants researched the effect of Article 27 of the Hague Rules, and they found it enacted the former customary rule that:

> **"In sieges and bombardments all necessary steps must be taken to spare, as far as possible, buildings dedicated to religion ... provided they are not being used at the time for military purposes."**

But since the Germans hadn't taken a blind bit of notice in the siege of Strasbourg in 1870 – or in the destruction of Rheims Cathedral in the First World War – they weren't likely to act differently in 1940. All the same, the Government agreed that church towers would only be used for observation.

The Bells

But the Military wanted something else too. It's not clear exactly how it started, but local commanders began to issue instructions to civilians – and they were instructions which they had absolutely no authority to issue. They summoned meetings of town councils, they gave instructions for public announcements to be made in cinemas and theatres, and – of most interest to us – they issued orders that church bells were not to be rung except as a warning of invasion.

It's unclear where this started and who thought of it, but we get a possible clue from Lord Geddes who was the *Commissioner for Civil Defence* for the South-East Region for most of the War. In the House of Lords in 1943 he said:

> **"It was at Tunbridge Wells. Lord Ironside, who was then Chief of the Imperial General**

Staff, was in my room, and there were also present General Thorne and, I think I am right in saying, my noble friend Lord Knollys. We had just got the first detachments of the Local Defence Volunteers formed, and the only part of the Local Defence Volunteers who had arms at that time were the Kentish and some of the Sussex Companies. The whole thing was very nebulous, and it was thought that at any moment we might see parachutists dropping down from heaven. I think it was the Chief of the Imperial General Staff who said: 'How are you going to get these Local Defence Volunteers together if parachutists suddenly appear?' and somebody in the room – not I, but I could not be sure which of the others – said, 'Why, we will ring the church bells, until we can think of something better.'

That was early in May 1940, and the War Office have been thinking of something better ever since. That signal at that time was supposed to be used only in the Counties of Kent and Sussex and in the rural areas, but somehow or other the order became more or less sacrosanct, and spread all over the country. It was trimmed and pruned, and sprouted new legs and arms, and it became one of the essential pillars of the defence of the country. It is a complete mystery to me why that should be so, but I am assured by War Office representatives that it is."

The Official Reaction

Lord Geddes had previously been a successful soldier, academic, diplomat, businessman and administrator, so he presumably wasn't making it up; but the person who'd said it, may well have been repeating what was already happening. Yet however the idea came into being, it quickly caught on and the Home Office found out about it.

And not surprisingly, they took a very dim view indeed. It wasn't just the fact that the Military had no legal powers to order any such thing, it was also that they thought it a completely daft idea. The War Office thought it a daft idea too, as did the military people attached to the Civil Service. Essentially, their view was that it was impracticable and confusing, and likely to go down very badly with the general public. And besides, other forms of warning were much more effective. The Home Office had discussions with Captain Stockwell – G.S.O.3 at G.H.Q. Home Forces – and on 20th May minuted:

> **"He also agreed with the main objections we have to such usage, which are –**
>
> **(a) They would probably be employed at the same time as an air raid warning and might well mask the air raid sirens :**
>
> **(b) They might in some circumstances be mistaken for hand-bells :**
>
> **(c) There is danger of confusion with the customary usage as fire alarms in certain places :**
>
> **(d) It would be necessary to prohibit the normal use of church bells throughout the**

country, so that they could be reserved for a parachute warning, and this would cause a tremendous outcry.

Captain Stockwell said he would have Eastern Command told that the use of Church Bells as a public warning is undesirable ..."

After which the War Office said on 24th May:

"We agree that the church bells suggestion is not satisfactory and that the police should be told that the use of church bells for giving local warning of parachutists is not to be adopted."

And so the Home Office then sent a secret message to local commanders telling them to stop it at once.

S E C R E T

All Regions and H.Q. Home Forces (for information) from Home Security.

For Regional Police Staff Officer.

War Office agree that church bells are unsuitable for giving local warnings of parachutists and should not be used. Please inform Chief Officers of police.

Manning L.2 Division

The Change

So essentially, all the civil servants said exactly what ringers subsequently thought. Nevertheless, and quite suddenly, on 5th June, the completely contrary decision was made. The Commander in Chief of the Home Forces had a meeting with Churchill, and Churchill over-ruled all his civil servants and ministers. Exactly *why* Churchill decided as he did, we'll explore in the next chapter; but once the decision had been made, the public had to be told, and as we saw in the last chapter, things now got a bit odd.

The plan was that the War Office should "**... placate the Archbishop of Canterbury and other ecclesiastical dignitaries**," while the Home Office would deal with the Fire Brigades. In fact, the War Office chickened out, and the Home Office had to write to the ecclesiastical dignitaries as well. But the *Fire Brigades Division* wasn't at all happy. In country districts many of the firemen were part-time, and church bells were used to " **... fetch them from their beds and benches**." But all the same, it had to comply.

The *ecclesiastical dignitaries* raised no objections at all. They obviously felt they'd got off lightly, and a ban on ringing – and having watchers on their towers – was little enough compared to having machine guns up there. Ringers, though, *did* raise objections, and the Secretary of the Central Council wrote suggesting that a single bell be the warning; but he got nowhere. Lord Halifax, the Foreign Secretary, suggested bells could be allowed on Sunday mornings, but he got nowhere either.

Clarifying the Rules

What exercised officials considerably, though, was what the rules for ringing church bells should actually be. Contrary to public belief, bells were never meant to be a warning of invasion, they were only meant to be a warning of the descent of German parachutists. Exactly how the wrong idea entered the public conciousness, isn't entirely clear – although the newspapers had a lot to do with it – but it certainly *did* enter the public consciousness, and it remained firmly fixed there despite all the Home Office's efforts to displace it. Indeed, it's still in the public consciousness now, and it appears over and over again in histories and novels.

From the outset, though, there was considerable worry about a chain reaction setting in. A handful of parachutists might be seen in one parish, and the bells rung – the purpose being to call out the Home Guard to deal with them until the Army arrived. But the next parish might hear and start ringing *their* bells too. And so on until the whole country was in ferment. Worse, the initial ringing might be a mistake, and if mistakes occurred on a regular basis – and the ringing was always passed on – no one anywhere would get any sleep at all, and industrial production and agricultural work would be disrupted.

The Instructions

Officials were much concerned about this, and the events of the night of 7th September which we read about on page 36, really brought it home. A good many clarification memos were issued, and this one to Southern Command was typical.

SECRET

Subject: - Ringing of Church Bells

H.F. 1/2817/Ops.

Headquarters, Southern Command

Reference your Z/5796/G(0) dated 8th September.

There appears to be some misapprehension about what the orders are concerning the ringing of church bells. They were given initially in L.D.V. Training Instruction No.

2, paragraph 2(1)(b), which reads :-

'Static observation may also be organised by watchers on church towers. They need not carry arms. Any such watcher himself seeing the descent of enemy parachutists in his neighbourhood will broadcast the alarm by ringing church bells. The bells will not be rung for any other purpose. He will NOT repeat the alarm given from a neighbouring church since this will only confuse the issue as to where the parachutists have landed.'

They have been recently repeated in Home Forces teleprinter 0.9 of 8th September, which reads :-

'Orders are that church bells will be rung only as a warning that parachutists have actually been seen to land in the neighbourhood. This signal will NOT be taken up by other localities where parachutists have not actually been seen'.

It is therefore clear that the ringing of church bells is in no sense a general warning, and orders are explicit that in no circumstances will church bells be rung merely because others have been heard ringing. It is considered undesirable to make any change in the instructions at the present moment which might lead to further confusion."

So for the moment everything was clear and simple.

Christmas 1940

Nothing ever stays simple for long, though, and less than three months later, Christmas was approaching. And what better time than Christmas for a short relaxation of the ban? "It would be good for public morale," thought the Archbishop of Canterbury, and the Germans were hardly likely to launch a full scale invasion in the cold and dark of mid-winter. So he made the suggestion to the Prime Minister in the third week of November and the Prime Minister agreed. The Military Chiefs then tried to backtrack, and Churchill was clearly annoyed. In a note with a red **ACTION THIS DAY** sticker, he wrote a **PRIME MINISTER'S PERSONAL MINUTE** to Sir John Anderson.

> **"LORD PRESIDENT**
>
> **Serial No M.572/2**
>
> **In my personal minute M.543/2 of November 23, I said that I was in favour of the Archbishop of Canterbury's request that the bells should be rung on Christmas Day and that I did not think that the invasion danger warranted the maintenance of this ban. I trust that C.-in-C. Home Forces is not raising objections on military grounds. If so please let me know immediately. I shall be seeing him before the week-end and would be very ready to put the position to him."**

Making Arrangements

The Home Office officials clearly knew a Prime Ministerial command when they saw one, and they immediately set about implementing it. But there were difficulties. A new *Control of Noise* Order was required and it had to be specific. The Archbishop wanted ringing during the hours of daylight but the Roman Catholic Cardinal wanted ringing from 6.00 a.m. So the officials drafted the Order to allow ringing between Midnight on Christmas Eve and midnight on Christmas Day.

Then they had to decide what to organise as a parachute warning instead of church bells; and the Military had a go at this too. The Home Office wanted a Home Guard soldier with a whistle in every police station throughout Christmas Day, but the Military wanted him to have a bicycle with him too so that he could cycle round his area whistling up his platoon. They also wanted bells only to be rung between 10.00 a.m. and 3.00 p.m, no matter what the Roman Catholic Church wanted.

Then there was the question of when to tell everybody. Initially, the Military wanted people to be told by word of mouth only – and no earlier than the day before. The Home Office pointed out that that wouldn't do at all, and suggested notification through the Press and BBC. The Military said that the Germans listened in to the BBC and would drop dummy parachutists just to cause trouble; and eventually, it was decided that an announcement would appear in the Press on the 23rd.

All for Nothing

Looking at the official papers now, it's hard to believe that most of the arguments put forward by the C.-in-C. could have been taken seriously at all, and we'll come back to that in Chapter 4. But whatever his real reasons, on 4th December Churchill reluctantly gave in and said there would be no ringing on Christmas Day after all. He may have had reasons that were too secret to be minuted, or he may have been appalled at the elaborate upheaval promised by the C.-in-C. He may also have wished to avoid creating public complacency.

But however that may be, an extraordinary amount of work by the Home Office and the Military had come to nothing, and the *Control of Noise (Defence) (Amending) Order, 1940* – which had been fully drafted and prepared for signing – was never issued. So ringers spent their Christmas Day entirely unaware that they'd come so extraordinarily close to receiving the official permission that "**... Church and Chapel bells may be rung at will during that day**."

Indeed, they came far closer than even the official papers show. "Jock" Colville – later Sir John Colville and Secretary to the Queen – was then in his mid twenties and one of Churchill's four personal assistants. Contrary to strict security regulations, he maintained a detailed diary which he kept locked in his desk at 10 Downing Street, and which remained secret until after his retirement. Here is his entry for 4th December 1940.

> **December 4th 1940.**
>
> **My time has been much occupied with the vexed question whether the church bells should be rung on Christmas Day. The P.M. was disposed to say yes in reply to a Parliamentary Question, but after much discussion the C. in C., Home Forces, has produced such overwhelming arguments against it that the P.M. has agreed to refuse. I was in a position to get the Question answered affirmatively before the contrary arguments could be marshalled, and I all but did so; but then the thought of the responsibility that would be mine if any disaster occurred on Christmas Day made me pause.**

And Onward

But all the fuss over the ringing ban certainly didn't stop there. Indeed, it was repeatedly reviewed and discussed over the next two years. It was discussed by civil servants, it was discussed by the Military, it was discussed in the House of Commons, it was discussed in the House of Lords, and it was discussed by the War Cabinet too. Indeed, although ringers never knew it, even the King himself entered into the discussions.

But how he did *that*, we'll be looking at in Chapter 7.

We've talked a lot about invasion in these chapters, and certainly the Government fostered the belief that the threat was a real and dangerous one. But did they and the Military really believe that a successful invasion – or even a half-decent attempt – was a serious possibility?

It seems that some of them did and some of them didn't, and Churchill himself – as we'll see in Chapter 4 – was among the didn'ts. *But preparations had to be made either way, and sea defences were constructed and plans made both for an attempted invasion and for a partially successful one. A second line of defence was constructed, and teams of soldiers disguised as civilians were trained in how to remain on the wrong side of that second line and engage in sabotage.*

But whether any invasion attempt ***could*** *have been partially successful, is something military historians are divided on; and as with all battles and military campaigns, there are endless analyses of what* ***did*** *happen and what* ***might*** *have happened. Certainly, Hitler wanted to take over the UK, and certainly he instructed his commanders to prepare for invasion. Certainly, too, he took all the major military decisions himself, even when his commanders and* *military advisers thought he was being completely unrealistic. Even more important, the Germans built up a huge armada of boats to ferry tens of thousands of troops and tens of thousands of tons of equipment across the Channel; and this German document states Hitler's intention explicitly.*

> **"i) General Aim**
>
> **The Supreme Commander has ordered the services to make preparations for a forced landing in England. The aim of this attack is to eliminate the Mother Country as a base for continuing the war against Germany, and, if it should be necessary, to carry out a complete occupation.**
>
> **The order to execute this operation depends on the political situation. Preparations are to be made in such a way that the operation can be carried out from 15th September.**
>
> **While continuing with its occupation duties in France and maintaining the security of the other fronts, the Army's task will be to land strong forces in Southern England, defeat the English army, and seize the capital. Other areas of England will be occupied as opportunity permits."**

But intending to invade is one thing, and successfully invading is another, not least because there were serious issues about the quality of the invasion fleet itself. In large part it consisted of barges taken from the canals of France and Holland – what the War Office papers refer to as a ***barge-borne invasion*** *– but although they were being adapted to carry tanks and equipment, there were serious questions about their strength, power and manoeuvrability at* *sea. Second, Hitler genuinely expected most of the British population to be in favour of surrendering. The invasion depended on* **the political situation**, *as the document put it. And third, since the barges would be travelling at extremely slow speeds, they would be very vulnerable, especially to air attack. So the* ***English Air Force*** *would have to be destroyed first as our German document went on to explain.*

> **"ii) General Plan.**
>
> **(a) The Luftwaffe will destroy the English Air Force and the armament production which supports it, and it will achieve air superiority. The Navy will provide mine-free passages and, supported by the Luftwaffe, will bar the flanks of the crossing-sectors."**

But of course, the English Air Force ***wasn't*** *destroyed – and the British general public weren't clamouring to surrender either – and it was immediately apparent, even to Hitler, that an invasion after losing the Battle of Britain just wasn't possible. What was more, the British* **knew** *that was Hitler's view, as Frederick Winterbotham of the* Secret Intelligence Service *recalled.*

> **"I think the most important signal we had decrypted through ULTRA right at the beginning of the Battle of Britain, was Goering establishing his strategy with his commanders. He told them that they were to fly over Britain and bring the whole of the Royal Air Force up to battle, because only in that way could it be destroyed in the time they had.**
>
> **That was the key for Dowding – to fight the**

> **battle with very small units every time they came over – gradually wearing them down and always having aeroplanes to send up. It became evident that Hitler and his generals wouldn't contemplate invasion unless they had absolute control of the air over the Channel."**

So by late September 1940, an invasion attempt had become very unlikely. But in June, the Battle of Britain hadn't even started – let alone been won – and it wasn't at all clear that it ***would*** *be won. So supposing it had been* ***lost****, could an invasion by sea have succeeded then?*

Well, military historians argue about that too, and of course, we simply don't know. But all the indications are that it couldn't, and that Churchill knew it couldn't. The essential point was that in the 1940s, invading anywhere by sea against strong opposition would have been extraordinarily difficult. Lord Louis Mountbatten of Burma – Head of Combined Operations *until October 1943 – recalled how Churchill summed up the difficulties in 1941 when he put him in charge of the preparations for D-Day.*

> **"In October 1941, I was recalled from Pearl Harbor to take up the job in charge of combined operations by Mr. Winston Churchill. The very first day I reported to him, he said, 'You are to prepare the invasion of Europe for unless we can land and fight Hitler and beat his forces on land, we shall never win this war. You must devise and design the appliances, the landing craft and the technique to enable us to effect the landing against the opposition and to maintain ourselves there. You must take the**

most brilliant officers to plan this great operation. You must take bases to use as training establishments where you can train the Navy, Army and Air Force to work as a single entity. The whole of the south coast of England is a bastion of defence against the invasion of Hitler. We've got to turn it into the springboard for our attack. There are three conditions necessary for a successful invasion. First, obviously, to get ashore against no matter what opposition. Secondly, having got ashore to stay ashore no matter what the weather conditions. Thirdly, to stop the enemy from building up his forces against you quicker than you can, otherwise he'll throw you back into the sea.' "

And indeed, although the D-Day landings were ultimately successful, they very easily might not have been. As the detailed records show, despite the massive British and American military resources and the extremely effective deception of the Germans by British counter intelligence – not to mention the very fortunate weather conditions – in the end, it was still very much touch and go.

But even if an invasion ***had*** *been possible in September 1940, by October 1940 Hitler had cancelled his invasion plans* ***until further notice****, and the British knew – although, of course, they didn't want the Germans to* ***know*** *that they knew. Certainly, Hitler could have changed his mind and perhaps he might even have been likely to, but preparations to start an invasion anew would have taken a good deal of time, and this March 1941 letter from the War Office to Norman Brook at the Ministry of Home Security makes that clear.*

"With reference to your letter of the 14th February to Colonel Hollis on plans for getting the public keyed up to a proper state of preparedness, I have held up the answer to your letter until the Chiefs of Staff have considered a report by the Vice Chiefs on the scale and likelihood of invasion.

The Chiefs of Staff consider that the Germans could not mount a full scale invasion without giving a number of indications of their final preparations. Starting from the position at the present moment, they think we shall obtain these indications during a period of about two or three weeks prior to the earliest date at which the expeditions could be launched. It must be emphasised, however, that the fact that all preparations have been made does not necessarily signify that invasion will be launched immediately, or even that it will be launched at all. It might be kept mounted for a considerable period, during which it could start at any time and at a few hours notice. We cannot be sure of getting information of the start of the expeditions."

So if invasion was so unlikely – and if an unexpected invasion was less likely still, why have a church bell warning system at all? Not surprisingly, there was a great deal more to the ringing ban than met the eye ...

4. The Truth!

I really love a conspiracy theory. I really love finding out we've all been hoodwinked. My idea of bliss is learning that a long accepted fact of history is total moonshine. Sad, I know, but there it is.

So what about that *church-bells-as-a-warning-of-invasion* business? Can you turn that into total moonshine too? Please make an old man happy.

John
Dorset

Well, I can't turn it into *total* moonshine, but I can at least let a good deal of moonlight in. And as you rightly suppose, it really wasn't as simple as it at first seemed.

May and June 1940

So just to recap, in Chapter 3 we saw that the idea of using church bells as a warning of invasion came initially from the Military; and to begin with, the Home Office, the War Office and just about everyone else, took a very dim view indeed. The disagreement arose because, in wartime, the Army and the Government have very different responsibilities. The Army are primarily concerned with attacking and defending; and although they're also concerned with getting supplies and maintaining supply lines, they're not much concerned about *winning the peace*, and they're inclined to see civilians as an irritation that gets in their way.

But the Government has to think of a great deal more than just winning battles; and although some of the greatest disasters of history arose when governments *didn't*, in the Second World War they *did*, and they did it extremely well. They realised that massive industrial production and massive agricultural output were needed every bit as much as soldiers; and to achieve that massive production and output, there had to be a vast number of willing and happy workers. And apart from everything else, those workers had to get enough sleep.

Interestingly, the Military had to be repeatedly reminded of this. Army soldiers were full time and received considerably more rations per head than the general population. Home Guard soldiers, on the other hand, got no pay and no extra rations, yet they worked very long hours at their day jobs in addition to their Home Guard duties. The church bell warning system looked likely to cause massive disruption to their sleep patterns and so cause a significant decrease in their effectiveness.

A Truce

But despite that, it was approved, and to understand why, we need to look at what else was happening in May and June 1940. The country was in a dreadful position. The British Expeditionary Force had been driven out of France; France itself was falling; Italy was entering the War; and the Germans looked set to discover that *Enigma* had been cracked. In every way things looked very grim indeed, and with an invasion attempt by sea now thought to be imminent, many wondered whether Britain could survive at all.

So a fair chunk of the population – including many in positions of authority – thought a negotiated surrender was the best option. A ***truce*** was what they called it, and the strongest advocate was the British Foreign Secretary, Lord Halifax. Halifax had been one of the two front runners to become Prime Minister in May 1940 when Neville Chamberlain had resigned, and he'd actually been Chamberlain's preferred choice. But he'd ruled himself out because he wouldn't have had a seat in the House of Commons, and because he didn't want a full time job as he liked to go fox hunting two days a week.

Halifax was also a devout member of the Church of England; and Clement Attlee – then leader of the Labour Party and Deputy Prime Minister – once mentioned to a friend, "**Queer bird, Halifax ... all hunting and holy communion**." But *queer bird* or not, Halifax and other senior ministers were so vehement in advocating a truce that the War Cabinet actually met nine times over the three days of 26th to 28th May 1940 to discuss it.

And although by getting the support of the Outer Cabinet, Churchill was able to continue the War, he fully understood the real danger of losing public support; and without massive public support he simply couldn't continue. And *that* meant he needed something strong, immediate and lasting to maintain the nation's morale and bolster the nation's will to resist.

Morale

With hindsight it's easy to underestimate this, but at the time it was an absolutely major issue. We've all been subjected to so much propaganda, that it's become part of our national identity to believe that morale was no problem and could never have become one. Since everything eventually turned out OK, the rose-tinted spectacles of hindsight seem to show that the whole country was behind Churchill and his *We-will-never-surrender* message.

But in that extremely dark time, the reality just wasn't that simple, and since the Government itself had been starkly divided, they knew that public support for resistance in the face of overwhelming military force could dissipate rapidly. So repeated boosts to morale were essential, and the suppression of dissent was essential too. A confidential memo issued on 11th June 1940 – the same week as the announcement of the ringing ban – makes this clear. It was sent by General Ironside, Commander-in-Chief, Home Forces, to his senior officers, and it shows how worried the Government was.

> **GENERAL HEADQUARTERS**
> **HOME FORCES**
>
> **The war has come closer to us owing to the German occupation of North-east France. This fact should be turned to advantage because the British people are at their best when faced with danger. We are now faced with danger. The attitude that there is little we can do against the invincible German war machine must be stamped out with the utmost brutality.**

Boosting Morale

There's a ruthlessness to this memo that scarcely fits the *we're-all-in-it-together-and-of-one-mind* idea that the Government was at such pains to foster. Certainly Churchill never made any speeches suggesting that public dissent would be ***stamped out with the utmost brutality***, but he *did* make speeches – and extraordinarily powerful and carefully crafted speeches they were too – which were expressly designed to boost public morale.

And put in that context, there's no doubt that the Order

banning the ringing of bells except in the case of invasion, was itself a significant and lasting morale booster. At a stroke, it not only brought home how immediate and personal the danger was, it also created a warning that was both supremely British and thoroughly *muddling through* at the same time. It had the feeling of being a signal *by* the people *to* the people.

And even more, it kept the threat of invasion constantly in the public mind. As far as the population was concerned, while the ringing ban continued, an invasion attempt was a possibility, and they had to keep working to prevent it. They had to be strong and determined in everything they did because Hitler could come at any time.

Put simply, Churchill fully understood the need to create in everyone's minds the idea that the War was not an overseas war but a home war. He knew the clear lesson of history that public support for a lengthy overseas war soon evaporates; and unlike the great majority of politicians, Churchill was supreme in understanding the lessons of history.

Jock Colville

For obvious reasons he never told the public he was playing up the invasion fear for propaganda purposes, but he certainly told people in private, and one of these was Jock Colville. We met Jock Colville and his completely unauthorised private diary in the last chapter, and in his entry for Friday 12th July 1940, he records how he has been at *Chequers* with the Prime Minister and others. During the course of a suitably alcoholic dinner, Churchill speaks of the War generally.

> **"He emphasised that the great invasion scare (which we only ceased to deride six weeks ago) is serving a most useful purpose:**

it is well on the way to providing us with the finest offensive army we have ever possessed and it is keeping every man and woman tuned to a high pitch of readiness. He does not wish the scare to abate therefore, and although personally he doubts whether invasion is a serious menace he intends to give that impression, and to talk about long and dangerous vigils, etc., when he broadcasts on Sunday."

So we've found a clear and solid reason why Churchill approved the ringing ban, and it has nothing whatever to do with the reasons given to the public. It explains, too, why Churchill went against the unanimous view of his Ministers and civil servants. What's more, Churchill – as with most of his major decisions – appears to have been absolutely right. The public were not only well and truly hoodwinked, they *remained* well and truly hoodwinked.

Indeed, one of the more remarkable facts about the War is that, while a great many people doubted whether the ringing ban was either practicable or sensible, they *never* doubted that the ban's very existence meant that invasion was a serious and ever-present threat. For nearly three years, regular discussions on the ban took place at the highest level – in the War Cabinet, by senior military chiefs, and even involving the King himself – but the risk of public complacency was always the major reason for keeping it going.

The Military

But what about the ostensible military reasons – was there some basis to *them*, particularly in the beginning? Well, it's not entirely clear what the Military *did* want in the beginning.

Their first idea seems to have been that church bells should be rung everywhere when parachutists started dropping; and faced with the possibility of a full-on invasion of 80,000 troops, that wasn't such a bad idea. Using parachutists as the advance guard of an invasion was a fairly new strategy, and when the Russians and Germans had used it, they'd been extremely successful. So in the Summer of 1940, parachutists were a serious concern.

Intelligence reports about invasion plans abounded too, and they all had to be taken seriously even when they were as preposterous as this one from 27th May 1940.

> **"Following message from CLOVER. Traveller just arrived here from Germany reports that as soon as Channel Ports have been taken Germans intend launching attack on English Coast under cover of darkness or fog as follows, each soldier is equipped with light Metal Cylindrical canoe electrically driven and capable of carrying one man with full equipment. Very large numbers will be employed working in connection with parachute troops and bombing planes. These operations have already been practised in the vicinity of Hamburg."**

Giving Warning

But even supposing a full-on invasion had actually taken place, what sort of warning would church bells have made? And here we meet all sorts of problems. First and foremost, why bother anyway? Most people either had a radio or they lived near someone who did; and they listened to it assiduously for War news. So a radio announcement would have reached the great bulk of the population very quickly indeed. Of course, that didn't cover the situation where parachutists were spotted in a particular area and the appropriate people needed to be notified quickly, but since the bells could only be rung following instructions from a senior officer, the appropriate people must already have known.

And then again, how would the bells be rung? Someone had to get into the church – which might very well be locked while the vicar was visiting his parishioners – and whoever that someone was, they also had to know how to handle a bell, if only to chime it. That would have been a real problem, and Dorothy L. Sayers – the author of *The Nine Tailors* and other Lord Peter Wimsey books – wrote to *The Daily Telegraph* saying so.

> **"... to order a completely raw hand to run along and ring a church bell is rather like ordering him to run along and milk a savage and reluctant cow; the net result would be much the same, except that the bell can kick much harder than the cow."**

And the Yorkshire Association wrote to the War Office making similar points – although in rather more sober terms – and the War Office took the letter very seriously, although without changing anything.

> **"I feel that points 3, 4 and 5 of the attached letter from the Yorkshire Association of Change Ringers, coming as it does from a responsible body who should be better informed than anybody else on the question of church bells, should receive consideration."**

What to Do

Then there was the problem that much of the country was not within earshot of a church bell – particularly during the day when factory and traffic noise was so loud. But the supreme difficulty was: what on earth were the public supposed to do when they *heard* bells? It was like coming across a sign saying, "Beware Falling Rocks." Everyone knew there was a problem but no one had the least idea what to do about it. On the many occasions when bells were rung by mistake this became obvious, and the experience of Harold Toms of Wareham was typical.

> **"I think it was in 1940 that my father came into my bedroom to wake me up. There was a bell ringing so we got dressed and went out to investigate. The bell was not a church bell but one at an old alms house which was just down the road from us. When we got there a load of people were milling around with no idea as to what to do and no idea on whose authority the bell had been rung. After a couple of hours dad and I decided to go back and catch up on our sleep."**

Indeed, no advice on what to do if bells were heard, was given until 1941, and even then, the public were essentially told, "Do nothing; stay where you are." Quite rightly, long columns of fleeing refugees would have been a major obstacle to the Army.

The Experts

But it seems that once the initial scare was past, the top ranks of the Army were as doubtful about church bell signalling as everyone else. In early 1943 Lord Mottistone reported these views of a senior officer.

> **"Of course, as a military expedient it is; frankly ridiculous. ... If you want a warning to warn you of the presence of the enemy, certain things are essential. The first is that you must know whence that warning emanated; secondly, you must know that the means of giving the warning are in good order. In the case of church bells, neither of these conditions is fulfilled. If I am to be asked to regard this as a serious matter, then I must ask that all the 12,000 churches shall be properly guarded by the military, in order to ensure at all moments that the bells are not rung by Fifth Columnists or reckless people. Secondly, I must be given authority to put those 12,000 belfries in order. ... I am advised that in a great number of cases either the ropes would break, or the bells would fall through the roof on to the heads of the people below."**

And apart from the last sentence that all made perfect sense. Indeed, even the last sentence made *some* sense in that many churches in London had been severely damaged by bombing, so attempting to ring their bells really *would* have been dangerous.

A Secret Change

But what the officer *didn't* tell Lord Mottistone was that a change of instructions had already been issued in September 1940 – or at least, a major clarification of the existing instructions had been issued. Previously, the great bulk of the Army – like the great bulk of civilians – thought that bells meant invasion, but the events of the night of 7th September convinced everyone that universal ringing, whether or not triggered by a genuine invasion, would be disastrous. Stirring up the entire nation in the face of a raid in a limited area would cause real and immediate problems, both to the Military and to industrial production, and stirring up the nation for no reason at all, would cause needless panic.

So although as far as the public believed, the arrangements for ringing the bells remained unaltered, they changed immediately. This memo of 12th September 1940 from Colonel White, the Fortress Commander at Newcastle-on-Tyne, to his three local Chief Constables, is typical.

SECRET.

SUBJECT:– RINGING OF CHURCH BELLS

To:– Chief Constable, Newcastle-on-Tyne.
Chief Constable, Gosforth.
Chief Constable, Gateshead-on-Tyne

Dear Sir,

The following instructions have now been received regarding the ringing of church bells.

G.H.Q. Home Forces have ordered that Church Bells will NOT be rung as a general alarm for the turning out of personnel of the H.G. in the case of invasion.

Church Bells will only be rung as a local alarm to indicate that an actual invasion by sea or by air is taking place in that particular locality.

The ringing of the bells of one Church will NOT be repeated by the bells of another

Church unless a landing is also taking place in that locality.

In consequence of the above order from G.H.Q. Home Forces all previous orders regarding ringing of Church Bells are hereby cancelled and the attached orders substituted.

Colonel
Fortress Commander, Newcastle

The Perception

It's clear from this memo that Colonel White and his Chief Constables – like the general public – had indeed thought that bells were to be rung everywhere or nowhere. The memo we saw on page 56 may well have *claimed* to be a clarification – and G.H.Q. probably even thought it was – but in reality it was nothing of the sort.

It's clear from a great many other papers that the various geographical sections of the army – the various *Commands* – had each been giving their own individual and very different instructions. So Colonel White and his Chief Constables hadn't got the wrong end of the stick at all. They'd simply been acting on local instructions.

But even if the Military were now of one mind and accepted that the bells only called out the Home Guard to deal with isolated incidents and small scale raids, the public still remained firmly convinced that church bells meant invasion. A War Office memo of February 1941 sums this up perfectly.

"The restrictions on the use of church bells are perfectly clear in our minds, but they

are not clear to the civil population taken at large. Conversations with people in all walks of life, articles in the papers, 'fan mail' and questions in the House, all go to show that people expect to be warned of invasion by the ringing of church bells. Nothing that we can do will remove this impression. People are keyed up to hear church bells as a signal of national alarm. This nation-wide expectation cannot be safely neglected."

The BBC

In fact I've been unable to find any evidence that the War Office *was* trying to *remove the impression*, and certainly there's abundant evidence that the Government was actively trying to maintain it without actually lying. But even those who fully understood the new rules couldn't see much sense in them, and in 1943 the Archbishop of York referred to them in a speech in the House of Lords. His point was that the ban was absurd because in large cities no one knew where one parish stopped and the next started, whilst in the country, much of each parish couldn't hear the bells anyway.

But what the Archbishop *didn't* know was that the Government understood this completely and had recognised it from at least September 1940. There was a good deal of discussion of what to do if there was a parachute raid on London – although it was always assumed it would be a limited raid designed to attack key installations rather than a prelude to invasion. All the same, church bells got only a perfunctory mention before being immediately dismissed as hopeless, and instead, this secret but never implemented message was drafted for broadcasting by the BBC.

SECRET

INSTRUCTIONS TO BE GIVEN TO THE PUBLIC THROUGH THE B.B.C. ON 'ACTION STATIONS'

This is a message for everyone who lives or works in London or may find himself there in the near future. By London is meant the Metropolitan Police District or the City of London.

If invasion comes, London itself might be attacked, perhaps quite suddenly, by air-borne troops landing on open spaces in or near London. If this should happen it might be necessary for a short time to stop all vehicles over a wide area in order that the Military Command, after getting some idea of how the attack was likely to develop, might have the roads clear to deal with it.

The signal for this traffic stop will be the sirens, which will sound their steady note for five minutes, instead of for one minute as they do for the 'All Clear'. On this signal all vehicles must stop, except civil defence and public utility vehicles on vitally urgent service. These must be ready to obey whatever orders the police give.

If you hear this signal, when you are driving a vehicle you must drive up on to the pavement, or, if there is no pavement, to the edge of the road, and wait until the police tell you what to do. Stay with your car, or as

near as you can with safety. Do not immobilise it unless told to do so. Buses and trams will stop as soon they get to the nearest collecting point, where they will await orders. Trains will go on running.

Pedestrians and cyclists need not stop, but should go on to their destinations. Passengers by train who have reached their stations, and passengers by bus whose buses have stopped should also go on to their destinations. If they cannot do this, they should ask permission to wait in a house or other building nearby – and in any case they should not wait in crowds at stations or bus stops.

If you are at home or at work, stay there; obey the 'Stand firm' orders.

The traffic stop is not likely to last long. As soon as the Military Command have sized up the situation and decided what area they want to keep cleared, traffic will be released everywhere else. The signal will be cancelled by instructions given over the wireless and by the police in person through loudspeakers."

So in London at least, an entirely effective but alternative communication system wouldn't have used bells at all.

In Parliament

And as the War moved on, the effectiveness of bells as a warning exercised many people. Not only did they write numerous letters to the papers, they also wrote numerous letters to their M.P.s, and even direct to the Government. Questions were frequently asked in Parliament too, and the reply was always a stonewalling one. Indeed, in many of the replies, the Minister of Home Security seems to have been as baffled as everyone else, and the responsibility was always passed on to the War Office – who simply replied that it was necessary. On one remarkable occasion the Deputy Prime Minister was asked in a supplementary question why it was acceptable for Big Ben to chime but not for bells to be rung. "I have no idea," he replied.

There were questions in the House of Lords too, and Lord Quickswood was one of many who pointed out that bells could still be used as a signal if rung in a different way to normal ringing. Although that said, he pointed it out in that intensely scholarly way then typical of the House of Lords.

> **"It certainly seems to me that people have overlooked ... that there is a great history behind the use of bells for purposes of alarm in cases of public danger or public excitement. In France, for example, it was the bells of Saint-Germain d'Auxerre which started the Massacre of St. Bartholomew, and we do not hear that there was any confusion. We do not hear that devout ladies arrived at the church expecting an early Mass, and accosted the verger and were informed 'No, ma'am, there's no early Mass, it's the Duke of Guise's people, I think, who are ringing the bells; some trouble with the Huguenots, I fancy,' and so the poor ladies had to go home unconsoled by devotion. We hear of nothing of that kind. No confusion arose; the massacre**

> **went forward with its usual businesslike efficiency, quite untroubled by any misapprehension as to the ringing of the bells."**

1941 and After

But despite all pleas, the ringing ban continued, and Government papers make it absolutely clear that the main reason was nothing to do with how effective a church bell warning would be. Instead it was to do with how complacent the public and the Home Guard might become if it was relaxed. The C.-in-C. Home Forces repeated this forcefully over and over again, and Churchill repeatedly agreed – albeit sometimes reluctantly. Indeed, even on 20th April 1943 Churchill wrote in a memo to the Home Security:

> **"Although the ringing of the bells will no longer have the significance of invasion, this idea has been so sedulously inculcated that unexpected ringing at unusual times might cause alarm."**

And yet the very forcefulness of the C.-in-C.'s opposition to lifting the ban – often with very feeble supporting arguments – leaves the impression that he had other, stronger reasons which he couldn't put in writing. So did he?

Aircraft Navigation

Well, just perhaps, he did. There are suggestions that he *may* have been concerned that enemy aircraft could use church bells for navigation; and if that sounds far fetched, the important issue would not have been whether German aircraft *could* have navigated that way, but whether they just *might*.

Conducting a successful war isn't a matter of guarding against *certainties*, it's a matter of guarding against *possibilities*, and the more catastrophic those possibilities, the more they need to be guarded against. So could German pilots have simply *listened* for bells?

Well, in the First World War pilots had certainly reported being able to hear church bells fairly clearly, but by 1940 planes were flying much higher and were much noisier. Even so, pilots just *might* have been able to hear bells if the Germans had manufactured special listening equipment or had manufactured special planes – or if they'd used gliders.

And gliders were seen as a significant threat anyway because Germany had invested heavily in glider technology following the restrictions placed on it after the First World War. The British believed that huge gliders could be released over France but still reach England easily, and there was a serious worry that a substantial invasion force could be delivered that way.

Radar

But the more likely concern was radar, which was then in its infancy. The British system was good and it developed quickly after 1939, but to begin with, it wasn't completely directional and it required considerable expertise to interpret the signals. Indeed, even in 1942 when the American radar team notified their High Command that Japanese planes were heading towards Pearl Harbor, the American High Command simply assumed the team were misinterpreting the signals and took no action.

Many countries were researching and developing radar independently, and the British simply didn't know what the German radar was capable of. Experts say it could *theoretically* have detected large bells being rung full circle, so although we now know that it couldn't, in 1940 it might have been a possibility the Military wanted to guard against.

Prime Minister's Questions

So it does indeed seem that for at least one reason – and just possibly two – the ban was completely sensible after all. And if there was some small incidental benefit concerning parachutists landing in country areas, so much the better.

But there is yet one more piece of evidence that the whole idea was just a smoke screen designed to keep public morale high. In April 1943 when the ban was being lifted in stages, an intriguing exchange took place in the House of Commons during Prime Minister's Questions. Until then, questions on the ban had normally been answered by someone other than the Prime Minister, but on this occasion Churchill was present when the M.P. for Ayr, Lieutenant Colonel Sir Thomas Moore, rose to ask a question.

> ***Sir Thomas Moore*:**
>
> **May I ask the Prime Minister what arrangements have been made to replace the ringing of church bells as a warning of invasion?**
>
> ***The Prime Minister*:**
>
> **We have come to the conclusion that this particular method of warning was redundant, and not in itself well adapted to present conditions of the War.**
>
> ***Sir Thomas Moore*:**
>
> **Will my right hon. Friend say what alternative arrangements have been made? Will he consider the use of sirens?"**
>
> ***The Prime Minister*:**
>
> **I said that we came to the conclusion that**

this particular method was redundant. Therefore replacement does not arise."

Of course, we now know that this last statement was untrue as a replacement signal via the BBC had been prepared years earlier. But all the same, the answer was completely uncontroversial and no doubt planned in advance. But then Churchill added what appears to have been an off-the-cuff witticism.

"For myself, I cannot help feeling that anything like a serious invasion would be bound to leak out."

And a very funny witticism it was, and even the Parliamentary reporter recorded that M.P.s laughed. But that must surely be the closest Churchill ever came to admitting that the whole *warning-by-bells* idea had always been no more than a cover story to conceal something far more important.

Struggling On

But intriguing as all that is to us now, in June 1940 it was of no importance to ringers at all. What *was* important – or, at least, what was important to those ringers who weren't in the services or engaged in war work all hours of the day and night – was something to take the place of normal ringing. And *that* is what we'll be looking at next time.

For me, the most fascinating aspects of ringing history are the ways ringing fitted into the major events and everyday life of the time. The Second World War was certainly a major event, but the history of everyday life is just as interesting, and nowadays, lots of attention is given to that. Even so, if we were suddenly whisked back into an earlier century, there would be lots of things that would hit us forcefully even though we were expecting them.

For example, if we went back to the time of Chapter 8 and rang with William Laughton in early eighteenth century London, we'd be forcibly struck that the great majority of women of child bearing age were pregnant; and we'd be horrified to see how very young many of those pregnant girls were. We'd be horrified, too, to find that child abuse and child prostitution were then considered entirely normal and acceptable.

In a more mundane way, if we went back to the time of Chapter 19 and rang in Sir Arthur Heywood's Midland Counties Association of the 1890s, we'd be much struck that many of the men not only wore hats and caps but were carrying walking sticks even though they had no real use for them. At that time, a single walking stick manufacturer in London had premises of sixty thousand square feet and employed five hundred skilled workers.

Similarly, if we went back to the time of Chapter 11 and joined the Oldbury ringers on their horse brake outing, we'd be much struck that they didn't just sing songs on the way home, they also recited poems to each other. And we'd be intrigued that they carried books of comic recitations from which they read extracts.

And in just the same way, if we went back to the time of the Second World War – or just after – we'd be struck not only by all the men still wearing caps and hats, but by the enormous amount of smoke everywhere.

There was smoke in the houses because it regularly blew back from sitting room fires. There was smoke in the streets because everyone heated their houses with coal, and because all the factories and power stations used coal too. And there was smoke by the railways because the coal fired steam locomotives created great columns of blackness and smuts that coated the line-side houses – and their washing – with a blanket of grease and dirt.

And yet most astonishing of all, on top of all the atmospheric pollution that was killing tens of thousands of people annually, most adults smoked cigarettes too. So there was smoke ***inside*** *public buildings as well as out, and it wasn't just a trace of smoke, but a thick, choking fog that made the eyes sting and the clothes stink, and did appalling damage to the lungs.*

Indeed, the fact that most people were content to make the air inside their pubs, cafes and church halls even more unbreathable than the air outside, seems to us modern, non-smoking ringers as daft beyond measure; but that was how it was.

So in the next chapter, when the ringers of 1940 are giving up their ringing for a ramble on the downs followed by a darts match in the church hall, do remember that the atmosphere in there was something shocking. So it wasn't just the absence of ringing that they had to put up with ...

5. Handbells, Billiards and Dinner Gongs

Last October I went to a chrysanthemum show. There were single blooms the size of melons, and one chap spent an hour telling me how he'd adjusted every petal on every one of his blooms the night before. So, jokingly, I asked what he did in the winter; and he spent another hour telling me about propagation.

Then he said, "But in November I *do* have a week's holiday." And lowering his voice he added, "You see, unlike the others here, *I* believe there's life *outside* of chrysanthemums."

And I thought, "I'm like that with ringing," and I couldn't imagine living without it. So here's a history question. Whatever did all the ringers do during the War-time ban?

P.B.
Sussex

A jolly good history question it is too. But something else comes first, because even before the ringers could think about what to do later, many of them faced an immediate and far more tricky problem. They all believed – because that was what they'd been told – that the ban had taken effect immediately. But they'd nonetheless left their bells *up* – as in those days a great many bands always left them up, often for months on end. Health and safety wasn't much of an issue then, and besides, everyone expected to ring on the following Sunday as normal.

Leaving them up indefinitely would have been a problem just by itself, but the ringing-for-invasion system added a much greater danger still. A non-ringer might be directed by the police or military to enter a ringing chamber without a clue of what was involved, and then simply pull a rope. And the result could be fatal.

In Mitcham

In some villages the ringers took the sensible course of telling everyone what was going to happen, and then ringing the bells quickly down. We now know that that was perfectly legal even though they didn't know it then, and the local policeman sensibly turned a blind eye. Other bands muffled their bells or tied the clappers – dangerous though that was with the bells still up – and then rang them down in silence. But a few churches sought official permission.

And although this seems curious to us now, in 1940 it wasn't curious. Another Order enabled factories to seek official permission to test the safety valves on their boilers – something they were required to do by law – as long as they notified the police and general public first. They had to notify the police directly, and the public through newspapers and by local announcements.

So the bands that sought official permission to ring down, were given it in the same way. The public had to be notified by announcements on the national radio and in the press, and everyone living nearby had to be told personally. Mitcham in South London recorded exactly this process in their parish magazine.

> **"All the world now knows that Mitcham Parish Church has a peal of bells. This has happened because the ringers at the end of their weekly practice left the bells 'up' on the night before a regulation was issued that church bells were not to be rung except in warning of invasion. Accordingly, notice that they were to be rung down had to be given on the wireless, in the newspapers and by word of mouth. The officials at the Ministry in London evidently like to think of Mitcham as still a place of lavender and liquorice, of camomile and the squirting cucumber, as their letter giving instructions about the ringing down speaks of 'Church bells at Mitcham *Village* Church.' Alas, we can hardly style Mitcham a village any longer."**

When Left Up

In many churches, though, no one was prepared to go to all that bother, and the bells were simply left up for what turned out to be an astonishing two and a half years. Indeed, in some towers, they were left up and unrung for more than five years. No one in those towers was apparently worried about the danger, and besides, there was a war on. It's possible that people were injured as a result, but if so, it was never publicised and there's no record of it.

All the same, leaving bells up and unrung for so many years had its own problems. Some of them filled up with rainwater which poured down through the ceiling when they were eventually pulled off, but in London there was a much more disturbing and spooky result. Many churches there were bombed during the Blitz, and many caught fire and burnt down. The stays and sliders – being made of ash – burnt far more quickly than the frames – being made of oak or cast iron; and once they'd given way, the bells rang themselves down before melting or breaking into pieces. So in the midst of the bombing, sheltering Londoners could hear bells ringing eerily in empty and burning churches.

Making the Best of It

But once the ringing down had been sorted out, ringers started looking to the longer term. They all wanted to ring, and for many of them the listening aspect wasn't anywhere near as important as the physical and intellectual aspects. *Those* were what they craved, and if their bells made no sound, so what?

So for many ringers the solution was simple; take all the clappers out and then carry on as normal. Or, at least, take all the clappers out but one. *One* clapper had to be left in to give the warning of invasion when the time came. So adverts started appearing in *The Ringing World* like this one from the North Staffordshire Association.

> **"A meeting will be held at Longton on Saturday, August 24th. Bells (7), without clappers ..."**

And this one from the Hertford County Association.

> **"Meeting on Saturday, August 17th, at St. Peter's, St. Albans at 3 p.m. ... 'silent' tower bells. Learners, here's a fine opportunity to learn ropesight!"**

And all that meant that a great number of silent practices took place throughout the War notwithstanding that – as we saw in the last chapter – swinging bells *just may* have been what the Military wanted to prevent. Many of these silent practices were very productive too, and many people not only learnt to handle a bell, they also learnt to ring methods to a high standard. Peter Rock recorded what happened in Eardisland in Herefordshire.

> **"By the time the war started the old band of ringers who only rang Grandsire Doubles, was beginning to fall apart and Leslie set about raising a band of youngsters. Sadly the ban was upon us before we started – but all was not lost. We removed the clappers from 1, 2, 4, 5 and 6 and made a wooden clapper stay to secure the third's clapper. It was nearest to the door and was maintained in availability to the Home Guard in the event of invasion. We practised several times a week, there were seven or eight of us altogether."**

A Dinner Gong

But although silent bells were a reasonable second best as far as ringers were concerned, they didn't do anything for congregations. Tradition had it that on certain occasions a real bell was essential, and when that was so, something desperate had to be done. The local newspaper of Alton in Hampshire reported an induction.

> **"When a vicar is inducted to his parish, he has to toll the church bell as part of the ceremony. Defence Regulations recently prevented the Revd. G. Hutchinson, the new vicar of Alton, from carrying out that part of the ceremony at his induction. Instead he pulled lightly on the rope, without sounding the bell, whilst at the same time striking vigorously on a dinner gong."**

In fact, one of the more peculiar side effects of the War was that Bishops gave special permission for new vicars *not* to ring a bell during their induction. Instead, they needed only take hold of a bellrope and then release it.

Association Alternatives

But whatever local bands did or didn't do, Associations were seriously worried. They all quickly agreed that members in the services needn't pay subscriptions, so finances were set to become tight. And besides, if attendances dwindled below a sustainable level, some Associations might have to fold completely, so they did their very best to think up attractive, non-ringing entertainments that would do instead of ringing.

By and large, a lot of those entertainments don't sound very inspiring. Here's one from the Yorkshire Association.

> **"Church House available during afternoon and evening for handbells, billiards, etc. Conducted ramble ..."**

And this Surrey Association meeting doesn't sound very exciting either.

> **"*The Surrey Association Meeting*. The ringers will meet at Boxhill Station at 3.30 p.m. and enjoy a pleasant walk through the country. Afterwards, each tower will supply a darts team. If wet, handbells will be available in the church hall."**

In fact, rambles continued to feature throughout the ban, and billiards and darts put in regular appearances too; but this meeting organised by the Norwich Diocesan Association really does seem to have been scraping the barrel.

"Business Meeting to discuss plan of campaign and incidental problems at 4.45, followed by social evening including the showing of a film in colour by the Rev. A. G. G. Thurlow, taken by him on his recent holiday in Norway and Spitzbergen, and the use of handbells."

Handbells

But although handbell sessions seemed like a good idea to begin with – and although they continued to feature regularly after business meetings – in most cases they met with only limited success. The *Ringing World* editor advocated them enthusiastically and repeatedly, and some local bands even started change ringing sessions with one bell per person, but these soon fizzled out. Some bands tried their hand at double handed ringing but very few met with success. The truth was that doubled handed ringing was a specialist activity which wasn't something that could be picked up easily, particularly when none of the band had any experience.

Various people put paragraphs of handbell advice in *The Ringing World*, but many of the paragraphs were only short and none of them were easy to understand. So although handbell sessions after Association business meetings existed in theory, most members just chatted. Indeed, some Branches admitted it openly – or *fairly* openly – and adverts appeared promising "**handbells and social intercourse**" or "**handbell practice and social chinwag**."

And meeting reports sometimes told the truth and sometimes didn't. The Bristol Rural Branch of the Gloucester and Bristol Association recorded that, "**Some members enjoyed handbells and others told stories of bellringing**

days," and the Furness and Lake District Branch of the Lancashire Association recorded that, "**Handbells were tried but everybody was out of practice, even the one-handers**."

The Hinckley District of the Midland Counties Association – who were never a group to shy away from confronting a difficult issue – reported that, "**Untiring efforts have been made by the district officers to make handbell ringing interesting ..**," but that showing a locally made film of members ringing doubtful Grandsire Caters – accompanied by the enthusiastic catcalls of the watchers – had been more successful.

The Yorkshire Association AGM interspersed musical items and a conjuring show with their handbell ringing; and reports of spontaneous darts matches, games of bowls and group singing, were common. Essentially, the frequently used phrase, "**handbells available**," accurately summed things up.

The Law

But when handbells *were* rung, there was an extra problem. As we saw in Chapter 2, when the War started and gas attacks were expected, separate warning signals were devised to differentiate gas attacks from bombing raids. ARP wardens had to whirl a rattle at the start of an attack, and ring a handbell to signal the *all clear*.

These ARP handbells were like school handbells but were inscribed with the letters "**A.R.P.**" They were manufactured by *Gillett and Johnston* who also manufactured school handbells and the handbells used by factories as fire warnings. So ringing a musical handbell in public – even though it produced a very different sound – became as much an offence as ringing a school bell. The Monk's Kirby meeting of the Warwickshire Guild encountered exactly this problem at *The Denbigh Arms* in August 1940.

"Just before the meeting the hotel proprietor informed the hon. secretary that the police had asked him to see that handbells were not rung as alarm might be caused. It was suggested that permission should be obtained from Rugby Police Station. A 'phone call was put through and permission sought. This was a real teaser. The constable said he would ask the sergeant. The sergeant wondered if we could possibly manage without the handbells. How loud were they? Could they be heard in the street? How long did we intend to ring? Finally the inspector was approached, who, after looking up regulation this and paragraph that, said that we might ring if we took every precaution against alarming the public.

All these precautions to ring handbells in the upper room at the back of a small village hostelry!"

Prosecutions

In fact, many Associations had problems. They arranged handbell practices in church halls and then had the local ARP warden come in and stop them. The bells, said the warden, could be heard faintly outside – especially when the door was opened to let someone in or out – and that wouldn't do at all. The fact that, if anything, handbell ringing signalled the *end* of a gas attack rather than the beginning, didn't seem to matter.

As far as we know, no Association member was ever prosecuted; but other handbell ringers *were*, and they were fined and imprisoned too. Occasionally the person was ringing a handbell as a prank – usually after drinking – but normally it was a tradesman.

The point was that before the War, bread roundsmen, milkmen, crumpet sellers, knife grinders and many other tradesmen, carried a handbell which they rang vigorously to let their customers know they were in the street. It was a system that worked well, and banning tradesmen's handbells inconvenienced both the tradesmen and their customers. And since it gave no real War benefit, many tradesmen just ignored it. But although most local policemen used their common sense and turned a blind eye, some prosecuted.

And prosecution for inappropriate noise-making could result in a serious penalty, especially if – in those extremely racist times – you carried the perceived extra stigma of being Irish. Here's a case from the Midlands.

> **"Sentence of three months' imprisonment was passed at Burton-on-Trent on Michael Dooley, an Irishman, for ringing local church bells. It was stated that alarm was caused, and the matron of an institution locked all the doors. When charged, he said, 'I was trying to see how loud it would ring.'"**

And here's an even worse example of racism from June 1941 when one blow on a bell was said to have threatened the morale of the entire town of Chadderton.

> **"For having rung a bell once at a church in Chadderton, Lancs, an Irishman named James Stewart, a twenty-five-year-old labourer of Oldham, was sentenced to a**

month's imprisonment by the Chadderton magistrates. The charge was brought under the Defence Regulations.

A police inspector said that Stewart was seen by the Rev. Peter Taylor coming down the steps leading from the belfry of the church after Mr. Taylor and others had heard the bell peal once. Stewart's action, said the inspector, might have caused a good deal of work among Civil Defence personnel, in addition to upsetting the morale of the public

Stewart declared that he went into the church to look round, and he touched the bell without meaning to ring it."

Whistle Blowers

And even an ex-soldier blowing a whistle could be fined a substantial amount. Later in the War, whistles were designated as the signal for incendiary bombs, but to begin with they had no special significance in most places although in some villages they were used as air raid warnings. Here's *The Times* from 12th September 1939 – less than a fortnight after the first Order came in. And since sexism was then as rife as racism, it was reported that the women "**ran through the streets**" whilst the men simply "**took shelter**."

"Stated to have thrown a village into a panic by sounding a whistle late at night. Arthur Smith, 60, an Army pensioner, of Shirrell Heath, was fined £5 at Fareham (Hants) Police Court yesterday. He was charged with 'sounding a whistle contrary to the Control of Noise (Defence) Order made on

September 1.' It was stated that as a result of the whistle women ran through the streets shouting that there was a raid and 200 troops in the district were ordered by their commanding officer to take shelter. Police-sergeant West said that in some country districts a whistle was used to indicate the approach of enemy aircraft. The defendant said he had got into an argument and feeling himself in need of police protection blew the whistle."

A Unique First

But getting back to what ringers could do legally, the one activity that *didn't* take place during the silence was peal ringing on tower bells. Or at least, it *probably* didn't. Peals on tied bells wouldn't have been thought right at all, and most ringers had strong views about inappropriate ringing then. But one or two bands of boys just *might* have rung a silent peal secretly, and a few silent quarters might have been rung too. Certainly, the band at Burnham in Buckinghamshire rang a silent 720 on their middle six and then sent an article about it to two local newspapers.

Of course handbell peals were rung, and handbell quarters too, and at Brasted in Kent a quarter in the ringing room provided an opportunity for claiming a unique ringing first.

September 22nd 1940.

Dear Sir,

I am sending you a report of what is, I believe, the first quarter-peal to be rung in an air raid. It was rung on September 21st in Brasted belfry and, as this is, under normal circumstances soundproof, the first

indication the ringers had of the raid was not the siren, but the noise of fighting planes overhead; nevertheless, they carried on, and special praise is due to the conductor, aged 14, who was calling her first quarter-peal of Major, and to the ringer of the tenors, who has been ringing handbells only since the ban.

Simulators

So business absolutely as usual there, and business as usual in other ways too. The ringing simulator as we now know it was decades in the future; but ringers are ever inventive, and quite a few immediately tried to create their own. Bill Gibbons – then a student at Oxford University and who we met in Chapter 2 believing the Germans were invading – recalled an attempt at an electrical arrangement.

"As the new term drew nearer, old acquaintances reappeared in Oxford, and we considered what could be done in spite of the ringing ban. Our first impulse was to devise some scheme whereby New College bells could be rung with clappers lashed but reproducing the sound in the ringing chamber by electrically operated strikers hitting handbells. We used an electric bell mechanism for each tower bell, activated by a metal strip attached to the bell wheel, which brushed past two contacts as the bell reached the balance.

Dick Post made us a beautiful frame on which we mounted the university handbells, each with its own electric mechanism. This

we wired up to the bells in New College tower, and on one Saturday afternoon, many campanological notables gathered for a trial ring. While the mechanism was by no means perfect, it showed distinct possibilities."

Seage's Apparatus

Sadly, this prototype no longer exists, and the same applies to a good many other prototypes which were discussed in great – albeit extremely confusing – detail in *The Ringing World.* Essentially, there were many good ideas but the electrical equipment to make them work properly either wasn't cheap enough or wasn't available in wartime. But there was already a *mechanical* simulator in existence dating from 1876. It was called the *Seage's Apparatus*, and some of those towers that had one, dusted it off and gave it a go.

The ***Seage's Apparatus*** was an extraordinary arrangement invented by a non-ringing Exeter man with the unusual name of Epaphras Seage. It enabled ringers to ring without annoying the neighbours, but it was cumbersome in operation and unsatisfying in result; and since noise abatement wasn't a big issue in 1876, it was decades ahead of it's time. But although it didn't sell well, it was nonetheless extremely clever, and in 1940 a fair number of towers still had one.

In operation, a large chunk of cast iron – shaped like a huge but elegant pair of cow horns – was attached to the frame next to each bell. It was fastened in such a way that it could rock slightly from one side to the other as a cast iron peg – fastened to the headstock – hit it's base as it went past. The result was that at handstroke the cow horns tilted slightly one way, and at backstroke they tilted slightly the other.

And *as* they tilted, a wire was pulled. The wire stretched down into the ringing chamber and it pulled back a little hammer which struck a handbell fastened to the wall behind the appropriate rope. It was undoubtedly very clever and it was reasonably accurate from a striking point of view, but the sound was necessarily thin and unsatisfying, and there was a good deal of rumbling to be heard from the belfry. But it *was* durable and there are still one or two in more or less working order today. Quite how many were used during the War, isn't clear, but *The Glasgow Citizen* sent a reporter up to Glasgow Cathedral to see one in action.

> **"As I climbed the steps I could hear the bells of St. Mary's chiming as clear as if we were back in the ringing days of peace.**
>
> **Behind an oaken door I found the bellringers in their grey stone chamber. Six men, shirt-sleeved, were pulling rhythmically on ropes that ran through holes in the high wooden ceiling above them.**
>
> **High on the stone walls I saw little bells. As the ringers pulled, a hammer struck each bell. But the real bells of St. Mary's, far above in the tower, were silent although they were swinging. Each has been gagged for the duration.**
>
> **The little bells sounded pleasant, though not impressive. But the band were taking them seriously. A campanologist has a lot to remember, and he can't take his mind off his ringing for a moment."**

By Hand

Curiously, though, the most obvious solution to clapperless bells seems only to have occurred to the Central Bucks Branch of the Oxford Diocesan Guild – and even *they* only appear to have tried it the once.

> **"The Central Bucks Branch of the Oxford Diocesan Guild held its annual meeting in the parish of North Marston on Saturday, June 14th. ... A novel experiment was tried with a new form of 'silent apparatus.' Each ringer was provided with a partner armed with a handbell, who struck his bell as the man with the rope pulled off at hand and back stroke. A six-score of Doubles was rung in this way, but the Oxford Guild does not contemplate worrying the Central Council to sanction the ringing of peals by this method."**

Success?

So with all this innovation and effort, how successful *were* Association and Branch meetings during the silent time?

And surprisingly, there's no general answer. A lot of ringers were in the armed forces or the merchant navy, and a lot more were working long hours on war work, both as employees and volunteers. Transport was extremely difficult too, so the numbers able to attend were certainly much reduced. But that affected different Branches very differently.

Some Branches cancelled meetings completely during the ban but others didn't. *Some* reduced their number of meetings during the ban but others didn't. *Some* carried on advertising in *The Ringing World* but others didn't. *Some* meetings were apparently extremely successful – both in attendance and enjoyment – but others apparently weren't. City Branches had transport advantages but air raid *dis*advantages, and rural Branches had transport problems but no air raids – although rural Branches had the extra difficulty that many agricultural workers were working extremely long hours.

So generalisations are hard, but it seems it was the attitude of the Branch Officers and members that made the biggest difference. If they approached the problems in a spirit of optimism and were determined to make the best of things, they succeeded. But if they felt they couldn't succeed, they didn't.

Sadly, though, the *Ringing World* reports contain very little that really illuminate the times. They're distressingly long on what the vicar said in his sermon – almost always the same thing – and they're distressingly long on who was elected to what post. They generally tell us that someone said that times were hard and that someone should do something about the ban, ***but*** they're distressingly short on anything of human interest. Most especially, they almost never mention the tea.

Teas

And that's a shame because providing tea against the backdrop of strict rationing must have been a real nightmare, and it's not surprising that many Branches went to cafes and pubs instead. But many Branches *did* provide tea, and yet they haven't left the slightest indication how. Perhaps they obtained their supplies on the black market or perhaps they went to a friendly farmer. Then again, perhaps the entire local band went really short for a couple of months beforehand. We just don't know.

We *do* know, though, that many Branches insisted on people bringing their own sugar – and often their own food too – but in all that long period, the content of a tea supplied by the local band was only mentioned twice. At Apsley the Western District of the Hertford County recorded that:

> **"Tea was the next item – sausage and mash – very well served, and received due attention."**

And at Tedburn St Mary the Devon Guild reported:

> **"Mrs. Cox [the vicar's wife] and her staff provided an ample tea, pasties, honey and what not. Her cook must be an adept in her craft, overcoming all rationing difficulties, and every hungry ringer was satisfied."**

Reconstruction

But behind an atmosphere that in many ways wasn't so far from normality, was a serious worry. And it was a worry that bothered more and more people as the ban wore on. Would ringing survive at all? Would it even be *allowed* after the War? Would the ban simply continue into peace time? And even if it didn't, would new learners come along?

After all, said the worriers, there were already people advocating that the "**useless bells**" should be melted down and their metal used in the war effort, and a great many bells had already been melted down in Germany. Indeed, the Germans were removing the bells from Holland too, and the German *Metal Mobilisation Board* later described their haul of 4,500 Dutch bells as "**A present from the Dutch people for the struggle against Bolshevism**." Couldn't something similar happen here?

The ban had already passed it's useful life, said the worriers, but it was nonetheless being allowed to continue.

The young male ringers had all gone into the services and many would never come back. And even those who *came* back, might well find better things to do. And on top of all that, the young people of the future probably wouldn't want to learn at all; and even if they did, the public wouldn't want to listen to them.

To some extent these worries had surfaced every twenty-five years or so for a long time – particularly the problems of recruiting – and they've continued to resurface regularly ever since. But in 1942 there was a feeling that *everything* was going to change after the War, some of it for the better and some of it not. *Reconstruction* was the word on the nation's lips, so ringers looked for reconstruction too.

And fortunately, of course, they never found it. But it was a very compelling idea for a while, particularly among younger ringers, and there was much discussion about whether all the territorial Associations should be abolished and replaced by a single national one. This would supposedly create new and improved standards of teaching, abolish the current overlapping of Associations, and "**... eliminate unnecessary expenses**."

Propaganda

The need for an improvement in advertising and public relations was much talked about too – although in those days it went under the rather unfortunate word *propaganda.* It seems that everyone thought propaganda was essential – although they generally thought someone else should do it – and a number of tower captains told of their own, often unsuccessful, attempts in their churches and parishes. To be fair, the Central Council Secretary had been working quite hard communicating with the national press and the Government, but no one seemed to acknowledge that.

And at the same time, non-ringers were active on the P.R. front too. A. P. Herbert, the Oxford University M.P. and author – later to become *Sir* Alan Herbert – wrote a splendid poem for *The Sunday Graphic* including these excellent verses:

> **"Bring back the bells. The bells are dumb**
> **Until the parachuters come:**
> **And even Huns may be excused**
> **For bombing belfries so abused.**
>
> **Bring back the bells: for there remains**
> **No music but the aeroplane's.**
> **But leave the little church in peace**
> **While we have soldiers and police.**
>
> **If we can not inform the town**
> **That parachutes are coming down**
> **Without inviting Huns to search**
> **For targets in the parish church,**
> **The old inventive British brain**
> **Had better, surely, think again."**

Getting Ready

But despite all the attempts at alternatives, for those ringers not in the forces and able to ring, it was a bleak and unsatisfying time – as it was for a great many people. What was more, although most ringers didn't realise it at the time, the absence of ringing added to the bleakness for the general public too.

Perhaps surprisingly in view of the vocal, pre-War opposition to ringing, the great bulk of the population missed the bells to a far greater extent than anyone had ever thought possible. Richard Church included a verse in his poem, *Wartime Christmas*, which summed this up.

"The bell-ropes hang unhandled
In steeple, tower, and spire.
This is the silent Christmas
Through every English shire."

But as we've seen, despite everything and despite the gloom of many towers, in *some* towers the bands were nonetheless looking ahead with determination and confidence. They were teaching bell handling on tied bells, and they were teaching method ringing too. And what the splendid result of that was, we'll be seeing in Chapter 7.

Distressing though it is, all wars bring with them a host of opportunities for unpleasant behaviour quite separate from the violence itself. If we're to look seriously at history we have to face up to that, but traditionally, with the Second World War, we simply haven't. We've had a national pretence that the country was absolutely united, all pulling together, and exempt from any kind of skullduggery except in the tiniest amounts.

But of course, that simply wasn't true. The black market flourished, profiteers profited, and theft increased substantially – particularly as the black-out afforded extra protection to petty criminals. Even many ordinary people turned to crime and stole from other ordinary people's vegetable plots, and buying on the black market was seen as entirely acceptable.

But sad to say, there was other behaviour a good deal more distasteful still. Wartime films and stories tell us of the citizens of occupied countries informing on their neighbours for money or out of spite, but the suggestion is always that it didn't happen here. But of course, it did. Certainly, no one was taken away and tortured – at least, not systematically –

but they were nonetheless subjected to severe fines, substantial loss of property, and even prison. And that happened because under the Defence Regulations all sorts of demands were made – and restrictions imposed – that were extremely hard for people to implement properly no matter how great their effort or honest their intention.

So old scores could be settled and petty spite satisfied by the simple expedient of shopping one's neighbours. Indeed, ARP wardens and other local officials could settle their own scores too.

The regulations on "committing an act prejudicial to the Defence of the Realm," and, "attempting to cause disaffection likely to lead to breaches of their duty among persons engaged under Public Authority in the performance of functions in connection with the Defence of the Realm," – what a mouthful! – were particularly tricky, and any sort of criticism in casual conversation could be construed as an offence.

If someone wanted to report someone, they easily could; and worse still, a study of some of the cases in the magistrates courts suggests that two or more people often ganged together and gave false evidence as a form of bullying. And since the mood of the times was to root out, ostracise and deal harshly with all offenders, it was a very pernicious form of bullying too.

In a different way, all sorts of unpleasantnesses and injustices occurred amongst farmers and smallholders as a result of the regulations dealing with the use of land; and even poor people in rented accommodation were vulnerable. Even though meek, punctilious and law-abiding, they could still find themselves tasked with some trivial and entirely inadvertent contravention of the black-out or noise regulations, often through no fault of their own.

Of course, **most** *ARP wardens and policemen were sensible and kind, and they simply pointed out the problem and saw it corrected at once. But if the warden was vindictive – or worse still, being leaned on by an influential person who was himself vindictive – financial penalties or prosecution could result.*

And anyone taken before the magistrates was likely to have a tough time. Stern punishments were handed out as a deterrent to others, and common sense flew out of the window. Even the rules of evidence and adherence to the law were put to one side. After all, said the magistrates, there was a war on.

So perhaps it isn't surprising that one Sunday morning a white-haired and deaf clergyman, sitting in his church and holding a bell rope, found himself in the most extraordinary situation ...

6. A Ringer Imprisoned

You've written before about ringers of past centuries going up into ringing chambers and ringing without permission; and even today *some* ringers do. So what about the period between 1940 and 1943? Did bands ring surreptitiously in remote churches and then make off before anyone could catch them? And if they did, was anyone actually caught? And if they were, what happened to them?

J.K.K.
West Midlands

As we saw a couple of chapters ago, there were a great many times between June 1940 and Easter 1943 when one or more bells were rung when they shouldn't have been. Sometimes they were rung on the instruction of an appropriate authority, sometimes they were rung on the instruction of a ***in***appropriate authority, and sometimes they were rung as a practical joke; but the great majority of those times only became generally known after the War, if at all. Whilst the War was actually in progress, the Government didn't want anything of that sort leaking out.

So it's *just* possible that a very few bands *may* have deliberately rung contrary to the regulations, but if so, they were very few indeed. Even this time later, no rumours have surfaced, and there's nothing in the Home Office papers to suggest it happened. In any case, the great majority of ringers have never been that kind of people.

In 1993 someone sent a letter to *The Ringing World* purportedly telling of a band being instructed to ring the warning, and then carrying on and attempting a long peal of Kent Major with the shutters closed. But the ringers didn't exist and the writer didn't exist either, and the letter was a complete hoax. The tower didn't even have eight bells. So the reputation of Wartime ringers remains entirely unsullied.

Yet despite that, there was *one* occasion when a ringer – albeit a vicar rather than a *real* ringer – was not only prosecuted for ringing a church bell but was actually put in prison for it; and this is how it happened.

The Background

But since we need to understand the background, we must first backtrack eight months to the late Autumn of 1939. As we saw in Chapter 2, at the beginning of September the *Control of Noise (Defence) Order, 1939* was made, and although it seemed alright at the time, it quickly became apparent that it had problems.

Most importantly, Guy Fawkes Night was coming up – something no one had thought about two months earlier – and if nothing was done, Guy Fawkes Night would mean fireworks, and fireworks would mean a great deal of noise, and a great deal of noise could mean disaster. So on 31st October the Government issued a second *Control of Noise* Order called, *The Control of Noise (Defence) (No. 2) Order, 1939*.

But this time the Home Office were intending to get it absolutely right, and a great deal of discussion took place. On page 8 we saw that before the War, an awful lot of different noises had been used for public communication, and although the Government had intended to stop them, they quickly found that that was by no means simple. A great many noises were required by law, and a great many others were required for safety. Others were essential if industrial production wasn't to come to a halt. So the Home Office files became packed with requests for clarification.

The Problems

For example, the *London Midland and Scottish Railway Company* were worried about the Runcorn Bridge. Section 18 of the *L. & N. W. Railway (Lines near Liverpool) Act, 1861* stated that, "**The Company ... shall direct that a bell be tolled on the said bridge in time of fog**," and in 1939 for four hours either side of high water on the Mersey a man still did that. He also did it during falling snow; so could he carry on?

The Chief Inspector of Factories had a problem too. Under the *Special Regulations for the Use of Locomotives in Factory Premises*, drivers were required to "**... give an efficient sound signal as a warning on approaching any level crossing over a line of rails regularly used by persons employed ...**," but with the black-out and noise controls, several workers in steelworks had already been run over by locomotives and waggons. So he asked for special permission for engine drivers to sound their whistles.

The Chief Constable of Barrow in Furness wanted special permission for Vickers-Armstrongs Ltd to sound their buzzers at the end of shifts as workers were leaving early with a consequent loss of production.

The *Central Association of the Lime & Limestone Industry of Great Britain* had the problem that their members could no longer give signals of imminent blasting; and the *Department of Health for Scotland* were concerned that market gardeners couldn't use bird-scaring guns. *The London Association of Public Wharfingers* reported that their members were much inconvenienced by not being able to ring their handbells "**... at the commencement and finishing times of the daytime working periods**," and so considerable working time was being lost.

In Lancashire, the members of *The Fine Cotton Spinners and Doublers Association* were concerned about the testing of their automatic sprinkler alarm gongs, and they got the Chief Constable of Bolton to intercede on their behalf. And *The British Engine Boiler & Electrical Insurance Co Ltd* reported that workers had been seriously scalded because the low water whistle alarms on water tube boilers had been taken out of commission.

The New Order

There were a great many other special cases too and none of them were straightforward. The fireworks issue *was* straightforward, though, so the new Order simply said:

> **"... no person shall, in any area in Great Britain, fire, or cause or permit to be fired any maroon or firework in such circumstances that the noise caused thereby is audible in any place to which the public have access."**

This was certainly clear and simple, and *The Times* reported it under the equally clear and simple headline, **No Outdoor Fireworks** – although they stressed that *indoor* fireworks were OK as long as they were quiet. Bonfires during the hours of darkness were already prohibited under the *Lighting (Restrictions) Order, 1939*.

So far so good, but what about all the other problems? Some of them could be addressed specifically and needed to be, so as well as permitting a "**servant of the Crown**" to fire "**any maroon or firework**," the new Order exempted:

> **"The use of a bell by a member of a fire brigade or ... as a fog signal by a duly authorised person ... or by the driver of an ambulance ... or in association with a burglar alarm."**

Church Bells

But specific exemptions in legislation are always a problem, and the Home Office wanted a clause which enabled them to maintain that whatever they *said* was exempted, *was* exempted. So Clause 1 simply – or at least, fairly simply – said:

> **"Subject to the provisions of this Order, no person shall, in any area in Great Britain, sound any instrument or cause or permit any instrument to be sounded, except –**
>
> **(a) for the purpose of making a signal, in accordance with directions given by the local authority or chief officer of police for the area, to indicate that an air-raid by the enemy is expected or is in progress or has ceased, or that noxious gas is present, or that danger from such gas has ceased; or**
>
> **(b) in such circumstances that the sound of the instrument is not liable to be mistaken for any such signal as aforesaid; or**
>
> **(c) for the purpose of testing the**

instrument, or carrying out any exercise, in accordance with directions given by the local authority or chief officer of police for the area."

And so church bells weren't mentioned at all. And that was entirely intentional, not because the Home Office wanted them banned but because they were entirely content that they were excluded from the Order under Clause 1(b). Initially they'd wanted a specific exclusion for church bells but the Parliamentary Counsel who drafted the Order convinced them otherwise.

"I enclose herewith another draft of this Order. I am afraid I have gone back on my promise to include an express exemption for clocks and church bells. I am still of the opinion (and I think you agree) that this exemption is quite unnecessary. On further consideration I suggest that the inclusion of this exemption would increase rather than diminish the troubles of your administrators who are likely to get any number of requests from other people for express exemptions, which they will want to turn down on the ground that they are covered by paragraph 1(b). They will be on much weaker ground in turning them down, if the order already contains an exemption which must be entirely unnecessary in view of that sub-paragraph. If, however, your administrators still insist on including an exemption for clocks and church bells, I suggest the following amendments of the draft:-

Paragraph 3(e). Before 'burglar alarm' insert 'clock or'.

After sub-paragraph (e) insert –

'(f) the ringing of any bell on or in any church or chapel by a duly authorised person'.

Re-letter paragraph (f) so that it becomes (g).

In this new paragraph (f) I have avoided the expression 'church bell' because, if it were used, I expect you would have people asking whether sacring bells, Angelus bells and other bells used inside a church in connection with the Roman Catholic ritual are covered: (this is a good illustration of the slippery slope on which an unnecessary exemption places you). I have also avoided the expression 'in such manner as is customary'. If the new vicar finds he can get a party of bell-ringers together when the late vicar couldn't, why shouldn't he ring his bells. Instead of these words I have used 'by any duly authorised person', which we have already used (though I do not much like them), to cut out mischief makers."

Clarification

All of which is just a single example of the enormous concern and consideration which the Wartime Government and the Civil Service had for ringers and ringing. The truly sad thing is that the ringers of the time hadn't the slightest idea, and put enormous effort into unfairly lambasting them.

Clarification was needed, though, and in correspondence with the Secretary of the *Central Council of Church Bell Ringers*, the Home Office quickly supplied it. *The Times* – then the pre-eminent newspaper in the UK and virtually an organ of the establishment – supplied it too.

> **"Church and chapel bells, clock chimes, and musical instruments, including bugles, are not affected by the restrictions."**

But most ringers didn't read *The Times*, and – without waiting for news from the Central Council Secretary – John Goldsmith, *The Ringing World* Editor, wrote to the *Ministry of Home Security (A.R.P. Department)* for clarification. He wrote on a Tuesday and this splendidly formal reply was posted back to him three days later.

> **"Sir,**
>
> **In reply to your letter of November 7th, I am directed by the Minister of Home Security to say that it is intended that the use of church and chapel bells should be excepted from any restrictions by virtue of clause 1(b) of the Control of Noise (Defence) (No. 2) Order, 1939.**
>
> **I am, Sir,**
>
> **Your obedient servant,**
>
> **R. L. Poland"**

Old Bolingbroke

So apart from all the difficulties explored in Chapter 2, ringing carried on well enough. But seven months later at Old Bolingbroke in Lincolnshire, something remarkable happened. It was 16th June 1940, and since there was no longer a local band there, the Rector, the Rev. Robert Grant Colvin Graham, was chiming a single bell.

We now know that he was acting perfectly legally. As we saw in Chapter 2 – the 1940 Order prohibiting ringing didn't come into effect until 19th June. But no one knew that then because the Archbishop of Canterbury, the BBC and the National Press had all told the country that the ban would take effect that weekend. All the Diocesan Bishops had written to their clergy saying that too, so the entire country – with the exception of the Government and a handful of civil servants – all believed that ringing a church bell on 16th June was a criminal offence.

The Arrest

And no doubt the Old Bolingbroke local policeman, P.C. Peck of the Lincolnshire Constabulary, believed it too. So when in pursuance of his duties, he entered Old Bolingbroke Church prior to the morning service and found the Rector sitting on a chair, in the very act of pulling the chiming rope, he thought he'd caught him red handed. So he had a brief discussion of the "*Now then, now then, what's going on here?*" sort, and arrested him.

A month later on 15th July, the case came before the Spilsby Magistrates. P.C. Peck gave evidence that Mr Graham had told him he knew nothing of the Order preventing bellringing but that it would, "**... save him the trouble of ringing them**." He also gave evidence that the Rector had said he'd heard nothing about the Order on the radio because he was deaf, and he'd had no letter from his Bishop.

More curiously, P.C. Peck also gave evidence that Mr Graham had announced in the evening service that he'd received a letter from the Bishop prohibiting the ringing of bells; yet unless Peck had attended the service himself, it was hearsay evidence and so inadmissible.

The magistrates weren't bothered about that, though, and nor were they bothered that the constable was clearly on intimate terms with at least one person who *did* attend the evening service. Equally, the magistrates weren't bothered that the evidence of P.C. Peck's boss, Superintendent Little, wasn't admissible either. *His* evidence was that the Bishop of Lincoln had written to all the diocesan clergy including Mr Graham – but he produced nothing to support that.

The Magistrates

And although at this remove we can clearly see a travesty of justice in the making, it probably wasn't justice that the magistrates were interested in. From their point of view, *there was a war on*. There were airfields in Lincolnshire, and the important port of Hull was very close; and an invasion attempt was imminent too. Many magistrates were former army officers and they saw their Wartime role as a quasi-military one, operating kangaroo field-justice without regard to procedures or common sense.

The previous month, for example, a mission pastor near Hull had been imprisoned for six weeks for agreeing that a bomb had fallen on Scarborough. "**This chatterbug business has to be stopped**," the magistrate had told him. In other places, severe penalties were being imposed for whistling in the street or showing tiny lights; and any form of criticism of the Authorities, no matter how privately expressed, could result in police action.

The Summer of 1940 was a time of outrageous prosecutions and sentences everywhere, and the Chairman of the Spilsby Magistrates, Mr F. L. Stephenson, was clearly a stern and serious man too. So having made his views about "**intentional and deliberate**" ringing completely clear, he sentenced the Rector to four weeks in prison.

The Fight Back

Even in July 1940, this was an extraordinary sentence for an elderly, white haired clergyman who was only trying to do his job. It was reported in all the national newspapers including *The Daily Telegraph*, and fortunately for the Rector, *The Ringing World* Editor was one of *The Daily Telegraph's* readers. All the newspaper reports suggested – although they didn't actually *say* – that Mr Graham was prosecuted under the 1940 Order; so since that Order was not in force on 16th June, our Editor immediately wrote to the Home Secretary.

His letter was short, clear and – in the manner of the times – suitably respectful, but the Home Secretary didn't reply as quickly as he had done to the Editor's previous letter. When he *did* reply, he said that Mr Graham had been prosecuted under the October 1939 Order not the 1940 Order, but he immediately released him from prison anyway. Probably he thought the sentence was monstrous, but he may also have sensed that the wheels of justice in Spilsby hadn't turned properly.

The Truth

And at this point things become really intriguing, and to get to grips with the true enormity of what *really* happened, we need to examine the various stages.

On 16th June, P.C. Peck no doubt genuinely believed that Mr Graham was committing an offence, and most probably both he and Superintendent Little continued to believe that for at least a week afterwards. They might even have taken the case before the magistrates under the 1940 Order without ever looking to see the date on which it came into force. It's not very likely, and it wouldn't have been very efficient, but it's *possible* and it would at least have been honest.

Indeed, all the evidence presented to the magistrates – and all the words the police and the Chairman of the Bench used – demonstrate in the clearest possible way that Mr Graham was prosecuted under the 1940 Order. If the police had prosecuted under the 1939 Order while reading out the wording of the 1940 Order, that would itself have been a major criminal conspiracy. In any event, the Clerk to the Court – a qualified solicitor – would almost certainly have spotted it.

The Home Office Papers

So how did the Home Office come to tell the *Ringing World* Editor that the prosecution had been under the 1939 Order?

And of course, this is one of those instances when we'd dearly love to read the Home Office file containing the correspondence. But we can't. The sub-file which probably contained the papers was reported as missing many years ago – which may or may not be suspicious. But a single sheet of paper still exists in an unrelated file, and it records a telephone conversation taken by a Home Office civil servant.

> **"Mr. Fooks, Chief Constable of Lincolnshire, telephoned to say that the Rector of Bolingbroke-with-Haresby, near Spilsby, was sentenced to 4 weeks' imprisonment at Spilsby yesterday for contravening the Control of Noise (Defence) Order, 1940. The offence was committed on June 16th and the Order is dated June 19th. Mr. Fooks wanted to know if the conviction could stand, on the grounds that Press and Broadcast publicity had been given to prohibition of the use of Church bells on**

June 13th and 14th, and that the Bishop had sent round a notification before June 16th.

I consulted with Mr. F. C. Johnson and Mr. Davie, and there is no doubt that no offence was committed, as the Order did not come into force until it was signed.

I advised the Chief Constable accordingly."

The Chief Constable

So the Chief Constable *knew* that Mr Graham had been wrongly convicted, and he knew it immediately too. His legal – and indeed, his moral – duty was to tell the Home Office of the Rector's imprisonment at once – something he *didn't* do – so that the Home Office could order an immediate release. Instead, the Chief Constable did nothing whatsoever, and without the *Ringing World*'s intervention, in prison the Rector would have stayed.

And once again, this gross violation of the law by a chief constable quite takes our breath away. Nowadays, it would lead to censure and compensation, and quite possibly dismissal too; but Mr Fooks was not a career policeman, he was a former military man who had been parachuted straight in at the top – like many chief constables then. And like the magistrates, he probably felt his duty in time of war was to operate kangaroo field-justice in a quasi-military way.

Besides, he had a strong personal belief that the lower orders should be kept in their place, and he no doubt saw the Rector as a lower orders person. Indeed, after the War he so vigorously – albeit unsuccessfully – opposed the formation of the *International Police Association*, that he was knighted for his efforts.

The Cover Up

But powerful though the Chief Constable was, his silence was no defence against the efforts of *The Ringing World* Editor; and the Magistrates were forced to answer to the Home Office. A simple admission of error would have been best, but instead – with the clear connivance of the Chief Constable and the Clerk to the Court – they actually went so far as to produce a completely false record of the hearing.

Put simply, in replying to the Home Office – and later in the papers they sent to the Appeals Committee of the Lindsey Quarter Sessions – they quite outrageously and quite obviously, lied. Even though they were the most senior local people, they entered into a criminal conspiracy for which they should all have been prosecuted and imprisoned.

But did the conspiracy go further? After all, the Home Office *knew* that the prosecution couldn't possibly have been taken under the 1939 Order, so why did they say that it had? We'll never know; but perhaps they simply thought it would be in the best interests of the War Effort to hush it up. After all, they'd let Mr Graham out, and in the context of the times, what was twelve days' wrongful imprisonment for one man?

The Appeal

But the *Ringing World* Editor was certainly *not* prepared for it to be hushed up, and he wrote to the Home Secretary yet again, this time with a copy of the Ministry's letter that we saw on page 119. And the result was that on 4th October 1940 the *Appeals Committee* of the *Lindsey Quarter Sessions* heard an appeal and quashed the conviction.

Sadly, the court papers are yet another set of documents that no longer exist – and the Lincoln Diocese have no papers either – so we have to rely on the Press. But before awarding costs, Judge T. W. Langham is reported as saying:

"It is clear that the Rector should never have been prosecuted or convicted. Even in times of danger the elementary principles of justice must be observed. It is clear that in this case, very much evidence was admitted which was not evidence at all.

The Rector has suffered imprisonment and all the odium of great publicity. That is a wrong which unfortunately cannot be undone in this court. All we can do is to allow this appeal with costs, which means the conviction is wiped out."

And Mr Graham's barrister, Mr N. Wing, was reported as saying that he wished the magistrates could be made to pay the costs out of their own pockets because the Rector was convicted "**... under gross irregularities**."

But of course, the magistrates *didn't* have to pay the costs out of their own pockets, and equally, although the Judge must have realised a criminal conspiracy had taken place, no action was taken. All the same, the case was reported in national and regional newspapers across the whole of the country, and Mr Graham was publicly exonerated.

In the Parish

Or at least, he *sort of* was. He was publicly exonerated as far as most of the country was concerned, but he *wasn't* publicly exonerated as far as some of the people of Old Bolingbroke were concerned. *They* knew – or at least, they *thought* they knew – that he was a Nazi; and certainly, the Magistrates must have been told that some of his parishioners thought that, because he is reported as telling them, "**I am loyal to the country. Do you think I would break any laws?**"

So did the belief that he was a Nazi have any foundation? Probably not. But very sadly, the parishioners had support for their suspicions because the week before Mr Graham appeared before the Magistrates, his wife, Bertha, had been detained and placed in a holding camp under Regulation 18B of the *Defence (General) Regulations, 1939*.

And very sadly, there was nothing either she or her husband could do about it. Regulation 18B was an extraordinarily draconian piece of legislation under which the Home Secretary could detain anyone indefinitely without trial and without producing any evidence. There was no effective right of appeal and no possibility of a court hearing; and Churchill later referred to it as being "**... in the highest degree odious**." But it was necessary at a time when fifth column activity was believed to be a serious national danger.

The Truth?

But was the wife of a rural Rector really a serious fifth columnist? Probably not. More likely, she was simply too free in her condemnation of the authorities following her husband's arrest. A great many completely loyal members of the public were detained under Regulation 18B, and she was probably one of them. Of course, the Government *knew* that loyal citizens were being detained, but they didn't want to take chances – and in any case, most Regulation 18B detainees were treated pretty well.

But there *is* another possibility. Many years ago, Professor A. W. Brian Simpson researched a large number of the detainees and established to his own satisfaction that Bertha was a member of the *British Union of Fascists and National Socialists* – i.e. one of Oswald Mosley's *Blackshirts*. He was a serious academic conducting genuine research, so he may have been right.

But having gone through the same research trail myself, I don't think so. The Home Office have no papers on her, and there are no records of her belonging to any Branch of the *British Union*. The emotional successors to the *British Union* have no record of her either, and they only claim her as one of their own on the basis of Professor Simpson's say-so. The Professor may just have *assumed* she must have been a member as otherwise she wouldn't have been detained.

It also seems unlikely that she could have been a member whilst her husband wasn't. And besides, most of the *Blackshirts* had been detained in the previous month, so even if she *had* had a connection with them, she'd probably never have been detained if it hadn't been for her husband chiming a bell by mistake.

But whatever the exact details, it's certainly a sad tale of injustice, conspiracy, persecution and – ultimately – a broken home; and it's yet another example of how the War destroyed many people's lives in many different ways. Yet it produced one remarkable and unique occurrence. In the whole of history, it was the one and only occasion when a copy of *The Ringing World* was produced in court as evidence.

Most ringers don't get too excited about tenor weights nowadays but it wasn't always that way. Time was, when size was important, and ordinary villagers took great pride in the fact that ***their*** *tenor was heavier than their neighbours'. In a curious and primeval way, a heavy tenor was seen as a measure of virility and manliness, and not just the virility and manliness of the man who rang it, but the virility and manliness of all the males in the parish. So local tenor weights tended to increase like the sizes of fish in fishermen's stories.*

A curious side effect of this was that many tenors were once said to weigh ***20 cwt approx*** *– the locals insisting that* ***their*** *bell weighed* ***at least a ton****. Most turned out to be substantially lighter when eventually weighed properly during a rehang, and indeed, the weight of one tenor in Gloucestershire went down from 25 cwt to 16 cwt. Even the modest tenor in my own tower, decreased from 10½ cwt to 8 cwt.*

So not surprisingly, with pride in the weight of the bell came pride in the ability to ring it. And men didn't necessarily want to ring it ***well*** *either, they just wanted to ring it at all. When bells went much worse than they do now, simply keeping them up was an achievement in itself, and many big, male ringers viewed a heavy tenor rather as they viewed a* ***test-your-strength*** *machine at the seaside.*

So back in 1885 when the tenor of St Paul's Cathedral – 62 cwt – was the heaviest ringable bell in the World, ringing it single-handed was certainly an achievement; and ringing it ***up*** *single-handed had never even been attempted. So when one person did indeed ring it up unaided – in October of that year – it merited a report in* ***Bell News****.*

> **"RAISING THE TENOR BELL AT ST. PAUL'S CATHEDRAL. – The pulling up of St. Paul's tenor generally occupies four, five or six men (sometimes more in hot weather), but on the last practice-night, Tuesday, October 6th, this feat was accomplished single-handed by Mr. Joseph Jones, a private in the Royal Horse Guards (blue), and a member of the Ancient Society of College Youths, in the presence of several well-known ringers and friends; the time occupied was a little over three minutes,**

and the tenor weighs 62 cwt. This is the first time she has been pulled up by one man alone."

A great story, certainly, and one that captured everyone's imagination; and until 1918 almost everyone assumed it was true. What was more, they thought it was a feat that was unlikely ever to be repeated. But towards the end of The First World War a rather different version came out.

It seems that Trooper Joseph Jones of ***The Royal Horse Guards (The Blues)*** *had become a London ringer after returning from The Egyptian War of 1882. He wasn't a change ringer but he was immensely strong – and a thoroughly nice and unassuming man too, apparently – and his one ambition was to raise the St Paul's tenor single-handed. So on 6th October he was given the chance, and having apparently succeeded in getting it up in a mere three minutes to the astonishment of all present, the report went into* ***Bell News****.*

But a few days later a couple of people realised that the report hadn't been quite right. While Trooper Jones was ringing the bell up, G. A. Muskett – the Secretary – and E. E. Clark were up in the belfry ready to put the clappers over of any bells that were rung ***up wrong****; and knowing nothing of the attempt below, they decided to lend a hand when the bell was half-way up.*

Apparently, they thought some "young chaps" were having a problem getting the bell "above frame-high," so they lent a hand on each side of the wheel. Once they realised what they'd interrupted, they were in a bit of a quandary – and especially after it became national news – and since Trooper Jones was such a nice chap, they decided to say nothing. And indeed, nothing at all was said until someone unkindly let the cat out of the bag in ***The Ringing World*** *in 1918.*

But here's the really sad thing. Trooper Jones would almost certainly have managed entirely unaided, and Messrs Muskett and Clark – like so many ringers both before and since – simply didn't understand what they were seeing. And they didn't understand the maths and physics of what was happening either. So by way of a short detour into the mechanics of bell raising, I'll explain.

Essentially, if the ringer gives one unit of pull on the rope, the centre of gravity of the bell rises by one unit-of-pull's-worth of distance. Of course, there are friction effects and such-like, and so some of the effort is wasted; but those apart, a pull on the rope means an equivalent rise in the bell's centre of gravity. That's true at any stage of the raise, ***but*** *– and this is a really big and important* but *– that* ***doesn't*** *mean that the bell will* ***swing*** *the same extra amount at every stage.*

Complex, I know, and if you don't want to be bothered with technicalities, you can just take my word for it and skip the next few paragraphs. But looking at the extremes of a raise, at the start, the bell has to swing a considerable horizontal distance if its centre of gravity is to go up at all. That's why you let out a lot of rope in your first few pulls.

But when the bell gets to be frame high, things are very different. Each unit of pull sends the centre of gravity up by the same amount, but to a watcher in the belfry, the bell hardly seems to be going up at all – even though it is – because the amount of increase in the ***swing*** *is so small.*

It's the same down below of course. You have to let out quite a lot of rope for each pull at the start of the raise, but when you're halfway up, you must let out very little indeed, and it feels as though you aren't getting anywhere.

So with this in mind, we can clearly see that Trooper Jones was actually doing very well. Otherwise he'd never have got the bell half-way up so quickly, and if Muskett and

Clark had just kept their hands to themselves, he'd have passed gently through the ***doldrums*** *stage and they'd soon have seen the bell palpably rising again. And besides, I doubt that their "help" on the wheel added much anyway.*

So myself, I'm completely satisfied that he genuinely achieved one of the greatest raising feats of all time; and even though it's now well over a century on, let's give Joseph Jones the credit that was genuinely his due.

But it's not just the strength and deception aspects of this story that make it interesting. Additionally, there's that Joseph Jones was almost always referred to as ***Trooper Jones****. He was seen in his twin roles as both a ringer and a soldier.*

And being both a ringer and a soldier is something that's always caught the public imagination too. We saw that four chapters ago in 1939, and we'll see it again in spectacular fashion in November 1942 ...

7. Egypt and After

Last year a very jolly group of ringers – who call themselves *The 43ers* – rang at our tower. They were lots of fun and great to talk to, but they were all rather elderly as they'd all learnt to ring in 1943 when the wartime ban on ringing was lifted. Thinking of it now, that must have been a tremendously exciting time and I'd really like to know all about it.

Emma
Kent

Certainly, it was a very exciting time, and we'll come to the details in a moment; but the first crack in the ban wasn't in 1943 but in 1942, and since it was such a truly momentous crack, we'll look at it first. On 11th November 1942 the Prime Minister made a speech in the House of Commons about the British victory in what we now call the Battle of El Alamein but which was then called the *Battle of Egypt*. He ended with these words.

> **"Taken by itself the Battle of Egypt must be regarded as a historic victory. In order to celebrate it, directions are being given to ring the bells throughout the land next Sunday morning, and I should think many who will listen to their peals will have thankful hearts."**

The Background

That was well expressed, without a doubt, and nowadays the memory of the El Alamein ringing has reached epic status – at least among ringers. But at the time, Churchill was taking a significant political gamble. Universal ringing for battle victories was then a tradition with a long pedigree; but most people saw the Second World War – with the horrors of the First World War still fresh in their memories – as a very different *kind* of war.

Unlike all previous wars, it wasn't just in some far off land or on the seas; it was on everyone's doorsteps and in their homes. And since the likely consequences of losing were infinitely more serious than in any war for nine hundred years, the jingoism wasn't there – and for most people, the blood lust wasn't there either. Everyone wanted the War to end, and everyone wanted Britain to win – and most people wanted to see Europe free of tyranny too – but they fully realised the human cost of winning, and they also knew that most Germans and Italians were simply ordinary people caught up in the same horrors as themselves.

So El Alamein was the last battle victory for which bells were ordered to be universally rung, and Churchill and the entire country made it clear that they were not ringing in a spirit of triumph but in a spirit of thanksgiving. The Editor of *The Ringing World* summed up the feeling superbly in his editorial of the following Friday.

> **"Never before throughout the ages have bells been more eagerly listened for, or more thankfully heard, than on Sunday last.**
>
> **Church bells had come into their own once more, and it was only possible because of their long history and the immemorial**

influence they have exercised over the people of this land. Nothing else could have had the same effect. Not the fluttering of flags, not the blare of trumpets. And those who remember what happened forty years ago, when the relief of the tiny garrison of Mafeking was announced, will be filled with a profound sense of gratitude at the contrast between the blatant vulgarity then and the ringing of Sunday last. Yet, widely different as were the issues involved, much of the root feeling was the same. The difference was in the form the news was celebrated and the greater sense of restraint, responsibility, and self control which England has learnt through years of peril and anxiety, as well as of success and victory.

But the voices of the bells were far more than an expression of joy at a great victory, or relief at the temporary passing of a great peril. They were an act of thanksgiving ..."

Getting it Wrong

But it wasn't just with the tone that Churchill was taking a risk. Battle results are not always what they seem, and British victories had often turned out to be far less of a success than they at first seemed. In the First World War, the Prime Minister, Lloyd George, had called for the universal ringing of bells after 381 tanks had broken through the German lines at Cambrai following the battle of Passchendaele. At first this had appeared to be a tremendous victory with all three German lines destroyed and five miles of land gained; but it came as such a surprise to the British

High Command that they hadn't the slightest idea how to capitalise on it; and ten days later – when the ringing had already taken place – the Germans got all the lost ground back again.

The Leak

So not unnaturally, Churchill felt he should get the approval of the War Cabinet before making his speech, and of course, he got it. The minutes of the Cabinet meeting on Monday 9th November 1942 record next to the side-heading "**CELEBRATION OF THE VICTORY IN NORTH AFRICA**":

> **"THE PRIME MINISTER thought that arrangements should be made for the Church bells to be rung on the morning of Sunday 15th November, in celebration of the victory in North Africa.**
>
> **The War Cabinet agreed in principle that, provided operations continued to be successful, this should be done, but decided that no announcement should be made on the matter until later in the week."**

And although that *seems* clear enough, unbeknown to most of the Cabinet, three days *earlier*, Police Sergeant Bowles – then on duty at the Redhill police station – had sent this message to his Inspector.

> **"Col. Hake, C.C. 8th Surrey (Reigate) Battalion, Home Guard, called at Redhill Police Station at 9.10 p.m. and reported that just previously a Canadian Dispatch Rider in possession of Pay Book and Identity Disc in the name of Sergt. Major Mills,**

Canadian Mobile Laundry 'Woodside', Linkfield Lane, Redhill, had called at the Colman Institute, reporting that Church Bells may be rung in the near future to celebrate the victory in Egypt. This had been suggested by the Prime Minister in the House of Commons today. Owing to the fact that the message had not been received through the usual Home Guard channels, Col. Hake was suspicious."

The Enquiries

And since Colonel Hake was quite right to be suspicious, he'd taken immediate steps to find out if Sergeant Major Mills was indeed a member of the Canadian Mobile Laundry, and he found that he was. So the Police Inspector then interrogated the rest of the Canadian Mobile Laundry, and took a copy of this telegram.

"From Ordnance. No.1. Canadian Corps. Secret message received from 'G' Canadian Corps. 'Due to success in Libya Prime Minister in address to House of Commons today may mention ringing of church bells. If, therefore, church bells ring today the action is not reference to enemy action or invasion. Warn Home Guard in area.' To inform. Signed. Lt. Col. Lake, Assistant Director, Ordnance Service, No. 1 Canadian Corps."

This was a serious leak because the Germans could have dropped dummy parachutes during the celebration ringing and caused major disruption. Besides, Churchill hadn't even decided, let alone made an announcement. So the Home

Office quietly investigated, and a hand-written note on a small slip of paper shows they traced the leak to a Brigadier who had sent a message following a meeting of Military Chiefs.

> **"SECO telephoned on Friday evening to say that the Church Bell rumour had somehow got out and they were receiving constant enquiries.**
>
> **He telephoned again first thing this morning to say that he had traced the leakage to Brig Mann who had sent out a message about it from London immediately after your conference.**
>
> **I told him of course that the proposal was 'off' and asked him to do everything possible to kill the rumours.**
>
> **Unfortunately the SECO duty officer telephoned our duty officer during the evening to ask if the rumour was true. Our duty officer foolishly rang up Home Security who asked the Secretary of the Cabinet who of course denied it."**

The Press

So it wasn't just the Canadian Mobile Laundry that had advance notice, most of the Press had advance notice too. All the same, they maintained their Wartime policy of never leaking, and they pretended complete surprise at the official announcement when it came. But they certainly didn't give it unanimous approval. Many thought celebration ringing would be premature and misleading, and others thought it would seem triumphalist. *The Dundee Courier*, was typical.

"The British people – and Scotland has her special reasons – are proud of the achievement of their soldier sons. But we cannot believe they will approve the decision to order the ringing of bells throughout the land on Sunday to celebrate the victory. It smacks of Hitler-Goebbels propaganda methods."

And *The Eastern Daily Press* said:

"Though there was a notable lightening of people's spirits yesterday when the news of the Eighth Army's success became generally known, we doubt whether more than a few will think ... that the time was ripe for a victory peal to be rung on church bells all over the country. People with long memories will recall with some bitterness the disappointments that so quickly followed similar exhibitions of exuberance ... in the last war."

But the severest criticism of all was left to *The Daily Herald* – then a big selling left-wing newspaper at a time when being a thorn in the Government's side was a risky business. Indeed, earlier in the year, the Government had almost closed down *The Daily Mirror* following the publication of a cartoon which was intended to be supportive of the War effort but which had been widely misunderstood. But thorn or not, *The Daily Herald* always wrote well.

Buts in the Belfry

'It is thought right,' Downing Street announces, 'that church bells should be rung throughout the land next Sunday

morning in celebration of the Battle of Egypt.' We do not know by whom this ingenuous demonstration has been 'thought right'. We do believe that if the proposal had been submitted to public and Parliamentary approval it would have been received with an indifference which would have abashed its author.

The public fully shares the mood of sober confidence in which the Prime Minister addressed the House of Commons this week. It shares no less his conviction, so eloquently expressed, that far sterner struggles lie ahead. Shall we be encouraged for those future trials by a gesture so studied, so artificial, as next Sunday's brief amnesty for bellringers?

It is not even an original idea. Hitler himself has more than once ordered the sounding of bells in Germany to celebrate military triumphs which have since proved illusions. The news itself, whether good or bad, is enough for us. Either way, it is a spur. We prefer to forgo ceremonial chimes, broadcast fanfares and victory parades until the result of the war is finally established.

Grim days yet await us. They will be grimmer for our enemy. He may need to titivate the spirits of his weary slaves by trumpetings and tintinnabulations. We, who are neither weary nor slaves, can dispense with such emotional indulgences."

But the majority of newspapers saw the ringing for exactly what it was, and *The News Chronicle* summed up the public mood under the simple headline, "**The Bells Will Ring.**"

The Press Anticipation

But aside from the editorials, the Press went at the story with a will. *The Evening News* accurately reported that the College Youths had been practising on tied bells at St Botolph's, Bishopsgate; and *The Evening Standard* – less accurately – carried the headline, "**St. Paul's Bells Cannot be Swung**," although of course, they could. Both *The Times* and *The Daily Telegraph* printed a statement from the President of the Central Council asking readers to be, "**... indulgent in their criticisms of any ringing**," as "**bands will be short-handed**," and, "**those that are left will do their best ...**"

Those local and regional newspapers that were printed late enough to catch the speech, carried the story too. Some, like *The Exeter and Plymouth Gazette*, just made a bald announcement; whilst others, like *The Western Daily Press*, resorted to overblown hyperbole.

> **"Tomorrow the church bells of Bristol, silent so long, will ring out merrily ... It was in this manner that our forefathers rejoiced in battles, won in the past at sea and on land. One can imagine how heartily the bells of St. Stephen's ... and other city churches rang out past victories."**

But most local newspapers stuck to those details likely to be of specific local interest.

> **"Recordings of famous chimes will be heard in Mid Craigie, where the radiogram**

> **connected to an amplifier on the church roof will be in use,"**

reported *The Dundee Evening Telegraph*. And, "**Nottingham people must not expect anything very remarkable,**" said *The Nottingham Evening Post* – before detailing the ringing to be expected in every church in their area. Indeed, even though the West Bridgford bells weren't safe ...

> **"... yet the people of the area will hear bells through radio and public address speakers housed on the top of the tower,"**

And in *Echoes from the Town* they explained about bellringers in general – albeit rather inaccurately.

> **"As a class they are nearly all elderly men, though in some families the business of campanology has endured for generations. Some have died, and some have been dispersed under the dictates of war, and some new recruits will have to brought in for the occasion. Like organ-blowing, however, it is not a task which calls for much skill."**

And necessarily for the time, some local newspapers – like *The Chelmsford Chronicle* – felt bound to bring sexism into their stories.

> **"Many women campanologists will help to ring the victory peals on the bells of Essex churches on Sunday morning.**
>
> **'The women are very keen ringers,' said an official ... yesterday. 'On Sunday they will line up with the older men ringers, and you**

may be sure they will put all they know into the job.' "

And on the morning of the Sunday itself, the less scurrilous Sunday newspapers – such as *The Sunday Times* and *The Sunday Express* – published appropriately Sundayish warnings about not getting carried away with euphoria, or concentrating too much on rejoicing and too little on thanksgiving.

The Occasion

But whatever the doubts beforehand, when the ringing actually took place, it became abundantly clear that, once again, Churchill had got it absolutely right. There were no unexpected reverses after El Alamein, and the ringing became the most publicly acclaimed in the whole of history. Indeed, it was almost certainly the greatest ringing event of all time.

People who hadn't rung for 40 years were brought out of retirement. People who'd had one tied bell lesson three years earlier, were given another and then told to get on with it. The Army, the RAF and the Navy all ordered serving ringers to attend, and a great number of people who'd learnt on tied bells during the ban, heard their bell for the very first time.

Of course, virtually no one at all was in practice, and most of the ringing must have been truly awful. But apparently no one minded a bit and the general public thought it was wonderful. The press coverage was massive and universal, and pictures of ringers in military uniform were everywhere. Jack Dear – then shore-based on a Naval Air Station near Burntisland – was in one of those pictures

"So with an early breakfast I was off on the first train to Auld Reekie and St. Mary's

Cathedral for my first ring for more than three years. The ringing room was full of notables and press photographers and reporters begging to be hung while we were ringing. I remember having a photograph taken with a soldier and an airman which duly appeared on the front page of an Edinburgh newspaper."

And Tom Fox of Horsham – who was able to ring as he was on short leave – had a similar experience.

"I was told to present myself at Westminster Abbey. Shortly after starting to ring a touch of Stedman Triples, a horde of newspaper reporters burst into the ringing room and made a bee-line for me. I was the only ringer wearing khaki. They pestered me with questions. I shouted at them to go away but they continued to demand information."

The Publicity

And whilst it was all happening, the BBC were broadcasting it on the radio – and not just on their Home service but also on their Empire, European and Transatlantic services. In advance they had promised that,

"... bells will ring out all over the globe ... their stirring sound will bring to the occupied countries inspiration and hope as the day of their liberation draws near,"

and they included ringing from all four countries of the UK as well as broadcasting the bells of Coventry Cathedral where only the tower had been left standing after the bombing.

The BBC *announcers* – as radio broadcasters were known then – were pretty good too.

> **"Did you hear them in occupied Europe? Did you hear them in Germany? After noon today they will be silent again, except for warning of invasion if needed, till they ring out for final victory."**

Virtually every newspaper in the country – national, regional and local – reported the ringing too, often at very considerable length with details of what was rung and who rang it. *The Hull Daily Mail* report was typical.

> **"The bells were also rung at Cottingham and at Hessle where three soldiers 'stood in' to make up the team. At St. Mary's [Beverley] soldiers and a policeman were among the ringers and a course of Grandsire triples was rung with treble and two leading."**

The Cornishman reported that the church was so full at Gulval that:

> **"... many were perforce unable to gain admittance, for, despite the use of every inch of space, including such places as the belfry, still there was not room for all."**

But all the same,

> **"The ringers played their part nobly after their enforced idleness, and it was a delightful experience to hear the mellow peal of the ancient bells across the meadows."**

Less poetically, *The Western Gazette* – a newspaper invariably fixated on the size of church collections – told its readers.

> **"The bells rang out joyfully from [Corscombe] Church tower on Sunday ... The offertory was £3 11s 2d. The bells at Toller Whelme were also rung ... and the offertory was 11s 6d."**

The Ringing

But most interesting to us as ringers, was not the publicity but the ringing itself. Most towers had problems in that many of their ringers were in the services or on war work elsewhere. The Government had thought of this and had encouraged all ringers to turn up at their nearest church with bells no matter how far from home they were. In particular they ordered all ringers in the services to be released from their normal duties.

And although that sounded a good idea, it naturally led to many servicemen turning up who couldn't ring at all. Some of them had once chimed, but most of them hadn't even touched a rope. But since it was a way of being excused all duties for the day, a good many free-loaders claimed an expertise they simply didn't have. Fred Hutt recalled how it was in *his* unit.

> **"Imagine the joy therefore on reading battalion orders that included an appeal for volunteer ringers among our ranks to give a hand with the ringing at St. Lawrence's Church, Hawkhurst. Such volunteers to make their own way to the church on Sunday 15th November. Plus the treat of being excused all duties for the day. I**

promptly volunteered, along with six or seven others and we presented ourselves to the ringer in charge at St. Lawrence's.

On commencing to ring up, it was soon evident that some of our numbers had no knowledge whatsoever of ringing."

And P. W. Cave who rang at Hereford Cathedral that day, had an experience very much along the same lines.

"Accordingly, the Officer Commanding requested any ringers who might be on parade, to take two paces forward and they would be excused from duty for the rest of the day. About a dozen took two paces forward.

***Two* arrived at the tower."**

And even when there were enough local ringers, they were generally so out of practice that the ringing was pretty awful. Church Kirk in Lancashire had long kept a record book of all their ringing, and their record for 15th November gives a dry but contemporaneous account of the standard.

"Ringing consisted of call changes and firing (once). One attempt at Changes was quite sufficient until more practice is available."

The Silent Learners

But the thing that's hardest of all for us to empathise with is how it must have been for all those ringers who had learnt on bells without clappers. Mary Lewis was one of these.

"My lasting recollection of the ringing for

the victory at El Alamein was going up to Bowdon Church for an hour or so on the Saturday with my grandfather (C. Edwards) and father (A. R. Elkins), tying three bells so that I could practise and be able to ring on the Sunday morning. I had had some experience way back in 1936 but only on tied bells so the El Alamein ringing was the first time I had heard my bell speak."

And even harder to appreciate is the experience of those bands who'd had months or years of silent practices and were now ringing on open bells together for the very first time. Jack Pryor witnessed exactly that in Londonderry.

"In the tower we were welcomed by the Tower Captain, but not invited to ring in the first touch. The reason being that he had taught a number to ring on the lighter bells with the clappers removed. What a thrill it must have been for these youngsters to hear their bells for the first time on such an historic occasion. Alas the touch was short, as we all know the problems of ringing in rounds for the first time!"

And in some towers, the learners had not just learnt to handle a bell and ring rounds during the ban, they'd also learnt to ring methods as well, sometimes to quite a high standard. Peter Rock – then of Eardisland in Herefordshire – was one of these

"We had learned Grandsire and Plain Bob by the time the El Alamein victory was celebrated and that Sunday was a day in my

life never to be forgotten. How excited we all were – we were very enthusiastic and rang so often – but had never heard the bells when we rang them. Even some of the old ringers turned up as well. I don't suppose the striking was very good – but a wonderful joyful noise was made."

And even more remarkable was that Peter Rock's younger brother, John, had learned to ring on silent bells with Peter. He later became Master of the College Youths before dying young, and yet he could ring touches of Grandsire Doubles before he heard his bell for the first time, and Kent Minor before he heard his bell for the second time.

The Ringing World

Needless to say, *The Ringing World* made much of the occasion, and a great many towers sent in details of their own ringing. The editor printed every one of them over several issues – even though they were generally very similar and rather lacking in human interest. All the same, with a foretaste of the great influx of women ringers to come, Burnham in Buckinghamshire reported that:

"Ten girls between the ages of 11 and 14, all trained since the outbreak of war, rang the bells at Burnham. Seven had never heard their bell speak before."

Sadly though, these tower reports – and indeed, the local newspaper reports too – show that the reception of servicemen ringers wasn't always as welcoming as it would be now. In many towers they weren't even asked their names, and in others they were only allowed to ring grudgingly or not at all. So whilst Leicester splendidly told us:

> **"At St Margaret's ... a special feature was rounds and call changes on the 12 bells by six serving members of the Forces from Durham, Stepney, Sileby, Handsworth (Birmingham), West Hartlepool and six ex-Service men."**

Earls Colne in Worcestershire disappointingly said:

> **"Touches of Bob Major by G. Bishop, O. Laver, J. Turner, F. Claydon, W. Scillitor, F. Ridgwell, C. Saywood, W. Arnold and E. Bowhill. Two soldiers billeted in the village took part in a few rounds."**

Official Reports

But having set up the ringing – and issued the *Control of Noise Order, 1942* to make it possible – the Government naturally wanted to know how it had gone. They wanted to know because it had been a propaganda exercise, and they wanted to know because bells might indeed be a good parachutist warning after all. So every Chief Constable in the country was required to make a report.

Even so, quite why the Government expected the reports to be truthful, isn't clear. Obtaining accurate information would have been extremely hard even if the Chief Constables had genuinely wanted to supply it, but their natural desire to show how patriotic and compliant their areas were, only made things worse.

A volume of ringing was reported that now seems completely impossible, and only a couple of West Midlands chief constables – who reported 35% of bells being rung in Birmingham and 50% in Worcester – seem to have told the truth.

Silence Again

But after all that excitement and public acclamation, it was back to silence. Certainly, ringers – and lots of the public too – clamoured for the ban to be lifted immediately, but they got nowhere. At a very late stage, ringing was allowed on Christmas Day 1942 – once again for three hours only – but it wasn't as widespread and it didn't fire the public imagination in the way the El Alamein ringing had. Indeed, many ringers seemed to treat it almost as *business-as-usual.* The entry in the Church Kirk record book reads:

> **"By permission of H.M. Government, the bells were rung from 9.40 a.m. till 10.30 a.m., 6 ringers present.**
>
> **Mr. Parr was late as usual."**

Lifting the Ban

But whatever was being said in public, behind the scenes a lot was going on. The El Alamein ringing was the crack in the ban that could never be resealed, and on 18th November 1942, the King himself raised the issue confidentially with the Prime Minister. He wanted the ban lifted immediately, and the Prime Minister agreed. But the C.-in-C. didn't, and a battle between the C.-in-C. and Churchill ensued. Both men accepted that bells weren't required as a warning of parachutists, but the C.-in-C. wanted to keep the ban to maintain Home Guard morale, whilst Churchill could see no merit in his arguments whatsoever.

Indeed, even at this remove it's hard to see any merit in the C.-in-C.'s arguments – something we looked at in Chapter 4 – but all the same, after writing a number of decidedly tetchy memos, Churchill eventually gave in. Four months later, though, he came back to the issue, and the War Cabinet minutes for 12th April 1943 record:

> **"Agreed that the restriction on the ringing of church bells should be waived so as to permit the bells to be rung on the morning of Easter Day and Whit Sunday, and invited the Home Secretary and Minister of Home Security to issue the necessary instructions."**

But for Churchill that still wasn't enough, and before the decision could be made public, he took the unusual step of preparing a printed background paper for the War Cabinet meeting on 19th April. We don't know what he'd said to the C.-in-C. but he'd clearly banged heads together in a major way because he finished his note:

> **"There is in my opinion no danger that the announcement that ringing the church bells will no longer play a part in our precautions against invasion, would discourage our Home Guard or induce a degree of slothful inertia among the regular forces. The Chiefs of the Staff concur."**

The War Cabinet gave detailed consideration to the note, and after a long discussion – also involving their plans to replace the signposts in much of the country – they ...

> **"Decided that the present restrictions on the ringing of church bells should be so modified as to enable the bells to be rung in all parts of the country on Sundays and other special days, to summon worshippers to church."**

The New Order

The Home Secretary was mandated to put the decision into effect before Easter, but since the meeting had been on the Monday of Holy Week he had to be pretty quick. Worse, for complex legal reasons – which would take several pages to explain – special legislation was required for which there simply wasn't time. So two days later he took the easy way out and issued yet another Order – the *Control of Noise (Defence) (No. 2) Order, 1943.*

Ostensibly it permitted bells to be rung for services on Sundays and other special days, but the Home Secretary and his Civil Servants secretly knew that it had no legal validity whatsoever. They just hoped that no one would notice; and in fact, no one did.

Still, it was good news without a doubt, and the Press was unanimous in welcoming it. Most newspapers expressed themselves with moderation but *The Daily Mail* went well over the top.

> **"Next Sunday and thereafter the bells will ring as they have always rung. Their sound, sweet with distance as it drifts across the sunlit meadows, strong as it shatters in the city street, marks not an isolated but a permanent victory. ... Henceforth the bells may fulfil their ancient function, 'those golden throats that call the world to God.' "**

But good news or not, why not also have ringing during the week? The Government's explanation that it was to "**... avoid misunderstanding from any ringing at times when the public do not expect it**," convinced no one, and on 27th May the ban was lifted completely.

Odd Aspects

Or at least, it was lifted *almost* completely, because, the ringing of a handbell remained an offence until January 1945.

In that month, blowing a whistle "**... worked otherwise than by mechanical power**" also became legal, but ringing any other kind of bell was *still* an offence. The ringing of an Angelus bell, for example, remained an offence until the end of the War.

And two other odd things happened in 1943, although they remained secret. The Government were so pleased with the success of the El Alamein ringing, they twice thought of ordering victory ringing again. On 10th May 1943 the War Cabinet minutes record:

> **"The War Cabinet considered a suggestion that the bells should be rung and a Thanksgiving Service held on the following Sunday to celebrate the victory of the Gulf of Tunis. [They] decided that this had better be deferred until enemy resistance in the Cap Bon Peninsula had been crushed, bearing also in mind that a special Thanksgiving Service on the following Sunday would conflict with the celebration of the Home Guard Anniversary already arranged."**

Similarly on 9th September 1943 when Italy surrendered, a discussion took place between the Foreign Secretary, The Lord President, the Home Secretary and the King as to whether they should order ringing to take place at 12.00 noon next day. Exactly how they thought that could be managed isn't at all clear, but in view of a counter attack by the Germans, they decided it was premature. Instead on the following day the Home Secretary issued a notice that the King hoped that clergy would include "... **a suitable prayer of thanksgiving in the services on Sunday**."

Things Changing

So with all normal ringing allowed again, did that mean that things went back to pre-War normality?

Yes and no. Rationing still made teas a problem, but more meetings and practices began to be arranged and more ringers went to them. Peals were rung again – although only a few as many ringers thought they were inappropriate in wartime. More significantly for the longer term, the quarter peal took its first steps into popularity and a number of bands rang quarters before services. *The Ringing World* started publishing them too – albeit under the heading "**Miscellaneous Performances**."

But something infinitely more important started to happen too, yet it happened so gently and quietly that for a long time most ringers didn't even notice. People were coming forward to learn, and they were coming forward in considerable numbers. Mostly they were young people, but not invariably so. Tower captains were certainly encouraging them, but there was more to it than that.

It seems that the ban and the El Alamein ringing had between them been the very best publicity possible. Ringing was now seen by young people and their parents as an entirely acceptable thing to do whatever their social class. It had become the epitome of *getting-back-to-normal*. It was an essential part of *all-that-we-are-fighting-for*, and *what-makes-us-British*.

Even more important, it was no longer largely boys who were learning. Social outlooks had been changed enormously by the War, and although sexism was still rampant enough, it had become a different kind of sexism. Girls no longer saw ringing as a boy-thing, and only the truly outrageous backwoodsmen – of whom there were very few – thought girls should be kept out of the tower. Suddenly a large number of young female ringers burst onto the ringing scene, and they brought with them an entirely new outlook.

In 1944 *The Surrey Mirror* – with typical media inaccuracy – reported a visit by the Bishop of Woolwich to the band of ringers of Godstone in Surrey – most of whom were girls.

> **"Their average age is 16, the youngest 14. They have been taught the mysteries of a famous craft by two members of the Oxted team of ringers and they have now become so proficient that they are starting to ring *Choral* Changes."**

Cowboys and Indians

And astonishing as this seems now, the tower captain of Godstone – Pauline Fairall – was not only a girl but only sixteen years old. She ran both the band and the *St Nicholas Youth Fellowship* – essentially, much the same people – and she kept a regular record of their activities. And unlike their predecessors, they'd clearly decided that sessions in the pub after practice nights were not for them.

> **"August 1st 1944.**
>
> **No sausages for the common [but] played cowboys and indians and chasing games for the evening."**

Indeed, frying sausages on the village green after ringing was apparently a regular occurrence, as were games and dancing. The games apparently included musical chairs, stations, winking, postman's knock and bigamy; and as Pauline recorded:

> **"Bigamy proved very popular."**

The Opposition

Yet while all these new ringers – who were to make such a difference in the decades to come – were appearing, the opposition was doing its best to gain support. Not everyone liked bells, and some shift workers, ARP wardens and fire watchers found them very troubling indeed. Letters of complaint started to appear in newspapers, so *Mass Observation* – the opinion sampling organisation – conducted a statistically sound survey to find out the public's views.

And although common enough now, this kind of survey was ground-breaking then, particularly as it tried to provide a breakdown of its results between social classes. The titles of those classes sound pretty snobby now, but at the time they were simply descriptive, and the survey results appeared in *The Manchester Guardian* in May 1943.

> **"The recent correspondence on the subject of the ringing of church bells suggested to 'Mass-Observation' that it would be pertinent to ascertain how feeling was actually distributed on the subject. A representative London sample was questioned, and results were as follows:–**

View Held	**Percentage Men**	**Percentage Women**
Like ringing of bells	**59**	**66**
Indifferent	**23**	**7**
Dislike ringing	**9**	**3**
Miscellaneous and vague	**7**	**14**
Unaware that bells were rung	**2**	**10**

> **Dislike of the ringing of bells is centered among the unskilled working class, though even here feelings were – Likes 50%,**

indifferent 19%, dislike 15%, miscellaneous 11% and unaware 5% – thus showing that a three to one majority like the bells even in the most critical class.

The following random selection of verbatim comments gives a good indication of the general tone of feeling:–

'I thought it was very pleasant. I was away for Easter, and they sounded quite charming across the fields – they made one feel positively sentimental.' (Man, 50, upper class.)

'I enjoyed it very much: it was delightful. Silly, of course, but it made one feel the war was as good as won.' (Woman, 40 middle class.)

'It's quite a good thing, I suppose.' (Man, 45, middle class.)

'I didn't know they were ringing again.' (Woman, 40, artisan class.)

'I think it was a very good idea. They do cheer people up.' (Woman, 40, artisan class.)

'I don't like the things. Never did.' (Man, 35, working class.)"

James Lees-Milne

So it appears that in May 1943 at any rate, bells were still overwhelmingly popular. But surprisingly, some people didn't even notice that they were now being rung. In the private diary of the author James Lees-Milne is this extraordinarily sad entry for new year's eve 1943.

> **"Having dined with Geoffrey I walked home and went early to bed. I read, but the Battersea church bells started pealing across the river, contrary as I thought to regulations. It was more than I could bear, so I went downstairs to put cotton wool in my ears. Still I heard them. ... The loneliness of this moment, wholly artificial though it be, harrows me."**

V.E. Day

But in May 1945, V.E. Day arrived. And the ringing had a local and low key feeling to it that was very much the shape of things to come. There were about 75 extra peals rung that month and they were published as *Victory Peals*, but they were mainly by local bands and in basic methods. And entirely in keeping with this local, low key feeling was Pauline Fairall's record of V.E. Day in Godstone.

> **"May 2nd 1945.**
>
> **On Monday 1st May at 7.45 p.m. the news was given out that the next two days would be celebrated as Victory in Europe Days. Within a quarter of an hour the bellringers were at the church and we rang for over half an hour. The next day, the fellowship spent most of their time together. In the morning, we distributed posters and tickets for the dance. Most of the afternoon was spent walking. After tea we went to the thanksgiving service at the church. The bellringers rang the bells before and after the service.**

Mr. Stokes (A.R.P.) kindly gave us some thunder flashes and incendiary bombs which we exploded on the Green before and after a game of rounders.

As it grew dark, we decided to have a bonfire. This proved a great success and everyone joined in, and sang popular songs around the fire until midnight. On the way home, we saw search lights circling round London; and Londoners' bonfires lighting the sky."

And After

So the War was over, and contrary to all the fears, the immediate post War years became a boom time in ringing. Ringers were far more active and far more adventurous in their ringing than they'd ever been before. Method ringing advanced by leaps and bounds, and meeting attendances boomed.

But the history of *that* must be left for another time.

Time was, when writers wrote ***complete*** *books. In 1653, for example, Izaak Walton wrote* ***The Complete Angler****, and in 1751 Vincent La Chapelle wrote* ***The Modern Cook's and Complete Housewife's Companion****. The public were keen on complete books too, and they still are.* ***The Complete Photo Guide to Cake Decorating*** *and* ***The Complete Book of Soups and Stews*** *are still available.*

But when you write history, no book can ever be remotely complete. The past is packed with such limitless detail – all of which interacts in such complex and fascinating ways – that untangling even the smallest aspect is the work of ages.

And even when you think you've untangled something entirely sensibly, someone comes along and untangles it in a completely different way.

So although these War chapters contain an enormous amount of information that's never been unearthed before, there's lots of stuff I've left out, because it just doesn't seem interesting enough. The ***complete*** *history of ringing would take up tens of thousands of pages – and would be deadly boring – and even then, it couldn't ever be* ***really*** *complete.*

So since we ***aren't*** *being complete, we can leap from one era to another without bothering at all. And that's how we're now going to step back two further centuries to the extraordinary early eighteenth century world of* **The Very First Tower Grabber**.

In Breeches and Braces

8. The Very First Tower Grabber

A while ago you wrote an article about the very first woman ringer; and while we were all talking about it in the pub, our newest learner – who's over sixty but with more than fifty towers under his belt – wanted to know who the very first *tower grabber* was. He said he'd write and ask, but he still hasn't, so I'm writing instead.

N.L.P.
Berkshire

Very fortunately, unlike most *how-did-it-all-start* questions, with this one we can be pretty certain. The term *tower grabber* – and indeed, compulsive tower collecting itself – only became general after the Second World War, so historically we're talking about intensive *tower visiting*; and certainly, we know that ringers had been ringing at different towers in the seventeenth century – and in the sixteenth century as well.

But they didn't ring at *many* different towers. The ringers of the labouring classes – and that was the great bulk of them – couldn't travel far because they had neither the means nor the time; and the well-to-do ringers – of whom there were comparatively few – only rang in the towers where their social equals rang.

Yet in 1733 in London, a man called William Laughton decided differently; and we know that because he not only wrote up his exploits in detail but his manuscript has been preserved in the Guildhall Library in London. Fortunately, he must have kept comprehensive notes throughout his sixteen months of tower visiting because afterwards – on Monday 10th March 1735 – he wrote this letter to his friend, George Carbery.

> **"You are not insensible (being one of those worthy members yourself) that a Company of us made an agreement to ring at all the peals of 3, 4, 5 and six bells, within the City of London, and bells of Mortality, which we should find Ringable, and to ring at a different place every time of meeting if we should think proper, likewise to ring a peal, sometimes upon eight bells, or take a walk into the country and divert ourselves with a peal, if our fancys should lead that way; for which the snarling criticks were pleased to call us the Rambling Club; the first time of this Honorable Society's meeting was on Thursday the 29th of November 1733, and their last on Satturday the 8th of March 1735 when this worthy body of members broke up after having rung at 35 different peals of Bells, and done severall extraordinary performances in this art."**

Social Class

So we know William Laughton's name and we know he felt sore about being looked down upon by *the snarling criticks*. And we also know he had occasionally eccentric spelling. But apart from that, who was he?

And here we must digress a bit because it's not just Laughton's personality that was important to what he did, it was his social class too. The London in which he lived was accepted almost everywhere as the biggest, most important and most advanced city in the World. It had at least 600,000 residents – nearly 50% more than at the time of The Great Fire sixty-five years earlier – and while some of them were extremely wealthy, most were very poor.

Indeed, a significant proportion of them were paupers who survived their very short lives by begging. And the great majority of those beggars were not *men* – as many polemicists would have had us believe – but women and children. When a husband died or ran off – or was taken by the press gang, or posted overseas as a soldier – his wife and children were left with no income of any kind and little chance of employment.

His Means

But Laughton was neither rich *nor* poor. He had enough money to ring and eat entirely as he wanted, but he wasn't a gentleman, and that meant he wasn't constrained by the social customs of the upper classes. He rubbed shoulders with both extreme poverty and extreme wealth on a daily basis but he almost never tells us about either. For him, the huge army of beggars was just a normal part of his world and so not worth mentioning. He probably gave them small sums on a daily basis, just as many men of his class did, but he never refers to them at all.

And Laughton's class was what we now call *the middle class* – although arithmetically there was nothing remotely *middle* about his income. And being middle class he had both the money and the freedom to go his own way and do what he wanted; and what *made* him middle class was that he was a comfortably off *tradesman.*

Watchmaking and Swimming

And naturally, we'd be very interested in the details of his working life too, but like most present day ringers, he gives us none at all. We can be pretty certain he was a watchmaker, though, from three compelling pieces of evidence. First, after ringing at Westminster Abbey he is so impressed by all the famous people buried there that he writes about them in verse, four lines of which run:

> **"There's one lies there, of my own trade,**
> **Who made as good work as e'er was made,**
> **The famous Tompion, that was he,**
> **As ingenious a man as e-er can be."**

And since Thomas Tompion was one of the greatest clock and watchmakers the World has ever known – indeed, possibly *the* greatest – it's clear that Laughton was a clock or watchmaker too. Separately, we know that a William Laughton – who had been apprenticed in 1712 and so was about the right age – was a watchmaker in Leather Lane – a street which then ran parallel to Hatton Garden. And lastly, if you trace Laughton's return journeys from his various ringing exploits – perhaps better described as pub crawls – Leather Lane is definitely the area he was heading for.

But he was by no means an introverted craftsman. Indeed, quite the contrary, and apart from his many remarkable ringing exploits, we read this of him in *The Grub Street Journal* of Monday 24 June 1731.

> **"On Tuesday Mr. Will. Laughton, Watchmaker, at the Wheat-sheaf in Leather-lane, swam from Billingsgate to Chiswick, which is 10 miles, without resting or swimming upon his back."**

The Opposition

But although Laughton wasn't a gentleman, he was close enough to being one that he was worth the notice of the well-to-do ringers of the time and their hangers-on – with whom he'd recently fallen out. And he started doing two things which, in their very snobbish way, they disapproved of. First, he rang at rings of three, four and five – which posh early eighteenth century ringers definitely *didn't* do – and second, he rang at towers where *paid* ringers rang – i.e. ringers of the labouring classes. Indeed, he and his friends got so much abuse from the ringing establishment that he placed this advertisement:

> **"'Tis well known that the first Design of this Club's meeting was not to affront any soul upon God's earth, but only intended for a little innocent divertion, to Ring at a few different peals of Bells; tho' some people has taken it very Hainously and bin pleased to call names, and endeavour to Ridicule folks behind their backs for it."**

The Rambling Club

Yet it seems likely that this very abuse both added to their popularity – they started with only seven ringers and ended up with forty-two – and also gave them their name. This was an era when groups of people were called rude names by their opponents and then gloried in them and took them to themselves. So the *Tories* had got their name from a group of Irish hooligans, and the *Whigs* had got their name from a group of Scottish hooligans.

So when their opponents called William Laughton's group, *The Rambling Club*, as a seriously offensive description, they started calling themselves exactly that. And in 1733 the word *rambling* was offensive because it implied aimlessness, vagueness and lack of purpose – with overtones relating to the sexual habits of rabbits and cats.

The Start

But *aimless*, the Rambling Club ringers certainly weren't, and their first grab was on Thursday 29 November 1733 when they rang at All Hallows, Barking and St Vedast, Foster Lane. Laughton recorded exactly what they rang everywhere – both in verse and in prose – and they were obviously accomplished ringers. Most of the methods in their repertoire we'd recognise today. Plain Bob Minor and Oxford Treble Bob were the mainstays, but Court Bob, College Single, Morning Exercise and Cambridge featured as well.

On rings of five they rang Grandsire, Old – essentially what we now call Bob Doubles – New Cambridge Delight and *Simonds*; and on eight they rang three full peals of Bob Major and several 1680s. Union Bob Major they rang once, and Grandsire Triples they rang occasionally.

But more interesting is how they gained access to the towers. It's never specifically stated but they apparently never wrote for permission in advance. In those days the incumbent had no control over the ringing, and a lot of ringing took place without any advance arrangement or consent. Indeed, Laughton's band often just went in and rang – something the local ringers probably did too – but at Broad Street they had a problem.

"At St. Peters poor in Broad St. next,
And there by a saucy sexton vex-d,
A nasty fat ars-d B-t-ch Godamnher,
She'd leggs as bigg as a paviors rammer,
I do believe she was three yards round,
But we brought her haughty stomach down,

For we went and asked the Warden leave,
And made pegg Crab give us the kyes."

Their Manners

That certainly makes for uncomfortable reading today. Not only were they very rude to the lady herself but they thought of her with such a complete lack of respect that it quite takes our breath away. Yet of note is that the sexton was a woman at all. The office of sexton was then a man's job, so she was either standing in for her husband or, in the way that we look at in Chapter 18, she'd been allowed to take over his job after his death.

And on a technical point, the workmen who laid cobblestones in the eighteenth century were indeed called *paviors*; and the heavy, four foot long, bottle-shaped mass of iron-bound wood they used to hammer them in, was indeed called a *rammer*.

But although the Rambling Club's manners towards women look bad to us today, their manners towards each other look very modern. It seems that the kind of shouting, insensitive, and just plain rude behaviour that was common in conductors until not so many years back, was very much the norm then as well, and Benjamin Annable, the leading conductor of the time and no friend of Laughton, was apparently particularly bad. Laughton, though, clearly disapproved.

"For when they know you're in the right,
They-ll contradict ye out of spight.
We had no swereing nor no grieving,
At any time when we were Ringing.
For whoever Rings as well as he can,
Ought ne'er to be blamed by any man."

And Laughton didn't just disapprove on the basis of politeness, he also saw that rude and shouting conductors made the ringing worse rather than better. Especially, he saw that shouting at someone who knew he'd just made a slip, only led to more mistakes.

"And what a pox signifies calling then,
When the person knows it as well as them,
It only serves to set 'em fretting,
And often causes more forgetting,
The consequence of which I've seen,
To often when I've bin Ringing."

A Happy Band?

Of course, with any of his writings we can't be sure of the balance between his true feelings and his desire to create a dramatic poem, but he certainly appears to have had particular conductors in mind when he wrote the next verse.

"Some men indeed are made by nature,
Directly fit to buff and vapour,
And Lord it over their companions,
Call filthy names and curs and damn 'em.
But how odious does sutch wretches look,
Hated, despised and i'th' end forsook."

Whether those conductors really were ***i' th' end forsook*** is doubtful, but there was certainly a lot of friction in the other London *companies* over the years, whereas the success of the Rambling Club suggests it may genuinely have been the happy band that Laughton claimed.

"There is no Company in the town
Free from those tempers but our own,
We ne'er allowed of any Railings,
For there's none on earth without their failings,

I wish all Companys would do the like,
'Twou-d put an end to a deal of spite,
For were backbiters taken up short,
'Twou-d put an end to all their sport,
To stop 'em in their hight of spleen,
Wou'd break their harts to keep it in,
Oh! that all other Ringers wou-d,
Take pattern by this Rambling Club."

Tower Maintenance

There was something else about The Rambling Club that was both very modern and rather odd at the same time. Having walked into towers without asking anyone's permission, they sometimes found the bells in very poor condition or unringable; but instead of telling the sexton or simply walking away, they set about mending them themselves – possibly with tools they'd brought with them. So at Camberwell they found a problem with the treble.

"But there the Treble was to mend
For she stood down in the frame on end,
Well up we got her and hung her true
But faith it was with much ado,
We unbraced the wheel and took it off
Before we could lift her up aloft."

Quite a lot of work, as it seems the bell wasn't in its bearings and the ringers had to take the wheel off before they could lift it back in. After that, they must have put the wheel back on again, all of which *should* have suggested there might be other problems, but apparently it didn't.

"Then another fault before we go
For every Sally was too low.
So we took 'em up and oyled the Bells,
And then we all went down ourselves,

To make us ready and pull 'em up
But then we found out more ill luck."

Yet in truth, this doesn't seem to have been *ill luck* so much as gross incompetence. Laughton was obviously a successful watchmaker, so it's odd that he didn't check all the bells over when he was up there the first time. Certainly, this was more substantial engineering than he was used to, but it wasn't so *very* different. Even so, each new problem came as a surprise.

"There was sutch a rawteling with the tenor
That we all thought the Dev-l was in her.
Says John Trendl she will not mount
Something's the matter without a doubt.
So up we went again to see
And found her disordered certainly.
One hoop was of, the gudg'on loose
And this I do believe is truth,
Before we could have rung a change out
She-d have tumbled through and dashed our brains out."

A Second Time

So they gave Camberwell up as a bad job, rang a peal of Bob Major at *Mary Maudlin's* instead, and had yet another big meal. But like modern day tower grabbers they weren't going to leave things at that, and a few weeks later they were back again. On occasions, they paid a workman to do work on difficult or unringable bells, and they may well have done that here because this time they rang 3,000 changes before giving up until the tenor was *mended*.

And in due course it must have indeed been *mended* because on their third visit they rang a full peal of Bob Major. Yet interestingly, they didn't attribute their success to the skill of the workman but to their finding a horseshoe shortly beforehand. Laughton appears to have been completely serious about this, and it demonstrates the deeply held religious feelings of the times, many of which are very difficult for us to empathise with.

> **"For by good luck we killed the witch**
> **A damn-d old cross-grain-d crabbed b-t-h,**
> **Full many a time she-d plaug'd us sore,**
> **But now she'll ne'er do so no more,**
> **'Twas by a horseshoe we did the feet,**
> **Nailed on the door as you may see't,**
> **For witch nor wizard cannot enter,**
> **Nor o'er the threshold dar'st they venter,**
> **Where-er that magic charm is nailed,**
> **Well known to us it never failed,**
> **'Twas great good luck to find the shoe,**
> **And better old then 't had been new,**
> **For 'till they're worn they will not do.**
> **'Twas found one night at almost dark,**
> **Upon the road by Mr. Clarck,**
> **As we was coming from that place,**
> **Which proved to us a lucky case."**

Foot Straps

And like modern towers grabbers, Laughton is critical of many of the towers he visits; and in doing so he throws light on the condition of eighteenth century ringing chambers generally. For example, at *St Botolph's Without Aldersgate* he's upset to find no foot straps, and the implication is that foot straps were the norm elsewhere.

Of course, there are almost none of these anywhere in the country now, but traces of them can still be found on a few old, fixed tenor boxes. They were quite simply two raised leather straps – one for each foot – fastened securely into the box or floor, and the ringers put their feet into them when they rang.

These days they seem a very daft idea indeed. You could only ever stand to ring in one position, and you couldn't move your feet while ringing. The potential consequences of a broken stay were horrendous too – and some bells didn't have stays anyway. But Laughton – and presumably other eighteenth century ringers – apparently found them essential, perhaps because the bells then required much more physical effort. Laughton also thought they helped him not to slip wheel on a bell that was inclined that way.

Lighting

Lighting was a concern to him too. St Botolph's was "**such a dungeon of a hool**" that even during the day there was "**no seeing to ring without a candle**." But where the candles were placed was also important. At Cripplegate – where Laughton was "**taken with the gripes**" and "**ne'er was worser in my life**" – the candle placing came in for particular criticism.

> **"To have 'em stuck against the wall,**
> **They gave hardly any light at all,**
> **For three that are hung in the middle,**
> **Are better than ten stuck round the steeple,**
> **Against the walls with dabs of clay,**
> **That nasty blackgard odious way,**
> **Each steeple ought to have a branch,**
> **Hung in the middle to advance,**
> **Higher or lower with a weight**
> **As men should fancy for to ha't,**
> **And at least to hold a dozen lights**
> **Which would look well on ringing night."**

A Long Length on Three

There were other bell problems too. On 10th October 1734, Laughton, Thomas Greenwood and James Benson rang on the three bells of Holy Trinity, Minories. The bells had been recast twenty-five years earlier with a tenor of just over two hundredweight, and the lightness was itself a difficulty.

But that wasn't all. The Minories was a wealthy parish and, from the time of the nunnery there, it had enjoyed the ecclesiastical status of a *Peculiar*. That meant it had ancient rights and its residents were exempt from various obligations. But although the extensive parish records show the churchwardens were assiduous in providing relief to paupers, they weren't nearly as assiduous in providing proper ropes for the bells, and instead, they provided thin ropes without sallies. Even so, the band still rang 1008 changes of plain hunt on three, conducted – or, at least, *counted* – by the non-ringing Tom Clark.

"In the Minories at a peal of three,
The church is called Trinity,
Where fourteen dozen we fairly rung
Of sixes all completely done."

Whether any band had ever rung such a long piece of plain hunt on three before, we don't know, but it seems unlikely. Certainly, the leading London societies hadn't, but perhaps the paid ringers had. What *is* clear, though, is that the band found the thin ropes and lack of sallies a problem, and to help get over this, they put chalk marks on the ropes where the sallies would have been. This, too, is interesting as nowadays, ringers of their skill and experience wouldn't need to look at the sally at all.

"The Tenor is so very light,
Two hundred one quarter is the weight,

The ropes were small, our hands they cut,
No sallys in them e-er was put,
So with some chalk we made a mark
Or else we'd all bin in the dark,
But that showed us whereabouts to catch
And stop in due time at full stretch,
But for all that we'd mutch ado,
To keep the ropes from slipping thro'."

A Quarter Peal

Laughton doesn't say *why* they rang 1008, and they may have intended to ring more but gave up as the bells were too difficult. Certainly, though, at St Bartholomew the Less, Smithfield they set out to ring 1260 changes of plain hunt on three, and at the second attempt they succeeded.

"By the hospital next was our lot,
Such a fine peal ought ne'er to be forgot,
Tho' my tale perhaps may make ye laugh,
We rang seventeen dozen and a half
Of sixes on that peal of three,
By Bennett, Benson and by me,
The longest peal that e'er was rung
On three bells and completely done.
Twelve hundred and sixty 'tis complete
Cast it but up and you may see't."

And although in 1734 the idea of a quarter peal as we know it now was still a very long time in the future, a quarter peal was certainly what they rang; and it was very likely the first ever quarter peal on three too. But although it was most definitely a considerable achievement, it clearly wasn't one that the establishment ringers of the day would have approved of; so even Laughton felt bound to offer justification.

"Perhaps it may be said by some
To be a childish thing as e'er was done.
All the answer I shall make to such,
It was our pleasure, and that's enough."

The French

But although Laughton showed considerable open-mindedness in ringing matters and *some* social matters, in others he was rigidly fixed in the common prejudices of his time. His racial prejudice was not only extremely strong, he expressed it in almost exactly the same terms that racial prejudice has been expressed in *all* eras. But his target was not the Jews, Irish, Welsh, West Indians, Pakistanis or Bangladeshis who were to be the targets of later eras, it was the Huguenots.

On two occasions the Rambling Club rang at Hackney, a village that was then a good walk from the city and, unlike today, it was a village of blissful rural tranquillity.

"For I think no steeple near the town,
Stands incompassed with sutch delightful ground,
There's orchards, Gardens and cornfields,
And meadows which charming propects yields,
And near the Church sutch pasture ground
No better in England can be found."

But having rung there – and having drunk a considerable amount of beer and spirits at various pubs – they had to walk home again in the pitch dark. The dark then would have been very dark indeed, and the drink wouldn't have helped, and they not only lost their way, they became separated from each other. Laughton and a couple of others ended up stumbling through the "**horrid cribs**" – i.e. the horrid *dwellings* – of

Spitalfields and Houndsditch. And to Laughton they weren't just horrid because of their condition, they were horrid because of the people who lived in them – the protestant *Huguenots* who had fled from persecution in France – or in Laughton's words, "**The French**."

Their Food

Like all immigrants to the UK both before and since, the Huguenots had brought with them skills, money and expertise that substantially benefited the UK economy for years to come. But also like all immigrants before and since, the bulk of the population took against them, and Laughton goes along with that entirely.

And he does so with that timeless xenophobia that's been applied against every immigrant population right up to the present day. He isn't concerned that France is the traditional enemy, and he isn't worried that the individuals might be spies. He simply attributes personal unpleasantness to them, typified by what they ate and the smell of their cooking.

"A pox on all such cribs say I
And all such nasty places
Where there always is a sluttish tribe
A turning up their arsses.
Whose food is nought but wretched fare
Harts, livers, lights, hogg's foot or ears,
Or stale red herrings, wretched things,
Or grunters, muns or chitterlings,
Stale sprats sometimes or neck of beef,
Or baked Ox cheek is their relief.
Rank bacon fried with addled eggs,
Cow heel and onions or sheep's heads.
Stickings or skirt(s) sometimes they chuse,
Or snails or frogs to make ragoos."

Indeed, he goes on at length in this vein, and herbs and "**stinking cheese**" come in for ridicule too. Yet looking back from today, what's so curious is that he sees liver and skirt of beef as disgusting whilst at the same time he is himself eating fried spinal cord and brains.

But how he did *that* – and how the Rambling Club finally drew to a close – we'll be looking at in Chapter 9.

Nothing to do with ringing, of course, but William Laughton's swim up the Thames to Chiswick is fascinating in its own right. He went in, we're told, at Billingsgate – which since it was below the old London Bridge, was itself remarkable. At that time, London Bridge was an extraordinary structure, and for centuries it had been one of the great wonders of the World. Among a great many other reasons, it was famous for all the houses built on it and it's many narrow arches.

*Indeed, the narrowness of the arches held the water back to such an extent that the flow at most states of the tide was very considerable. "**Shooting the bridge**" by boat was therefore a skilled and courageous undertaking, and in Laughton's time an average of thirty watermen a year lost their lives while failing to manage it. Indeed, as Thomas Pennant tells us, bridge drownings for all sorts of reasons were extremely common.*

> **"I well remember the street on London Bridge, narrow, darksome, and dangerous to passengers from the multitude of carriages: frequent arches of strong timber crossed the street, from the tops of the houses, to keep them together, and from falling into the river. Nothing but use could**

preserve the rest of the inmates, who soon grew deaf to the noise of the falling waters, the clamours of watermen, or the frequent shrieks of drowning wretches."

So Laughton must have swum up through London Bridge at the turn of the ebb tide – the flow would have been too great otherwise – and then ten miles further. Yet the river would have been extraordinarily busy. Quite apart from the mass of commercial traffic and ferries, there were literally thousands of watermen carrying passengers up and down the river and from one side to the other. Putney Bridge had just been completed in 1729 but since that was the ***only*** *other bridge, most crossings had to be made by boat; and the popular estimate was that over 12,000 men were working then as watermen.*

So simply swimming through the traffic would have been dangerous enough, but the health problems would have been considerable too. The Thames had not yet become the dead and choked sewer it was to become a hundred years later, but it was still enough of a sewer to be extremely hazardous. Indeed, one of the great advantages of living in one of the many houses on London Bridge was that you had an immediate outlet for your personal sewage, and you weren't infected by your neighbours'. Referring to the great plague of 1665 – what he called "the visitation" *– a doctor named Baynard wrote about this in 1709.*

"I remember that I heard an Apothecary say (I think it was Mr. Thomas Soaper) who lived then on London Bridge (an ingenious, sober Man) that there were but two Persons died on the Bridge in the whole time of the Visitation. The Truth of this may easily be inquired into, there being many Men now

> **alive, that then lived on the Bridge, or near it. And I have been lately told, by several Eminent Men, living on London-Bridge, that they have observed, that for the quantity of Houses, that the Bridge scapes better than other parts of the City, in any Contagious time whatsoever."**

So Laughton's swim showed him to be strong, macho, foolhardy and a man with a mind of his own. But what it ***didn't*** *show was his passionate interest in the forerunner of the ringing tea ...*

9. Piths and Brains

The bits I like best in your writings are the ones about food. Ringing teas are especially fascinating, and I'd dearly like to know all about what was in them hundreds of years ago. You must have researched all that sometime, so please tell all.

Emma
Hampshire

Indeed. And certainly, what people ate when, interests me as much as it does you. It's practical, it's cultural, and it's fundamental to history too, yet it's astonishingly hard to get reliable information. During any period, most people never record the *detail* of what they eat because, for them, it's so routine. They sometimes record exceptional meals and they sometimes record exceptional items – they sometimes even record the main item of a particular meal – but they almost never record the whole thing.

So they'll put in their diary that they had a ham salad but say nothing of what the salad consisted of. Or they'll write that they had roast lamb but tell nothing of the vegetables. And ringing tea reports – rare though they are anyway – are even worse. There might be a reference to the *excellent strawberries* or the *superb chocolate cake*, or even – going back further – to the *pigeon pie per person*, but there'll be no details of the entire spread.

Early cookery books don't help us much either. There aren't many, and most were written for the upper classes or the servants of the upper classes. They rarely give quantities, and they assume a knowledge of long extinct vegetable varieties and animal breeds. Essential details such as how close to the fire to put your spit, and how fast to turn it, don't get a mention at all. So it's just as well that – ringing wise – William Laughton, the country's first ever tower grabber, comes to our assistance.

A Good Hang-Up

And although in 1733 *ringing teas* were still a long way in the future, a good feed after ringing was still very much the order of the day. A good *hang-up* Laughton called it – a term that's completely disappeared in the UK although it's still used occasionally in parts of America – and he recorded his *hang-ups* in considerable detail. Indeed, in his tower grabbing writings – which, as we saw, are still preserved in the London Guildhall Library – he rather engagingly records each hang-up twice, once in verse and once in prose. So for example:

> **"For Harrington & Saunders hung us b' the teeth,**
> **With a legg of mutton and three Ribs of beef,**
> **'Twas in Milk Alley at the Waterman's Arms,**
> **Such a supper ev'ry night wou-d do us no harm."**

And

> **"Witness Will Coster's large sea pie,**
> **Enough for twenty men at least,**
> **Who dar'st say 'twant a noble feast"**

The Vegetables

And very fortunately, he doesn't just tell us about the main item, he also tells us about the vegetables. So after hiring a waterman to row them to Rotherhithe, and then two 720s later, row them back again, he records:

"The boat that carried us brought us back,
To Milk Alley, where at first we met,
Where beans and bacon boyling hot,
Was taken smoaking from the pot,
And Collyflow-rs and legg of mutton,
Was provided for us there to sup on."

And since seventeen sat down to the meal – well over a boatful – it's clear that, as with ringing teas nowadays, rather more ringers came to eat than ring. And on a technical note, the bacon was probably a flavouring to the beans, while the mutton was the central item.

The Roots

And although that's the only time we hear of *collyflow-rs*, not surprisingly root vegetables feature strongly in the winter. So on 17 October 1734 they meet at *The Sive and Last* in Haydon Yard after ringing a quarter peal on three in The Minories.

"We met at the Sive in Haydon Yard
Where a supper for us was prepared
Of good Roist Beef, and horse rhadish
A root which has a charming rellish,
Two dishes heaped with buttered turnips
Which proved agreeable to our stomachs."

And it's just possible, albeit unlikely, that the *turnips* they were eating were really swedes, since although they're generally thought to have been introduced into the UK later in the eighteenth century – and called *turnips* or *swedish turnips* then – it now seems that some Londoners were eating them rather earlier. But whatever, two months later on 12 December 1734 they meet at Will Coster's and were eating turnips once again.

> **"We met at brother Coster's next,**
> **And there we had a supper dress-d,**
> **It was indeed two leggs of pork,**
> **And a belly piece o' the same sort,**
> **Peas pudding, potatoes, parsnips, turnips,**
> **Various sauce for various stomacks,"**

And here's an extra point because Will Coster was both a ringer and an innkeeper; yet although he or his servants actually *cooked* the meal, Laughton himself paid for it. Indeed, the food for many of the meals was clearly bought by the provider but cooked by the innkeeper; and since Laughton had bought the meat, he was able to tell us in a later note that the "**two leggs of pork and a piece of the belly piece**" weighed 24 pounds and that there were 24 men to eat it all. So we get an idea both of the size of the joints and the amount of food consumed by each man.

And since pigs were generally slaughtered larger then than now, it seems that the word *legg* must have meant only part of the full leg. But more important, since eighteenth century pig breeds had a far greater proportion of fat to lean than today's breeds, a pound of meat per person was a very considerable amount of fat and calories, and certainly far more than the great majority of the population could afford.

Greens

But lest that gives the impression that their meals were unbalanced, the Rambling Club ringers didn't just eat meat, potatoes and root vegetables, they ate a great deal of cabbage too. We learn in Laughton's notes that the *roist beef* in *the Sive in Haydon Yard* was also accompanied by cabbage; and after yet another unsuccessful attempt at the bells of Camberwell, Laughton tells us:

**"At the Crown we met and had to eat
A legg and shoulder of good meat,
Cabbage well boyl-d and store of pickels
We had to eat with this good vittels.
After which we played a game at skittles."**

And after one of their rare full peals of Bob Major, they not only eat some kind of cabbage but they also have lettuce with their hot meat.

**"A leg of veal well boiled with bacon
And charming greens if I'm not mistaken
As e-er was eat and nice raw saleet,
Food very delightful to the pallet
To eat with lamb and there was plenty
Two lordly quarters did not look scanty,"**

At Mitcham

But the most detailed greens information we get is during a visit to Mitcham – a trip involving twenty miles' walking, a deal of drinking, a threatened fight with a "**brazier**," and a night in a ditch. It's July, the weather is superb and they're making a full day of it. But the pub – *The Stag's Head* – although clean and very well cared for is by no means posh, and the meal reflects this.

**"Beef, bacon, cabbage, in one dish,
Served up as good as man could wish.
And in another I was glad to see't,
As good french beans as e'er was eat,
And charming roisted leg of mutton**

Good as ever knife made cut on.
The gravy ran amongst the beans,
Which we eat with them and other greens,
And with good butter intermixed,
Made as good sauce as could be wished."

So in this inn – which evidently catered primarily for the labouring class – there was a considerable variety of green vegetables. But at the same time, the main item – presumably prepared to be eaten by the regular clientele – was *beef, bacon and cabbage in one dish*, or put simply, cabbage stew, the chief food of the poor for centuries.

The Toilet

And as an aside, Laughton was very impressed by the standard of cleanliness of *The Stag's Head* – and no doubt his opinion had considerable weight since his experience of pubs was extensive. So in addition to writing about the excellent wooden plates and bowls that the food was served on, he also wrote what was probably the world's first ever poem about a pub toilet.

"A nessisary or convenient
There stood quite at the further end on't,
O-er spread with woodbines fenced with roses
Delightful smells to most men's noses,
For honysuckels when they're blown
Have a charming sent it is well known,
And nothing more proper can be found
To spread over a privy all around."

And lest you're wondering whether the toilet was really covered in cigarette ends, *woodbine* was a word then used for honeysuckle – although other varieties of creepers were sometimes given the same name.

Other Dishes

But getting back to food, Laughton gives us an insight into the eating habits of a social class of which there is little other record. He's not eating as the labouring classes because he has far more money, but he's not eating as the gentry either. So although nothing remotely like this appears in Hannah Glasse's ground breaking 1747 cook book, he tells us:

> **"Next at Will Costers, and there Jo Haynes,**
> **Gave us a Hang up of piths and brains,**
> **Some was boyl-d and some was fry-d**
> **And nice crisp parsley laid by the side,**
> **And very good eating let me tell ye**
> **As I'd ever desire to put in my belly."**

And as you've probably never eaten piths and brains yourself, I can tell you that *piths* was spinal cord, so they were eating fried and boiled spinal cord and brains. What's more, they were apparently cooked by Will and his servants while the other ringers went off to ring.

Recipes

But Laughton didn't just enjoy *eating*, he was very interested in food preparation and cooking as well. So he gives us some very detailed recipes, one of which – leg of mutton stuffed with pickled herrings – certainly isn't in Hannah Glasse's cook book either.

> **"We met again at Brother Ned's**
> **And had for supper two noble leggs**
> **Of weather mutton fresh cut up**
> **And both with pickled herrings stuffed."**

And as with all their meals, this doesn't appear on the table as a surprise. The whole band knows what the meal is going to be, and collectively approves it even though one of their number makes the initial decision and pays for it. Innovation in eating doesn't bother them, and since this dish will be new, they even invite six women – very probably prostitutes – to share it.

> **"We'd half a dozen dames came there**
> **To taste of this new fashioned fair**
> **And were all well pleased with this odd dish**
> **But would scarce believe anything of fish."**

But for Laughton, a simple description of the dish wasn't enough. He clearly studied exactly how it was put together and cooked, and then he sampled each aspect separately to learn the result. And having done all that, he broke free from the constraint of rhyming, and set out this remarkable recipe in plain but very specific prose.

> **"We met at the George in Houndsditch where Mr. Greenwood and Mr. Davis gave us for supper two leggs of mutton roisted and stuffed with pickled herrings, which was as fine eating as ever was eat. The stuffing was composed of pickled herrings, sweet marjoram, penny royal, time, parsley, onions, beef suet, crumbs of bread, grated nutmeg and whites of eggs; the herrings mixed small and mixed with the other ingredients. 3 herrings is enough for a legg of 12 pounds and 4 for one of 15 or 16. Ours weighed 12 pounds each, so there was 6 large herings used to them both. They were stuffed without cutting of holes in the meat, as they do in a buttock of Beef or a fillett of Veal, for the stuffing of them was crammed down by the knuckles where there is a cavity to be found in the middle of the leg**

near the bone though not quite at it. The stuffing of these went down quite to the bottom of the legs and so up to the knuckles, that when they were stuffed they looked half as big again as they did before. As they roisted the herrings dissolved among the other ingredients and left not the least taste of fish behind, but gave the stuffing the finest flavour that can be imagined, nor was there the least taste of fish in the dripping for we had several sops made in it to taste."

Allamode

But the Rambling Ringers ate standard upmarket dishes too. Beef à la mode appeared on the best tables in both town and country. Curiously, Hannah Glasse tells us that there is the French way of preparing it and the *standard* – presumably English – way of preparing it – which is odd for a dish called *à la mode*.

Essentially, beef à la mode is beef boiled with bacon, herbs and wine. A good deal of meat was boiled then because the cast iron oven had only just been invented and was not yet in general use; so roasting wasn't very easy. Besides, boiling is an extremely good way of cooking meat, albeit now unfashionable. Interestingly, it was common in the eighteenth century to put an extra weight on the pot lid – ostensibly to keep the steam in – the cooks of the time apparently not realising they were increasing the cooking temperature by creating a primitive form of pressure cooker.

Beef à la mode continued to be a popular dish for over two hundred years with very few changes, but Laughton's recipe – for what he refers to as beef *allamode* or even *allamonde* – is pretty standard.

"At the George in Houndsditch on Thursday the 7th of November 1734, where Mr. Davis gave us for supper a buttock of beef dressed Allamonde fashion, that is larded with Bacon and stuffed with several sorts of herbs, spice, and other ingredients mixed together. The way of cooking it is as follows, viz: After the meat is seasoned 'tis put into a large pot with a quart of Claret and water mixed together to keep it from burning to the bottom, then it is set over a slow fire and the pot lid covered down as close as possible and weights laid on it to keep it from rising up to let the air in, and so it stews for 12 or 14 hours successively; this was 12 hours a stewing and when it was taken up there was 4 quarts of liquor though there was but one put in. It happened to be a little overcharged with salt or else the soop would have been exceeding rich and delicate, but the meat was very Rellishing."

The Last Meal

But in March 1735 The Rambling Club came to an end, and Laughton's meal descriptions came to an end with it. For the very last meal, Laughton paid for the meal in its entirety and arranged for them all – now increased from just seven to forty two – to go out in grand style. There was no ringing this time, just eating.

"The house where first this club began,
Agreed at first by seven men,
But now increased to forty two,
Strange tale to tell, but very true.

We met not for to ring a peal
But to eat a piece of good roist veal.
'Twas a shoulder stuffed with savory herbs
Good suet and some crumbs of bread,
And eat exceeding rich and good,
For 'twas a noble dish of food.
Likewise we had a pair of puddings
Well filled with suet eggs and currens,
As big as a middling pair of globes,
Plum puddings a food by most beloved."

And splendidly, just like most modern ringing teas, it was the *sweet* course that got the final mention.

When you're looking at the history of food, there's nothing quite so fascinating as class-specific items. Oysters, for example, went from being food for the extremely poor to being food for the extremely rich simply as a result of scarcity and fashion; and stodgy puddings were once enjoyed by both the upper and lower classes but not by those who had pretensions to being middle. *Yet amongst all the examples, none are quite so fascinating as cabbage.*

If you're a classical scholar, you'll know that the Ancient Greeks prized cabbage as the supreme vegetable. They thought – and indeed, they've now been proved right – that its health giving properties were numerous and considerable; and the Romans were very fond of it too. It was also widely eaten in various forms throughout the ancient World, both in the West and the East.

And apart from its health benefits, cabbage has many other advantages. It matures very quickly, it adds considerable flavour to stews, and it can provide an enormous quantity of edible matter per unit area of ground.

So since it also grows exceptionally well in our own climate and can stand in the ground for long periods, it's not surprising that it was a staple food of the English and European poor for centuries.

And because the poor could normally only cook by boiling on an open fire, it was mostly eaten in the form of cabbage stew – with other vegetables and a little meat added if and when they were available or could be afforded; and that was what Laughton was eating in Mitcham.

But human nature being what it is, since the poor ate cabbage in enormous quantities, the rich turned their noses up at it; and what's more, they did that for many centuries. So in 1653 when the herbalist, Thomas Culpeper was writing his massive work, ***The Complete Herbal****, he acknowledged that everyone knew what cabbages looked like but added – completely wrongly – "***... they are but seldom eaten in our days***;" because they are,*

> **"... extremely windy, whether you take them as meat or as medicine: yea, as windy meat as can be eaten, unless you eat bag-pipes or bellows,"**

which even for a man with a marked pre-occupation with wind, was a bit over the top.

And in the eighteenth century the class prejudice was just as strong. So when Hannah Glasse published her magnum opus, ***The Art of Cookery, Made Plain and Easy*** *in 1747 – a book that was so popular, it went through many editions until well into the nineteenth century – cabbage gets hardly a mention; and when it* ***does****, it's combined with copious amounts of meat, butter and cream.*

So we can see that when Laughton was enjoying cabbage in a stew with meat, he wasn't eating posh food at all but ordinary people's food – albeit with much more meat than most of his contemporaries could afford. Indeed, the indications are that it was ***only*** *the gentry who turned their noses up at cabbage. And just as an aside, Laughton – although not shy about mentioning his bodily functions – never mentions wind.*

He never mentions the ***taste*** *of cabbage either, but we know that the old varieties contained far more sulphur than present day varieties, so it would have been far more strongly flavoured, especially after long stewing.*

And just in case you're wondering what happened after Laughton's time, not much changed during the nineteenth century. Cabbage stew continued to be the staple food of the poor, and the upper classes continued to look down on it. But by now there was a burgeoning middle class too, and since they were following the normal course of "aping their betters," they had to look down on cabbage too.

So Mrs Beeton in her 1861 ***Book of Household Management*** *was as uninformative about cabbage as Hannah Glasse; and in 1886 when the publicity-shy Major Landon wrote* ***The Pytchley Book of Refined Cookery*** *he advised:*

> **"Especially in a small house, prevent the horrible smell which arises from boiling greens, fumigating and stinking out your guests ..."**

although as a member of The Pytchley Hunt *and a close friend of Lord Spencer, his idea of a* ***small house*** *was probably rather different to ours.*

But by the nineteenth century a curious class-based twist had come to stay. Red cabbage had been developed in the early eighteenth century, and – as is still true today – the flavour was almost indistinguishable from white cabbage when cooked in the same way; it was just a little bit blander. But being red made it a novelty, so it was braised with red wine, apples, spices, stock and suchlike instead of being just plain boiled. And in that form it could – and did – appear on all the best tables.

And even today, nearly three hundred years after this solely colour-based fashion started, the separation still exists. Red cabbage and hard white cabbage are almost identical in taste – ***sheep's food*** *as the farmers used to say – yet white cabbage is cooked one way and red cabbage is cooked another, and a great many people genuinely believe that the two vegetables have an inherent flavour difference.*

Of course, the twentieth century saw a substantial increase in the living standards of the poor, and as a result ***they*** *started to look down on cabbage too; and so a general cultural prejudice developed that's been passed from one generation to the next ever since. So while the Russians now eat an average of 44lbs per head per year,* **we** *eat less than an eighth of that.*

But getting back to post-ringing food, whether the ringers of the time liked cabbage or not, it was always more acceptable when it came as part of a free meal.

And ***free*** *meals were exactly what nineteenth century ringers sometimes got ...*

10. How Ringing Teas Began

For me, one of the greatest pleasures of being a bellringer is the ringing teas. It's not just the supreme quality of the food and the opportunity to sample a multitude of different cake recipes, it's also the feeling of taking part in a continuous living tradition that goes back centuries. It's like stepping gently back into the reign of Queen Victoria or Elizabeth I. So what I'd like to know is: how did they begin?

Richard
Leicestershire

History has it – or, at least, folklore has it – that Anna, Seventh Duchess of Bedford invented afternoon tea – or at least, she invented afternoon tea in the form we know it now. She did that around 1840. Dinner was getting later and the previous meal was getting earlier, and she found herself becoming distressingly hungry in the late afternoon. Of course, being a duchess, she could order any food she wanted – as long as no one but the servants knew – so she arranged for a pot of tea, together with small sandwiches and cakes, to be served to her privately in her boudoir.

But shockingly – although folklore doesn't tell us how – she was found out. Yet instead of being ridiculed, she was applauded by all the other equally hungry aristocratic ladies who promptly joined her in her boudoir. Then later, they all decamped to the drawing room and ate their tea there.

Snobbery came into it too. The Duchess was a *Lady of the Bedchamber* to Queen Victoria, as well as being the Queen's lifelong personal friend; so she had a good deal of clout in society, and upper class ladies naturally followed her lead. Quite soon everybody who *was* anybody was taking afternoon tea too, and at the Duchess's suggestion, Queen Victoria herself started hosting afternoon tea parties in the 1840s. And since if Queen Victoria did something, the middle class immediately had to do the same, the Queen's support gave the custom the ultimate social *imprimatur*.

So put simply, folklore has it that *afternoon tea* in the form of tea, sandwiches and cakes dates only from the 1840s, and certainly, a study of British porcelain manufacturing confirms that the modern day *tea service* only came into being then.

Tea Dances

But although it's a splendid story and although it definitely has a great deal of truth to it, the origin of any social custom is never quite that simple. *Tea dances* were already being held in London before 1820, and these were late afternoon events at which sandwiches, cakes and tea were served between the dances.

But although they certainly *were* tea dances, they weren't actually called that until several decades later. Instead they were called *Thé Dansants* because they had been imported from France – although even then, they most probably originated in Morocco. So rather distressingly, although the Duchess undoubtedly popularised it, afternoon tea almost certainly pre-dated her and wasn't an English invention at all.

Patriotic English people need not despair, though, because even as early as 1738, the word *tea* was being used in England to describe an afternoon meal at which tea was served; and besides, what we now see as *afternoon tea* has undoubtedly become a solidly British tradition that tourists from all over the World come here to experience. And in that form, the Duchess of Bedford and Queen Victoria were jointly responsible.

Contrary to popular belief, though, the one thing they *didn't* invent – or even *eat* – in 1840 was the cucumber sandwich. In the early nineteenth century a good many people still thought eating cucumbers was dangerous, and they were more often eaten cooked than raw. They weren't easy to grow either, so the cucumber sandwich only came into vogue several decades later.

Social Class

But all that said, tea – the drink – was for nearly two centuries an important part of the working class diet. It was drunk much stronger and more stewed than today, and the caffeine boost – as well as the sugar boost – helped both men and women maintain their performance in their heavy physical labour. So a great deal of tea was drunk at *tea time*, and the working classes ate cooked food then too if they could afford it. This was called *high tea* from the mid-nineteenth century until not that long ago, probably because it had to be eaten from a high enough table for the eaters to be able to use knives and forks without too much trouble.

And very splendidly, *ringing* teas in Lancashire, Yorkshire and some surrounding areas were *always* high teas until fairly recently. Lancashire hot pot served with mushy peas and hot beetroot was a favourite, as was meat and potato pie with mushy peas and pickled red cabbage. And that is itself one of our great ringing traditions even though the Duchess of Bedford and Queen Victoria never ate Lancashire hot pot in their boudoirs. Indeed, a Wartime advert for a Yorkshire Association meeting tells us, "**Plain tea 1s. 6d.; meat tea and chips 2s. 6d**."

When

But with *high tea* there were timing issues. It couldn't be eaten until the working man came home, so it was naturally later than *afternoon tea*. But even afternoon tea didn't have a set time across the whole of society. The upper class took it at around 4.00 p.m. but the middle class – who in this as in all else, at least *attempted* to "ape their betters" – were forced by circumstance to take it later. Indeed, even in 1969 the short crosswords in both *The Times* and *The Daily Telegraph* had the same clue – *Tea Time?* But while the answer in *The Times* was four o'clock, the answer in *The Daily Telegraph* was five o'clock.

Ringing Teas

So with all these influences, how *did* ringing teas in their present form become the norm in most of the country?

Well, they certainly don't date back to the 1840s, and since the great bulk of ringers were working men then, they wouldn't have been bothered with what Duchesses were doing in their boudoirs anyway. A good feed was what interested them, and there's plenty of evidence of them having exactly that after ringing, especially when someone else was paying. Essentially, they fortified themselves with a proper meal; and as we've seen, some Northern ringers continued that tradition long after the rest of the country became more genteel. Equally, pasty teas remained – and still remain – common in Devon and Cornwall too. But what about those areas that *did* change? Why did they do that?

And sadly, evidence about that is distressingly thin. Of course, Association Saturday meetings traditionally started at 3.00 p.m. so that working men had enough time to get to the meetings after doing half a day's work in the morning. So by 5.00 p.m. they were ready for major sustenance. Perhaps most would have preferred something substantial, but sandwiches and cakes are very sustaining too – as well as being a considerable treat – and it seems likely that the middle class *vicarage garden afternoon tea* moved smoothly across into ringing.

Quite likely, vicars wives had a lot to do with the change because vicars were then very wealthy and it was common for them to supply tea to all the visiting ringers – especially as there normally weren't that many. No doubt their wives arranged for their cooks to provide what they thought was socially appropriate, and when the ringers' wives themselves supplied the tea, they no doubt followed the lead of their social superiors

The Very First

So we simply don't know when the very first ringing tea was served in its current form, and since so few records of Association eating exist, we're probably never going to find out. But it's clear that afternoon teas and high teas existed side by side for a long time, with high teas being generally preferred. So on 22nd February 1881 when the recently formed Essex Association met at Witham they recorded:

> **"At half-past five the members assembled at the 'Albert,' on invitation to tea by Mr. W. Bindon Blood. Tea is generally associated with something 'water luke,' and a weak infusion, dry cake, etc.; not such was Mr. Blood's entertainment: the commission**

to mine host was evidently to do his best, and provide a substantial meal for his visitors; and though the 'cup that cheers and not inebriates' – no weak infusion – was there, John Barleycorn was not forgotten. The activity of thirty-seven pairs of knives and forks and suspended conversation evidenced that recruitment of the inner man was being most satisfactorily proceeded with."

And we can see from this that tea and cake must have been supplied at some meetings – although there's no mention of sandwiches – so ringing teas in approximately their current form must then have existed. Possibly they were indeed as faint-hearted as the writer suggests, but equally possibly, he simply disapproved of a new fashion.

But more importantly, we can see that the meal was served in a pub and it was eaten at *high tea* time. Mr W. Bindon Blood paid for everybody's food out of his own pocket too, rather in the way that a single person paid for the meals we looked at in the last chapter. And we can see also that it was a substantial meal – with beer – and no doubt the working men with limited means were very glad of *that*.

Sandwiches

But in Lancashire in July 1881, ringers definitely *were* eating sandwiches. A monument to a deceased ringer and member of the *Independent Order of Oddfellows* was unveiled in Mottram, and detailed instructions were given.

"Before dispersing, the procession will be re-formed, and march back to the Market-place, when the band will play the National Anthem. A Sandwich Tea will be provided

in the National-school room, at 5 o'clock, price 1s. 3d. each. The order of procession will be: the Band; then Ringers and Friends; followed by the District Officers of the Mottram District I.O.O.F., M.U., and the Officers and Brothers of the various Lodges in the district."

And certainly we can see that a sandwich and cake tea was easier to prepare and serve than a hot tea – or indeed, than a knife and fork *cold* tea – but the really sad thing is that evidence is so very hard to come by. The one thing that all Association Secretaries in the country had in common for decades was an overwhelming predisposition to bore the pants off everybody whilst giving no useful information. So while their minutes record the discussions of entirely trivial issues in the minutest detail, the make-up of the tea goes completely un-noted. The *ladies* were always recorded as being thanked, but that was that.

So, very sadly, we'll just have to content ourselves with speculation. All the same, for the benefit of future historians, what about getting your Branch Secretary to break free from the traditions of over a century, and write some really *interesting* minutes?

This chapter has been about tea, the meal, and we haven't said much about tea, the drink. And the drink is actually much more fascinating than the meal because, after air and water, it's the most widely consumed substance on the planet. All the same, until the second half of the seventeenth century, no one in this country had even heard of it. Samuel Pepys had his first cup in 1660, and although he doesn't say where he got it from, he does say. **'I did send for a cup of tee' (a**

China drink) of which I never had drank before.*" Also in 1660 Charles II had a cup when he was given two pounds and two ounces by* The East India Company.

But thereafter it took off in a truly astonishing way. Although the first legal imports weren't until the second half of the seventeenth century, in the first quarter of the eighteenth it took the country by storm. In 1700 only 100,000 lbs were imported, but in 1750 imports had reached 5,000,000 lbs. And even more astonishing, no one at the time had the remotest idea why. It was nice enough, certainly, but it was very expensive; and the teapot to brew it in was expensive too. Equally, no one knows why everyone started drinking it with milk and sugar.

Of course it was far easier to prepare than drinking-chocolate but its great attraction – especially to the poorer classes – was probably the caffeine lift it produced. Indeed, it became so popular that servants began to insist on tea as part of their remuneration. In 1776 Parson Woodforde recorded these details of the new maid he'd just taken on.

> **"A very pretty woman she is and understands cookery and working at her needle well. I am to give her per annum and tea twice a day – 5. 5. 0."**

And since wherever there's trade, tax quickly follows, the economic effects of all that tea drinking soon became profound. By 1780, the customs duties on tea provided a staggering one sixth of all government revenues; and unsurprisingly, that led to smuggling and adulteration on a grand scale. Indeed, it's estimated that in 1780 two thirds of tea consumed was either smuggled or adulterated or both. Even Parson Woodforde, pillar of the establishment though he was, obtained his supplies nefariously. He tells us on 29th March 1777:

"... Andrews the Smuggler brought me this night about 11 o'clock a bagg of Hyson Tea 6 Pd weight. He frightened us a little by whistling under the Parlour Window just as we were going to bed. I gave him some Geneva and paid him for the tea at 10/6 per Pd ... 3. 3. 0."

*And by way of comparison, Parson Woodforde paid his other maid – who's duties were "***... to milk, etc***." – only three pounds and ten shillings for the entire year – and* ***she*** *didn't even get tea added in.*

The enormous commercial and political effects of all this tea drinking weren't just felt in the UK either, but over the whole world. The Chinese weren't interested in our main exports – woollens and such – and there was public opposition to them being paid out of the UK's silver reserves, so interlinked trading arrangements came into being involving sugar, the slave trade and – eventually – the establishment of tea plantations in India. It's all very complex, but essentially, the World would be very different today if we'd stuck to drinking water and weak beer.

And even in the Second World War the Government saw tea as so essential to national morale, that it became a vital strategic commodity in its own right. So the nation's supplies were moved immediately on landing from the London dockside to secret locations.

Yet most of us don't see tea as a substance that created fortunes, destroyed lives and changed the political map of the World for ever. We see it as no more than a quiet cuppa on a Summer's afternoon. And quiet cuppas on Summer afternoons were exactly what nineteenth century horse brake outings were all about ...

11. Horse Brakes and Charabancs

Last Saturday I went on a tower open day. We raced from tower to tower, queued for hours on spiral staircases, rang quick bursts, and raced off again. It was *awful*; and I hankered to be back a hundred years ago when ringers had leisurely outings on horseback.

Anthony
Huntingdonshire

Well, it sounds nice, certainly, but I'm afraid it wasn't quite like that. In Chapter 8 we saw that even three hundred years ago William Laughton and *The Rambling Club* only went tower grabbing on foot or by boat; and since few eighteenth century London ringers owned a riding horse, horseback outings weren't an option. For that matter, neither then nor since can I find *any* record of a horseback outing. One or two *individuals* went tower visiting on horseback, certainly, but organised groups apparently never did.

And that's not surprising because very few people, either in town or country, *ever* owned a horse as a means of transport. Contrary to popular belief, the number of *private and pleasure* horses was far less in 1900 than today; and the chance of six ringers living near each other, each with enough money to own his own horse, was vanishingly small.

Trains

But as ringers became less poor, non-walking outings became a possibility; and by the mid-nineteenth century, trains were an option. All the same, ringers were slow to use them, mainly because they couldn't afford them. The comfort and safety for third class passengers was horrendous too. They travelled in open, shoddily built carriages directly behind the engine, and deaths and injuries were part of the normal routine. At Sonning in 1841, two third class carriages were crushed between the better carriages and the engine, and twenty-five people were killed or mutilated; and in other incidents, whole carriage-fulls of passengers were burnt to death.

And the railway companies' belief that accidents were a matter of normal routine, was chilling. Here's an extract from the daily record of *The North Midland Railway* from January 1843.

> **"Jan 6th. – The passenger train which leaves Leeds at 5.30 p.m. was standing at Barnsley Station when Edward Jenkins, driver of a luggage train, ran into it. The usual signals had been given to Jenkins, but from some cause or other were not observed. There were only three carriages in the passenger train, and fortunately only one passenger. The carriages were all smashed to pieces and the head of the unfortunate passenger was cut completely off."**

The Cost

It helped a little when trains became less expensive from 1844 with the passing of *The Railway Regulation Act*. All railway companies then had to run trains that travelled at not less than 12 mph, stopped at all stations, and charged no more than one old penny per mile. These trains were certainly cheaper, but they still weren't cheap enough for most ringers. If the journey was less than ten miles, they'd just as soon walk. If it was fifteen or more, the fare was beyond their means.

Special Fares

But as the nineteenth century wore on and wages rose, train travel became an occasional possibility. It was still very expensive, though, and ringers wanted special fares – something that wasn't unreasonable because in those days, there was a vast number of special fares for all sorts of travellers. Golfers and fishermen, for example, got special fares – as, at times, did ship-wrecked mariners – but ringers generally didn't. Some companies would charge them the same rate as brass bands, and they could always get group discounts, but as the Secretary of the *Gloucester and Bristol Association* complained in *Bell News*, that wasn't enough.

> **"... when one is travelling for pleasure he has a rooted objection to paying full fare, and this he has to do unless he can get seven others to travel with him, and then he can claim to travel for three-quarter fare. The Central Council must again endeavour to persuade the Railway Clearing House to re-classify church bellringers. At present they are classed with brass bands, who, when they travel, take their instruments and music stands with them carriage free, and the classification is therefore obviously unfair."**

The Committee on Railway Fares

In fact the Central Council did indeed set up a *Committee on Railway Fares* in an attempt to get cheaper rates, but they were completely unsuccessful. All the same, *some* ringing outings travelled by train, although they were really social outings rather than tower grabs. In 1891, for example, the Ashby-de-la-Zouch ringers recorded:

> **"The Annual outing of this Society took place on Wednesday June 24th, when ... a comfortable table saloon for the ringers was attached to the special train which left Ashby-de-la-Zouch at 9.30 a.m."**

Indeed, even by 1882 there were sufficient ringers taking their outings by train, that a stern warning was deemed necessary in *Bell News*.

> **"As the excursion season is now approaching, the attention of excursionists and travellers by rail generally is directed to the dangerous practice of throwing ginger-beer bottles out of carriage windows."**

Horse Brakes

But even if most ringers couldn't afford trains, some could at least afford a *brake* – which sounds splendidly old-world and relaxing but in reality was nothing of the sort. A *brake* was simply a two-horse cart used for carrying things during the week. For weekend outings, it was cleaned out and had seats put in. Brakes were slow, with no protection from the weather; and two horses were little enough pulling power for a long day out. All the same, an outing was an outing, and the Oldbury ringers certainly enjoyed theirs in 1901.

"On Saturday August 31st the members had an outing by brake to Bridgnorth. Starting about 8.30, Wolverhampton was reached, where the horses had a little rest. Away at full speed again, a drizzling rain having ceased and the sky become clear, a first-rate spin was made all the way to The Bardon Arms ..."

The horses had another rest here while the ringers did some ringing, and then they set off again. But as was usual with a brake, they all had to get out and walk when they got to any kind of hill.

"The horses were again put to, and after a walk up the hill, which is a rather heavy one, seats were taken for the return journey, pipes were refilled, and away homeward we went, the journey being enlivened by song and recitation until Oldbury was reached."

Certainly, a brake full of ringers singing and reciting does sound rather fun, but brakes had problems. Trains might be expensive but they generally arrived on time whereas brakes often didn't. So London-area ringers – who were generally rather better off – normally took the train. Here's the Haverstock Hill outing of September 1896.

"On Saturday, September 12th, the above Society held their outing, the place selected being Southend-on-Sea. A start was made at 8.43 a.m. from Kentish Town by the Midland Railway, Southend being reached at 10.15 a.m., and after refreshing the inner man we parted for a stroll round, some going on the Pier, others along the shore, all

meeting at 1 o'clock sharp for dinner. ... a move was made for Prittlewell ... arriving there about 4 o'clock ... ringing ... tea ... a walk back to Southend ... home was reached about 11.15 p.m."

Horses

And when compared to a steam engine, a horse was a very variable thing. Horse brake hirers never knew what horses they'd get or how fit they'd be, and the organiser didn't know the state of the roads either. Worse still, even in the nineteenth century, outing organisers were already displaying that unrealistic optimism about travelling times, that they've been displaying ever since.

Essentially, the horses were expected to travel very long distances at impossibly high speeds. The ringers naturally wanted to make a very long day of it as they had few enough outings of any kind, and they wanted to get their money's worth too. So their outing normally lasted from first light till gone midnight, and that was very hard indeed on the horses. This experience of the Kidderminster ringers was by no means uncommon.

"The wagonette was again brought into use, and a move was made for Morville, a pretty little village about three miles north-west from Bridgnorth, on the Wenlock Road."

So far so good, and tea-time went well too, but:

"Kinlet was the next place to be visited, but the member who arranged the time-table had evidently not calculated on the roads. Hills were expected, but not the sort we encountered, and Kinlet was not reached

until 9 p.m. The local ringers had waited about for us until 8.45, but had then given up all hope."

And what's also interesting here is that the local ringers were apparently quite happy for a visiting band to start their – presumably quite long – ring at 8.45 at night.

Penny Farthings

But towards the end of the nineteenth century the bicycle came along, and it brought with it a freedom that most people had never known before. Roads were much poorer then and punctures were much more frequent, but ringers could now travel tens of miles for free – as long as they could afford the bicycle to start with. Indeed, in the very early days of cycling, some ringers actually went on outings on their *penny farthings* – then often known as *high bicycles*. George Williams – a famous peal ringer whose wife was the first woman ever to ring a handbell peal – recorded his various cycling outings in his private record.

> **"A week was also spent amongst Guildford friends in August ... Holt's original at Godalming lost in last 3 leads by 7th man being done up as we were travelling about then on high bicycles."**

Indeed, it's not surprising that the *7th man* was *done up* as penny farthings were very hard work and George and his friends clearly travelled huge distances on them.

> **"Well do I remember friend Harry tumbling into the nettles when attempting to dismount at the last hill fairly done up ... we had ridden over 60 miles in addition to the peal."**

Rowing Boats

But while some outings travelled on bicycles, others travelled in rowing boats. In Chapter 9 we saw how *The Rambling Club* sometimes travelled by rowing boat, but that was a different kind of rowing boat. *Those* boats were essentially river taxis rowed by professional watermen – rather like the pedalled rickshaws of the East – but the Edwardian rowing boats were hired, *row-them-yourself* boats.

Rowing and boating had now become very fashionable, and since people had more money, and transport had become easier, rivers and lakes were popular places to visit. Boating on the Thames was so hugely popular, that on Sunday afternoons the river was literally jammed by thousands of hired, rowing skiffs. Men were expected to be able to row – or at least, to *claim* to be able to row – and women were expected to lay back on the cushions holding their parasols. So the Plymouth outing to Fowey in July 1911 was absolutely the modern thing to do.

> **"Boats were hired, and a nice row up the river brought the party to Lanteglos, but time being short they could only ring 120 each of Grandsire and Stedman Doubles, and then off to the boats again"**

Indeed, some towers arranged entire weekends based on the river. Here's the Chelsea ringing weekend, also in July 1911.

> **"The annual outing took place on Saturday and Sunday, the party, consisting of twelve members, making their headquarters at Marlow. After an admirable lunch, it was decided to make Hurley the destination, and, boats being requisitioned the journey**

was thoroughly enjoyed by all. After a short stay at Hurley the return journey was made by easy rowing. Dinner being disposed of, some of the party went for a quiet ramble, and others for further exercise, in the shape of rowing."

Steam Boats

And from late Victorian times until well after the First World War, outings on steam boats were very popular, and ringers made use of them. Often the boats were vastly overloaded, and the UK's biggest ever peace time disaster occurred in 1878 when the Newcastle collier, *Bywell Castle*, cut the excursion steamer, *Princess Alice*, into two pieces in the River Thames. At least 640 people died, and although nothing like that ever happened on ringing outings, unexpectedly rough seas could cause the best laid plans to go astray. The Cardiff ringers had this trouble in 1911.

"The St. John's Guild had their annual outing on Saturday, Sept. 30th. Meeting at the pier head, they left by the pleasure steamer 'Lady Ismay' at two o'clock. A rather rough voyage across the channel was experienced. It was intended to ring at Minehead, but owing to the rough sea the boat did not stop there, so the party had to content themselves with another couple of hours roll on the beautiful waves until Ilfracombe was reached, at 5.50. ... The party landed at Ilfracombe, but now had just an hour and a quarter's stay, so owing to the distance of the church away from the pier, the idea of having a pull had to be abandoned."

Charabancs

But the really big change in ringing outings came with the advent of charabancs. These had arrived before the First World War but they became much commoner after; yet although they improved outings enormously, there were problems.

In their early days, most charabancs weren't the elegant and beautifully made *toast racks* that still exist in vintage vehicle collections; they were simply lorries – typically, war surplus lorries bought cheap by former soldiers with their gratuities – and like the horse brakes we looked at earlier, they were used for carrying goods during the week. On Friday nights they were scrubbed out, seats were put in, and they became charabancs until Monday morning.

So they had loose seats and no roof, and no way of getting on board except by way of a short ladder leant against the side. Their engines were often extremely unreliable – particularly over anything other than a short distance – and they were normally substantially overloaded too. Having hired the vehicle, the organisers packed the maximum number of people into it, as photographs of the time clearly show.

Road Accidents

The roads were extremely dangerous too. In 1928 when road deaths were first recorded, there were well over twice as many deaths as today even though there were less than a tenth as many vehicles on the roads. Each vehicle travelled far fewer miles too. So with the overloading and unreliability combined, this 1921 experience of the West Didsbury ringers was typical.

> **"Setting out at 1.45 p.m. in a 12-seater motor charabanc, we were soon moving**

very smoothly through the prettiest village in the county. At Lawton, on the outward journey, two of the local ringers were picked up, and the 12-seater became somewhat overcrowded."

But even so, everything apparently went splendidly until they turned for home.

"The party left for home at 9 p.m., but the journey was not without incident. After a few miles the lights failed, but a short stop enabled this to be rectified. Then some 20 miles from home a thorough breakdown occurred through the exhaust having gone wrong. It was an isolated part of the country, but fortunately within 50 yards was found a place 'within the meaning of the act,' where the party were enabled to refresh themselves. After about an hour's stoppage, and failing to be taken in tow with any passing motor, the driver, with the aid of some of the excursionists, eventually got the motor in working order again, and the destination was reached after midnight when, the [tram]cars having ceased running, some of the members had a two and three miles walk home."

But were they downhearted by two breakdowns and a three mile walk after the trams had stopped for the night? Certainly not! The West Didsbury ringers were clearly made of stern stuff; and they ended their report,

"Verdict – a most enjoyable time."

A Disaster

But if the West Didsbury ringers had an enjoyable time in *their* charabanc, the Barnstaple ringers in July 1913 certainly didn't.

> **"A merry party, numbering 14, left the town in a motor char-a-banc for Exeter, and all went well until the neighbourhood of Oakford was reached. The excursionists had been enjoying the exhilarating ride, but the car got into difficulties on a very steep hill, and, to the alarm of the occupants, began to run backwards. The brakes failed to act, and, the driver losing control, the vehicle crashed into a hedge and overturned. It was quickly obvious that several of the party were badly injured. One of their number, Mr. William Goss, aged 60, and for many years a ringer at Barnstaple, was terribly crushed, and died soon after being dragged from under the car."**

And Later

As far as we know, William Goss was the only ringer to die in a charabanc accident on an outing, but there may well have been others who went unreported.

But reverting to happier matters, once the Second World War was over, outings took off in a very big way indeed, and *The Ringing World* became packed with cliché ridden reports, all sounding exactly the same except for the different towers. But something *extra* happened. Lists of the leading tower grabbers started to appear each year – albeit initially known as *tower visitors* – and tower grabbing became a matter of personal pride and competition.

And once that got going, people wanted to grab *subsets* of towers – all the sixes over 20 cwt, for example, or all the eights in Berkshire – and in the 1970s, Peter Devenish wrote a splendidly funny, but sad, poem about a man attempting to achieve the tower grabbing alphabet. Not much to do with history, of course, but here's "**The Tower Grabber**."

He'd rung at Abbotskerswell,
Altarnun, Ash and Arley;
At Bootle, Bishop's Itchington –
At Baltonsborough and Barley;

At Chedzoy, Chipping Sodbury
And Cromhall (12-1-7)
At Dodderhill and Dodleston
And Dittisham in Devon.

He'd grabbed Egg Buckland, Egremont,
Egloshayle and Eltham,
Flookborough, Fishtoft, Finchingfield,
Farthingstone and Feltham;

Then Groton, Massachusetts
And Groton, Suffolk, too –
And Horsington and Hoylandswaine
And anti-clockwise Hoo.

Ipplepen and Ightham,
Inveraray, Ipswich town,
Jarrow, Jersey, Jacobston –
Rang them up, then wrote them down.

Kirby Malzeard, Kirby Lonsdale,
Kirby-on-the-Moor;
Llanfihangel,Llandefaelog,
Llangyfelach. (That's a four)

Mucklestone, Much Marcle,
Messingham and Mere;
Nempnett Thrubwell, Nether Wallop –
Just you name it: he'd been here!

Oswaldtwistle, Ombersley,
Old Cleeve in Somerset –
Longing for the day when he'd
Complete the alphabet.

Penge and Perranzabuloe,
Queen Camel, Quinton, Quorn;
Raunds and Ratley, Rampisham,
Sibbertoft and Shorne;

Tydwardreath and Twickenham,
Ubley, Upper Boddington;
Victoria and Veryan,
Wangford, Wapley, Waddington...

Then, with sinking heart, he searched
From Gwent to Middlesex.
The fact was inescapable:
He couldn't find an 'X'.

He never touched another rope,
Never raised another tenor;
Nevermore called "Treble's gone.
They buried him ... in Zennor.

Sometimes when I'm giving ringing history talks I say what someone paid for something years ago – so I might mention that Fabian Stedman paid five shillings a ream for paper in 1677. And whenever I do, someone always asks, "So what's that in today's money?" And although on the face of it that ***seems*** *a very good question, in many ways it* ***isn't****, because prices are never really comparable between one era and another.*

Partly that's because some things go radically ***up*** *over time whilst others go radically* ***down****. So for example, paper prices are now only a few times what they were in 1677, whilst oyster prices are thousands of times more. But more important, some things – baked beans, for example – are a staple food now whereas they didn't even exist in 1677; and many common foods then – pigs' heads, for example – are virtually unobtainable now.*

Of course, you could try to compare the price of a seventeenth century pig's head with a twenty-first century tin of baked beans, but somehow that wouldn't feel very satisfying; and indeed, the people who compile the ***Retail Prices Index*** *have had exactly that problem for decades. It's certainly fascinating to see what was included in the very first* ***Index*** *in 1947 but which nobody at all buys now – table mangles, lamp oil and detachable shirt collars, for example.*

Average wages ***might*** *seem a good basis for comparison, in that you could calculate how many minutes a man earning the average wage would need to work to buy a dozen eggs now, and then you could compare it to the equivalent figure for 1677.*

But that doesn't work well either. Eggs were once so expensive that working men in towns could rarely afford them at all, and besides, wages have always varied significantly between different parts of the country. Worse, those variations have ***themselves*** *varied.*

And on top of all that, you can't compare wages in any meaningful way anyway. The difference in taxation is a factor, as are the current universal benefits such as ***The***

National Health Service *and free schooling. And even if you could get round all those, you'd be completely scuppered by the fact that the* ***discretionary spend*** *margin is now so much greater for most of the population than it ever was.*

A bit subtle this, but for most of history, ***most*** *people lived – or, indeed,* ***didn't*** *live – at the very margin of existence. Their income was entirely used up – or* ***more*** *than used up – in paying for the basic costs of survival. Food, clothing, rent and a limited amount of fuel took all or most of their income, and only a very little – or nothing at all – was left for even the simplest discretionary spend. So in 1677 a working man would never have been able to buy paper at all – quite apart from the fact that he wouldn't have wanted to as he'd never learnt to read and write.*

And to make things worse, what's thought of as ***essential*** *– rather than discretionary – changes over time too. So in 1925 it was* ***essential*** *for an urban working class housewife to pay for the materials to whiten her front step every morning, whereas patched and darned clothes were nothing to be ashamed of. But in the twenty-first century, front steps are an irrelevance whilst clothes are supremely important. So for children today, the right trainers are a social necessity, but in 1925 they could have gone to school barefoot without comment.*

And on top of all that, is the problem of simple common sense. A century and more ago there was such a vast difference in income between the bulk of the population and the income of the middle class – let alone the upper class – that in reality there were several completely different commercial worlds in operation.

It's rather like the difference now between ordinary people and the super-rich. A genuine designer handbag can cost over a thousand times an almost identical handbag on a market stall, yet most of us can hardly tell the difference. But you can't simply average the two prices in order to compare handbag costs now with handbag costs fifty years ago. Still less can you use handbag costs to compare the value of money generally.

So when a newspaper tells you that a sum of money two hundred years ago would be such and such *today, take no notice. It always sounds impressive but when you get right down to it, it's nonsense. There's been inflation, certainly, but historical comparisons are far too complex to be expressed in simple numbers.*

All the same, for many sums, I know you'd like a rough idea. So on an **average wage comparison** *the ringers in our next chapter will actually be competing for hats worth over £1,600 each ...*

12. Laced with Gold

You've written about the World's first woman ringer and the World's first tower grabber, but what about the World's first striking competition? They're not a big deal nowadays, I know, but someone once told me they used to be. Is that true?

Simon
Hampshire

Well, it sort of is and it sort of isn't. For most of the country, striking competitions as we know them today are a fairly recent phenomenon. Modern ones generally date from well after the Second World War even though there's a popular misconception that they go back much further. Indeed, even the term *striking competition* is fairly modern. But ringing competitions of a rather different sort were common throughout most of the eighteenth and nineteenth centuries, and they were known as ***prize ringing***.

The Gloves Off

And if you see in that term a similarity with the equally popular eighteenth and nineteenth century activity of prize *fighting*, you're absolutely right. Competitions of any kind have always attracted people, and the more the competitors feel personally antagonistic to one another, the more the public like them. *Needle matches* are always compelling, and since business-savvy promoters make good money from providing alcohol, food and gambling, they play them up for all they're worth. The eighteenth century was no different, and although we don't know when the very first open-to-all prize ringing match took place, one of the earliest adverts appeared in *The Norwich Gazette* of the 12th January 1712.

> **"On Monday the 28th Instant there will be Five Pairs of Gloves rung for at Acle in Norfolk, and Seven Ribbs of Roast Beef given for the Ringers Dinners at the Kings-head in the said Town."**

And immediately we have the essential elements that were to feature in all prize ringing. First, there had to be – or at least *appear* to be – prizes of sufficient value that any group of working men would fantasise about winning them. Second, alcohol had to be plenteously available to the spectators. And third, a good entry had to be encouraged by the provision of free or cheap meals to all the entrants – in this case a share in thirty pounds of beef.

Naturally enough, no one actually *mentions* gambling, or even hints at it, but we know from numerous other references that it certainly went on.

Ongoing

And since this was such a simple but winning formula, it continued virtually unaltered for well over a century. So over fifty years later *The Ipswich Journal* of Saturday 13th March 1762 advertises very much the same thing.

> **To all Gentlemen Lovers of RINGING.**
>
> **On THURSDAY the 25th of this Instant March, being the first Day of the Fair, there will be at the CROWN in MALDON, SIX HATS of Half a Guinea Value each, to be**

rung for at the Parish Church of St. Mary, by any two or more Companies of Six Bell Ringers: To ring two eighteen Score; one a plain Course, the other a dodging Course: To be at the Belfry by Eleven in the Forenoon.

N.B. There will be Dinner provided at the Crown: where all Persons shall have a hearty Welcome, from their humble Servant, T. Brand.

Here, though, the inducements are more specifically stated. It's now clear that all the ringers will get a full meal rather than just an unquantified share of seven ribs of beef, and more importantly, the hats are specifically valued at ten shillings and sixpence each.

And to put that into context, an agricultural worker of the period – assuming he didn't live close to one of the up-and-coming industrial towns – received only about six shillings a week. So since almost all of that had to be spent on necessities, ten shillings and sixpence was riches indeed.

And Elsewhere

And just to show that prize ringing was happening in a great many places, here's *Jackson's Oxford Journal* of Saturday 30th April 1763.

Notice is hereby given,
To all Gentleman RINGERS,

THAT there will be given gratis, by William Roman, at the Sign of the Chequer, in Beaconsfield, Six Silver Stock-Buckles, to be Rung for in Beaconsfield Church, on Whit-Monday next, to them that ring the best

Round Peal, which is to be determined by proper umpires: No less than three Sets to ring, but as many more as will. The ringers of Beaconsfield to be excepted from Ringing.

N.B. There will be an ordinary at Two o'Clock; and the gentlemen who propose to Ring, are desired to give their Names, on Wednesday in the preceeding Week, to their humble Servant, William Roman.

And this advert makes it absolutely clear that the competition was being sponsored by the publican himself. And just in case you're not acquainted with the eighteenth century patois, an *ordinary* was a set meal with no or very few alternatives, and available to anyone who paid. It was a kind of Georgian *table d'hôte.*

Fairs and Rejoicing Days

But if the publican was going to make a profit, a large number of spectators had to attend, and in the eighteenth century that wasn't straight-forward. Agricultural workers got very little time off, and when they did, they'd only be able to travel to events by walking; so competition dates had to be chosen carefully. And that's why William Roman at *the Sign of the Chequer* in Beaconsfield organised his competition for Whit Monday, and T. Brand at *The Crown* in Maldon organised *his* for *the first Day of the Fair.*

But when the day was well chosen it seems that large numbers of people did indeed attend. Some publicans even employed a couple of local bruisers as bouncers – normally referred to as *constables* – to keep order and deal with trouble makers. There was lots of cheering and booing as well apparently, and it was probably well informed cheering and booing as the spectators then would have been much more knowledgeable about ringing than most people are nowadays.

The Prizes

But although in two of our adverts, the prizes were gloves and buckles, most often they were hats, generally valued at half a guinea or a guinea each. Exactly *why* hats featured so strongly is complex, but since the historical, cultural and economic background of hat wearing and hat manufacture – fascinating though it is – has nothing to do with ringing, we'll skip it.

All the same, it helps to know that a *hat laced with gold* gave the wearer a particular, if rather odd, social status, so a fair few of the prizes were *hats laced with gold*, as in this Devon folk song.

[First Verse]
One day in October, neither drunken nor sober,
O'er Broadbury Down I was wending my way,
When I heard of some ringing, some dancing and singing,
I'll always remember that jubilee day.

[Chorus]
'Twas in Ashwater town, the bells they did sound,
They rang for a belt and a hat laced with gold,
But the men of North Lew rang so steady and true,
That there never were better in Devon I hold.

[Second Verse]
'Twas misunderstood for the men of Broadwood,
Gave a blow on the tenor ne'er ought to 'a been,
But the men of North Lew rang so faultlessly true,
A difficult matter to beat them I ween.

[Third Verse]
They of Broadwood being naughty then said to our party,
We'll ring you a challenge again in a round,
We'll give you a chance at St. Stephen's by Lan'son,
The prize to the winners a note of five pound.

[Fourth Verse]
When the match it came on at good Callington,
The bells they rang out o'er the valleys below,
And old and young people, the hale and the feeble,
They came out to hear the sweet bell music flow.

[Fifth Verse]
Those of Broadwood once more were obliged to give o'er,
They were beaten completely and done in a round,
For the men of North Lew pull so steady and true,
That no better than they in the West can be found.

In fact, I was going to spare you the last three verses but I thought you might like to know how the story ended. Besides, the best tune – and as it's a folk song there are several possibilities just as there are with the words – is quite catchy and compelling. So I've put it on the next page in case you'd like to sing it at your next Branch meeting.

Jubilee Day

And just as a curious aside, this is one of the few folk songs we can date with reasonable accuracy. The writer was walking *one day in October* when it was *jubilee day*, so we need to find an eighteenth century monarch who came to the throne in October and ruled for a long time. And that was George III, who became King on 28 October 1760 and reigned for over fifty years.

One day in Oct-to-ber neither drunken nor sob-er,
O'er Broadbury Down I was wending my way,
When I heard of some ring-ing, some danc-ing and sing-ing,
I'll al-ways re - mem-ber that jub - i - lee day.
'Twas in Ash-wat-er Town, The bells they did sound,
They rang for a belt and a hat laced with gold,
But the men of North Lew rang so steady and true that
there ne- ver were bet-ter in Dev-on I hold.

Yet curiously, his *jubilee day* was neither in 1785 nor 1810. It wasn't in 1785 because a jubilee then came after *fifty* years not twenty-five – *jubilee* being the fifty year period under Hebrew Law at the end of which all debts and other obligations were written off. The idea of a *silver* jubilee didn't catch on until Queen Victoria's silver jubilee in 1862. Equally, George III's *jubilee day* wasn't in 1810 because it was celebrated at the *beginning* of his fiftieth year rather than at the end. So the song dates from 1809.

The Con Trick

But getting back to the action, even though large numbers of ringers entered prize ringing competitions, often walking considerable distances to do so, could it be that the prizes weren't really what they seemed? After all, three guineas for a set of hats was a huge sum then and a publican would have had to sell a vast quantity of beer and spirits to pay it; and even the gambling profits seem unlikely to have covered that amount. So could the prizes have been a con trick?

Well, we can't be sure, but they probably were; and the ringers probably *knew* they were – just as modern-day fair-goers know the cuddly toy prizes are really absolute rubbish. Certainly, this excerpt from the *Taunton Court Report* of 31st March 1737 shows that the publican didn't always play fair.

> **"On Wednesday a Cause was try'd between a Set of *Sherbourne Ringers*, Plaintiffs, and one Perret and Baker, Defendants. The Plaintiffs brought their Action for Six Prize-Shirts which they had won at a Ringing-Match at Mudford, and which the Defendants refus'd to deliver to the**

Plaintiffs, and a Verdict was given in Favour of the Plaintiffs against both the Defendants."

Sadly, we don't know whether the Sherbourne ringers ever got their shirts, but there's other evidence to suggest that everything was not always what it seemed. Here's an advert from *The Ipswich Journal* of Saturday 21st June 1760.

"This is to acquaint all Lovers of Ringing. THAT on MONDAY the 30th of June instant; there will be FIVE PERUKES, value Five Pounds, to be rung for on WIVENHOE BELLS, by any ten Ringers, putting in Five Shillings each. Those five Men that ring the best four Peals (as shall be allowed by Judges appointed) to have the Wigs; which shall be worth Twenty Shillings each, according to the Judgement of any Peruke-Maker.

N.B. Dinner will be provided at the FALCON at Wivenhoe aforesaid, by their humble Servant, THOMAS CORDER."

Perukes

So what they were competing for here was a set of five stylised wigs of the kind now only worn by barristers and judges; and you only have to say that, to realise what a ridiculous prize it must have been. A stylised wig worth a month's wages was very little use to a farm worker who'd have neither the reason nor the opportunity to wear it, except perhaps, in church on Sunday.

But highly fashionable though wigs had been, in 1760 wig wearing was decidedly on the wane, and wig makers everywhere were being made redundant. So presumably Thomas Corder of *the Falcon at Wivenhoe* had either picked up a job lot for a song, or he'd received them in part payment of a bad debt. Either way, they were largely valueless except as spurious ringing prizes. Yet for many country people there would still have been a feeling of satisfaction in owning one.

The Context

And to put these prizes into the context of the times, competitions for clothing were common in other activities too. For example, the *Watermen* of London – i.e. the men who rowed the rowing boats that operated as river taxis and private ferries – competed in an annual rowing race for *Doggett's Coat and Badge.* And Parson Woodforde describes a women's race in his diary of 23rd September 1769, in which the first prize was a *shift* – i.e. a plain linen under-dress – and the second prize was some *ribbands*.

> **"Great doings again to-day at Cary in the Park. At one o'clock there was a shift run for by women. There were five that started for it, and won by Willm. Francis's daughter Nan of Ansford – her sister Pegg was second and therefore had ribbands. I never saw the Park so full of people in my life. The Women were to run the best of three half mile Heats: Nan Francis run a Heat in three minutes ..."**

The Opposition

But popular and successful though prize ringing was, in time it attracted increasing opposition, particularly during the middle and late nineteenth century. The cultural and religious forces behind this were many and complex, but the idea of working class men enjoying themselves in a rumbustious fashion was itself a cause of anxiety. Drinking and gambling was too, even though the alcohol consumption was way below modern levels. But in addition, a different attitude towards ringing was developing among ringers. They began to see bells more as Church property and less as public property, so an anonymous contributor to *Bell News* apparently spoke for many when he wrote:

> **"... considering that they are in our Church towers – placed there as instruments of the Church for a definite purpose in connection with its public services, that their use is most egregiously perverted by these ringing matches seems to me incontrovertible."**

So by 1890, prize ringing had almost completely vanished from most of the country – although in the South-West it was gently metamorphosing into a cross between a modern striking competition and a ringing festival. But we *do* have some remarkably detailed first-hand accounts of one of the last major events of its dying days, in Liversedge in Yorkshire.

Liversedge

It took place on Whit Monday and Whit Tuesday in 1891 – and since, in those days, all clergy had the day off on Whit Tuesday, that may have been the reason for the dates. Our first report comes from an unknown ringer from the South who went there by train to witness it – and although not relevant to our story, a very slow journey he must have had, since the additional Whitsun railway traffic in the nineteenth century was very considerable.

He arrived to find good quality ringing already in progress – but was then much surprised to learn it wasn't the competition he was listening to but the practice pieces. The eight competing *companies* – as Yorkshire local bands were then called – were all being allowed an hour's practice; but even so, there were already plenty of spectators, and he listened all day before taking a room in an inn for the night.

The competition itself was due to start at 7.30 next morning but it actually started an hour late at 8.30. Each band had to ring a half peal – 2,528 changes – of Kent Major; so with eight bands competing – not to mention the swapping over between bands and the extra practice time allowed – there was clearly going to be a lot of ringing. Astonishingly, though, the ringing actually lasted continuously from 8.30 a.m. on the first morning until 3.00 a.m. on the next. Noise abatement wasn't a big thing in 1891, and long periods of ringing weren't particularly uncommon, but even so, our visitor was clearly taken aback.

The Arrangements

He comments on the general arrangements too. Apparently there was plenty of drinking and plenty of betting, but nonetheless everything was entirely orderly, and most of the attendant crowd were genuinely knowledgeable about ringing. They were there to listen as well as drink and gamble; and indeed, people stood listening intently to the best ringing for long periods – something that rarely happens at striking competitions nowadays. The Dewsbury band, although coming on late, impressed everyone.

> **"This band commenced a little before ten o'clock at night. All around was 'as still as a funeral;' scarcely a breath of wind, even, seemed to be stirring; and though the night was chilly, for an hour and a half I listened to such ringing as I think I never heard before for such a length of time. The**

changes came out like clockwork; in fact, it seemed like one long piece of mechanism from beginning to end."

And although it was now getting on towards midnight, not only did everyone stay to hear the end of *that* piece but they listened to the next two bands as well.

"There were yet, late as it was – past eleven o'clock – two more bands to compete, and I imagined the affair would in consequence be adjourned till the following day. But no; Brighouse took possession of the belfry, and after about an hour's essay, collapsed, and retired with their task unfinished. Mirfield came on the scene, and somewhere about three o'clock brought their half-peal home, thus finishing the programme."

Yet even now the proceedings weren't finished, and at this remove it's not easy to understand why. Almost certainly, none of these men had any kind of personal transport except – for a few of the better off ones – a bicycle. And equally certainly, nearly all of them would be starting work only a few hours later – most likely between 5.00 a.m. and 7.00 a.m. Yet even so, they didn't leave before hearing the results.

"You might well imagine that at this 'unearthly hour' everybody had been long gone to their respective homes, and were soundly asleep. But in this you would have been mistaken, for their was quite a numerous assembly in and about the 'pub' where the committee had conducted operations. About an hour afterwards, some

one appeared at one of the windows and proceeded to read out the judges' decisions."

The Judging

And here's another interesting point. How on earth did the judges *manage* to judge? And who on earth were they anyway? The mind simply boggles at the idea of attempting to listen attentively from 8.30 a.m. on the first morning to 3.00 a.m. on the second; and our visitor's mind clearly boggled too.

> **"... the Liversedge contest occupied some nineteen consecutive hours, during the whole of which time these judges were *supposed* to be incessantly engaged in their duties. Now, will any reasonably-minded person dare to assert that these men could keep themselves 'in condition' (excuse the phrase) for this lengthened period, and maintain one uniform status of censorship from beginning to finish? It is contrary to human nature: and thus from a purely secular and contestant point of view, this 'judging' lays itself open to very well-grounded objections."**

But on this point another anonymous person comes to help us. He's a Yorkshire prize ringer of more than thirty years experience, and he's clearly proud of both the system itself and the high quality of ringing it fostered. He tells us:

> **"In this case, the promoters appointed three of the Liversedge company as judges, than whom they could not have appointed three better qualified men in England ... They sit**

> **in one room the whole of the contest, listening to the ringing and calling the faults as they are made, with a writer to put them down as they call, ... it is usual to divide the peal, for the purpose of judging, into three parts, when each of the three judges takes his own part for each company in judging the peals ..."**

And once again, we get a brief glimpse into an entirely different world. These three judges – who may or may not have been the ***three best qualified men in England*** – sat in the same room all day but only one of them judged at any one time. And when his turn came, each judge didn't make notes or put ticks on a piece of paper; he just sat back and listened for an entire half-hour, simply dictating faults to a writer. And who was that writer? How many writers were there? And what age and sex were they? Sadly, we'll never know.

The Culture Clash

But what *is* clear is that we're witnessing a perfect example of the culture clash between the old and the new that was a feature of the last quarter of the nineteenth century. We can see that whatever those stuffy and prejudiced, ecclesiastical ringing historians of the time liked to pretend, the Yorkshire prize ringers were a group of people who rang to a very high standard and who behaved perfectly properly in every way. Indeed, even our man from the South felt compelled to point out what clearly surprised him.

> **"I have attended a considerable number of ringers' gatherings in various parts of the country, and certainly on the score of respectability, this Liversedge contest would bear comparison with any of them. "**

Although as a prize-ringing opponent he felt bound to add:

> **"But for all that, had any radical-teetotaler been desirous of making out a practical case in support of the old charge regarding the close affinity between Church and 'pub' he might have found material here."**

But nonetheless, the prize ringers and the whole culture that went with them were now an endangered species. The Yorkshire Association had been formed almost sixteen years earlier with a different approach to ringing, and it was flourishing. Not everyone was happy with the idea of a county-wide Association – particularly for such an extremely large county – and many groups and small Associations remained independent. But prize ringers saw the Yorkshire Association as the fount of all evil, and Thomas Stead of Huddersfield wrote to *Bell News* to say so.

> **"... and on this subject (the poor ringing), it is altogether the fault of the Yorkshire Association, who for the last fifteen years have never done anything to make good ringers, but have done everything they could to retard them. I hope there will be many more contests as pleasant as the one at Liversedge, and if your correspondent should pay us another visit, he will be able to hear the improvement Yorkshire ringers have made in the meantime."**

And another anonymous Yorkshire prize ringer not only felt the same way but struck a decidedly twenty-first century note in his desire for competition and excellence.

> **"When contests were more frequent, you could scarcely go into a town or village for**

miles around here but (if there was a peal of bells) you would find a first-class company of ringers, able and willing to compete against all comers on any peal. In conclusion, it is the honour each company strives for. Take away competition in anything, and what becomes of any attempt to excel?"

But whether it was sad or not, he was shouting in the wind. The world of ringing was changing, and he and all the other prize ringers, were going to be forced to change with it.

I've never been keen on competitions myself, but when I was twelve years old I was chosen to represent my class in the discus throwing. I wasn't exactly ***good*** *at discus throwing –* ***none*** *of us were – but I could at least get the thing to travel in approximately the right direction, which was a definite plus on health and safety grounds.*

And once I'd got used to the idea, I was even looking forward to my Sports Day appearance. So I was all the more disappointed to find the event re-scheduled – also on health and safety grounds – to the preceding Thursday evening with no one there to watch. Apparently, an unfortunate accident during the previous sports day had something to do with it.

Still, as I'd done absolutely no training – nor even thrown the thing more than a couple of dozen times – I wasn't much bothered, particularly as it was such a sunny evening. When my turn came, I just picked up a discus, stepped into the circle, drew my arm back and chucked it as best as I could.

Bizarrely, though, something very strange happened. Instead of just landing a few feet away as normal, it soared up into the sky and went spinning and floating through the air in the most extraordinary and poetic fashion. I watched mesmerised as it ended up a truly vast distance from where I was standing. The sports master – being the only adult present – got very excited. He unreeled a long tape measure, strode out to where the discuss had landed, and announced in a suitably awed voice that I'd just achieved a new under-13 school record. What was more – his voice became shrill with emotion – the Headmaster would announce it in assembly, and my name would be entered on the school's records board for everyone to read for years to come.

Not surprisingly, the other five competitors were as underwhelmed as I was; but all the same, fifteen seconds of fame and the Headmaster's momentary approval, weren't to be sneezed at; so I was happy enough.

But not, unfortunately, for long!

The next competitor – who although not yet thirteen had biceps like a lumberjack – stepped into the ring and nonchalantly tossed ***his*** *discus about twenty feet further than mine. So even the Headmaster's gracious, "Well done, Coleman," never materialised, and to this day, my one claim to athletics prowess is holding an obscure school record for just under 3½ minutes.*

And it brought home to me, there and then, that unless you're a regular entrant in pub quizzes, records don't count for much. And they only tell a small part of any story anyway. They can be easily fiddled too, yet they're the kind of seemingly authoritative information that's so easy to rely on when you engage in historical research.

So no matter how good any historical source seems to be, you still have to ask – as S.Y. from Norfolk did – ***Is it true?***

Getting a Grip on the Past

13. But Is It True?

The bits I like best in your books are the historical bits – the little stories and snippets; the brief glimpses of the past when you reveal some aspect of the days of yore that sheds entirely new light on the whole business. But much as I enjoy them, I'm still troubled that they're so entertaining and intriguing, they might not be – well, how shall I put it? – true. So, forgive me asking, but – your history stuff: is it *true?*

S.Y.
Norfolk

Of course, the simple answer is, yes, it most certainly *is* true. Or at least, it's as true as I can manage to get it; and hours of painstaking research go into even the tiniest bits. But that said, when it comes to history, nothing is anywhere near as simple in the researching as it is in the telling; so how *do* you make sure it's correct?

Facts

And we'll start by looking at problems with *facts*. After all, *they*, at least, should be straightforward. Either something *is* a fact or it isn't. If it is, you can put it in a history book. If it isn't, you can't. *Simple*.

Well, no, unfortunately it *isn't* simple, because how can you be sure that something you haven't personally witnessed *is* a fact? Someone long ago may have written it down as a fact – or perhaps he got someone else to write it down for him if he was illiterate – but that doesn't necessarily mean it was true.

He may have been deliberately lying to mislead others, or he may have been deliberately lying to mislead *himself.* He may have been confused or mistaken, or he may have been misled by others. He may have been embellishing things to make a good story, or he may have been innocently mis-reporting what someone else told him. He may have been engaging in wishful thinking or he may even have been completely deluded.

After all, there are a good many first hand reports of people being abducted by aliens and then experimented upon in flying saucers. It's even been established by psychological testing that most of those people genuinely believe they're telling the truth, but you'd be pretty disappointed if I recorded flying saucer abductions as facts.

In Authority

So would it help if the person reporting a fact were someone in authority? An official scribe, for example, or a king, politician or government officer?

Well, it might – just a little – but generally, not all that much. Of course, official scribes, kings and politicians don't *just* tell lies, and indeed, they speak the truth a great deal more often than they lie; but they *sometimes* lie – and at other times they seriously distort the truth – and the more important or startling the fact, the more likely it is to be unreliable.

The classic cases are reports of wars, battles and the goings on of previous administrations. It's a truism that history is normally written by the victors, so when there are contemporary reports of the same battle or campaign written by both the victors and the vanquished, they're often startlingly different.

For example, most people's idea of the character of the last Plantagenet King, Richard III, is based on Shakespeare's play of the same name. Yet Shakespeare had to write the play in the way that would please the powerful people who would watch it – or who would hear about it even if they didn't see it – and *they* were the Tudors who had defeated Richard III at the Battle of Bosworth. So it *had* to be biased.

Equally, anyone else writing at the time had to consider the wrath of the ruling house. So saying nice things about Richard III, whether true or not, just wasn't acceptable. Indeed, throughout history there are countless examples of absolutely authoritative – but completely impossible accounts – of recent happenings. Put simply, when retelling anything, truth almost always comes second to personal survival.

Newspapers

So what about newspapers reports? They're *supposed* to tell the truth after all, so shouldn't we be able to rely on *them*?

Well, obviously not. Indeed, in general, newspapers and the media are the biggest liars and distorters of the truth of all, and they always have been. Even in countries with a supposedly free press, such as the UK, the proprietor of any newspaper exerts a strong control over both its political direction and how its stories are portrayed. So even if facts aren't actually manufactured – and often they are – they're still arranged in a selective and distorting fashion with the intention to mislead.

But much more important – and considerably more subtle – newspapers need readers if they're to make money, and potential readers will only buy a paper if they can use it to bolster their own prejudices. So newspapers simply can't *afford* to tell the unvarnished and unbiased truth even if they can bring themselves to recognise it.

And that creates a vicious circle. Certain types of stories are appealing to a newspaper's readers, so reporters find more of them. And if they can't find enough, they slant or create stories to fit what their readers want to read. And equally important, they *don't* report stories that contain facts that don't fit in with their proprietor's and readers' prejudices. And besides, obtaining correct information takes a lot of time, so points of detail are often wildly inaccurate, as every ringer well knows.

All the same, as with recollections written in private diaries, and statements made by politicians, not *all* newspaper facts are untrue. Indeed, a great deal of media reporting is substantially correct. But the *absolute* accuracy of it can be very hard to establish, and only the very gullible look to newspapers to give them a true and complete picture of anything.

Academic and Scientific Reports

Still, there's one group of people you *should* be able to rely on – academics and scientists. After all, you'd suppose that when eminent scholars are writing reports and scientific papers, they wouldn't have any political or personal axe to grind, so you *should* be able to rely on them to tell the whole truth and nothing but the truth.

But unfortunately you can't. *Most* try to tell the truth, of course; but not all. Some academics and scientists have been far more interested in their reputations and careers than the truth – and after all, they're only human – so they've falsified supporting evidence while suppressing and destroying conflicting evidence. And although that has never applied to the great majority of researchers, wishful thinking has always been a major problem.

After all, once you come up with an idea, you grow fond of it; and the more startling – and so, reputation enhancing – the idea is, the fonder of it you become. So the evidence in support seems far more compelling – and so far more worthy of repetition – than the evidence against.

At the same time, if your life's work and reputation has been built on old ideas, you're naturally very disinclined to put them aside and accept new ones. So you repeat and accentuate the evidence for the *old* ideas more than you repeat and accentuate the evidence for the new ones. So even when academics are doing their very best to be objective, a natural bias insidiously creeps in.

Consensus

But there's a far bigger and more subtle problem than either of those. At any given time on any given issue, there's always an academic or scientific consensus. And that consensus is very slow to change. The history of science is packed with instances of scientists proving conclusively that an element of the prevailing consensus is wrong, but then seeing their work immediately rubbished by the entire scientific establishment.

And that rubbishing doesn't come so much from people trying to protect their reputations, as from an instinctive tendency to hold on to things learnt in one's formative years no matter how compelling the later evidence. Looking back with twenty-first century hindsight to the nineteenth century, for example, many of these instances appear quite astonishing. The failure of the medical establishment to accept that cholera was a water borne disease, for example.

Even trickier is scientific research that not only challenges the prevailing consensus but goes against social and religious prejudices. In those cases it isn't just the research that gets rubbished, it's the scientist himself who gets rubbished and personally vilified too. In times past, the theory of natural selection was one such example, but there have been plenty of others.

And Today

And for that matter, the rubbishing of good quality research and the vilification of researchers – particularly by the popular press and politicians – is just as prevalent today as it ever was. Added to that, blatant scientific untruths can easily be placed on the web, from where they get picked up, believed, and repeated over and over again by people using the web as their primary source of scientific information.

But even for that great majority of scientists who are trying to get things right, the current basis of research funding and the "peer review" system for the publication of papers in scientific journals, still pushes them towards remaining within any current consensus.

Statistics

But what about statistics? Surely they don't lie?

Well, of course, a large proportion of the population believe they most certainly do – although as I'm a numbers man myself, I'm very fond of statistics. I find they frequently give an insight into history that other evidence simply can't get anywhere near, and I'm never happier than when pouring over tables of employment, consumption, industrial production, etc.

But although statistics may *look* splendid and authoritative, they always need to be compiled from raw information; and raw information needs to be supplied by lots of people before being collected and collated by lots of others. The collectors and collators are themselves often a problem. As a Viceroy of India once acerbically pointed out, the British Indian Government sent out detailed forms to many thousands of local officials, but those officials just, "**... filled in what they damn well chose**."

Yet even when the collectors are being punctilious, there can be real problems with the information suppliers themselves.

Census Returns

Take census returns, for example. You can look at the very detailed 1861 tables of employment and think you're getting good information. And although in many respects you are, in many respects you aren't. After all, we all know how hard it is to fill in forms and how difficult it is to get to grips with what we're really being asked. So we can spend many minutes wondering what the questions really mean, and even when we know what's wanted, we're often reluctant to tell the truth despite knowing that the information will be treated as anonymous or confidential.

So until fairly recently, the question, "Religion?" to a white, middle class Englishman, generally got the answer, "Church of England," even though the answer, "Atheist," or, "No religion," would have been far more correct.

Likewise, in 1861, a man who ran a small flock of sheep and a couple of cows, might describe himself as an agricultural worker even though he earned as much or more by making nails in the winter. Equally, his wife who made as many or more nails as he did, might not be described by him as a worker at all because saying she was a housewife gave both of them a higher social status. Similarly, the couple's children – who probably also made nails for tens of hours a week quite apart from helping with the livestock – weren't recorded as workers either.

And status produced all sorts of other distortions too. No one wanted to reveal that their main source of income was prostitution, for example – indeed, no one does now – and there were plenty of other socially unacceptable occupations too. People didn't want to admit to *themselves* what they did for a living, let alone reveal it to the census collector.

And they were actively discouraged from suggesting they'd stepped outside the social norms anyway. So while Queen Victoria could put down that she was the head of the household at Windsor Castle, a woman in Portsmouth caused a minor scandal by claiming that *she* was the head of *her* household, and by describing her husband's occupation as, "**He turns my mangle**."

Corroboration

And if all of that seems very discouraging, don't despair, because if we dismissed all factual reports as valueless on the grounds that they might be unreliable, we'd get nowhere at all. So like the Courts and the Police, when faced with "facts," we seek corroboration.

And first we look for other witnesses. After all, in general, the more people who report a fact, the more likely it is to be true. Indeed, a number of people independently confirming the same fact, is a pretty good basis for believing it.

Or at least, it *normally* is. But you need to beware of reports that are identical or very similar. The main facts should be very much the same but they should always be expressed differently or alternatively. To be convincing the different reports should contain *extra* but *differing* points of detail.

That's because two people witnessing the same event always describe it rather differently – indeed, sometimes *very* differently. That's partly because they'll have been standing in different places or looking in different directions, but it's mainly because they'll have *perceived* it rather differently. They're different people with different personalities, so whatever happened will have had a different effect on each of them.

So slight differences between reports of the same event are evidence of reliability, while identical reports are suspicious. Identical reports have either resulted from collusion, or – more likely – from one being a first hand report and the others being unattributed repetitions.

Group Mis-reporting

Of course, there's still the possibility that a whole *group* of people may have reported incorrectly. They may have thought it socially unacceptable to say what really happened, or they may have thought that telling the truth would have imperilled their personal wellbeing or their lives. Mass hysteria, especially at an event of deep religious significance, may cause many people to think that something happened when it didn't, or that something didn't happen when it did.

Different Sources

And that's where different and unconnected sources can be very helpful indeed. If the same fact is confirmed by a number of different sources which apparently have no connection with each other and which haven't been subject to the same political, social or religious pressures, the chances of it being true substantially increase. And best of all is corroboration that comes from completely different *types* of sources. If eye-witness statements, government statistics, annual reports of commercial companies, medical records, etc, all say essentially the same thing, you can feel pretty confident.

Consistency

But there's also another form of corroboration, and that's historical consistency. Nothing ever happens in a vacuum. Whenever one thing happens in the world, a great quantity of other things are happening at the same time. No single event ever stands alone, and any particular occurrence can only happen in the way it does because of the social, political and religious pressures that surround it or have preceded it. And that means we can test any record for *consistency*.

So the first question is: is a record that was apparently made by a particular person, consistent with their other records? Is it written in their style? Is it the sort of thing they might have witnessed or known about? Does it follow on from their earlier records and activities?

Then more important, is it consistent with the way things were done generally at the time? Is it consistent with the records that other people made in similar circumstances? Is it consistent with the social and religious pressures of the period? Does it contain elements of the social and religious prejudices that we would expect of someone of the class and occupation making the record? Or on the other hand, is it more consistent with statements made at the time which we now know to be false?

The Great Myths

And once you start investigating consistency, all sorts of new insights come along, because, like scientists, historians always build upon the work of their predecessors. So you can come across things that were incorrectly accepted as facts long ago – and have then been repeated over and over again – because the social pressures of the time weren't fully understood or investigated. There are a good few examples in this book, and if you're looking for one, try **The Great Myth** on page 307.

But that said, consistency issues are never easy to explore, and they require much harder work and a much deeper knowledge and understanding of general history than some of the early ringing historians were prepared to bother themselves with.

Your Question

So yes, the simple answer to your question all those pages ago is that, to the best of my knowledge and belief, the ringing history I write is factually true; and I certainly do my very best to test and validate the facts involved.

But even when we're satisfied with the facts, there are still two monumental problems in trying to write accurate ringing history. The first is how the two of us – you, the reader, and I, the writer – can arrive at a common understanding of the period we're looking at. And the second – and even more important – is how we can arrive at a common understanding with the people who lived, worked and rang at the time.

And *that* is what we'll be looking at next time.

One of the fairly well known "facts" of ringing history is that Fabian Stedman – the inventor of the method and the author of the second ever ringing book, **Campanalogia** –

was born in Cambridge and spent some time there as both a ringer and Parish Clerk of St Bene't's church. You can read this on a plaque in the church, on local websites, and in all sorts of other places too; but authoritatively though it's stated, it just isn't true.

There's no evidence at all that Stedman ever spent any time in Cambridge, and there's a good deal of evidence that he didn't. Most certainly, he wasn't born there. What's more, it isn't entirely clear where the idea originally came from, although a ringer called John Alfred Parnell – who wrote extensively to newspapers in the early nineteenth century under the pen name, **The Gothic Traveller** *– probably started it. Another man, Charles Henry Cooper – when rewriting* ***Memorials of Cambridge*** *in 1866 – then turned Stedman into the St Bene't's parish clerk.*

But however the whole thing started, once this "fact" had appeared in print, it quite naturally got widely repeated; and it then appeared in a good many other published histories too; and by the time people had read it in lots of places, they very reasonably assumed it was true.

Of course, there wasn't much harm in that because where Stedman was ***really*** *born is of no importance to anyone except nit-picking historians, the parishioners of St Bene't's, and the parishioners of Yarkhill in Herefordshire where he* ***actually*** *came from. But all the same, the parishioners of St Bene't's were sufficiently proud of having employed such an illustrious person, they rehung their bells on the 300th anniversary of his birth.*

That was in 1931, although unfortunately, the histories had got Stedman's birth year wrong too, and the true tercentenary wasn't actually until nine years later in 1940.

So in this case, the historical mix-up did nothing but good, and since most of the parishioners of St Bene't's are probably still unaware of the truth, if you know any of them, you'd best not show them this book – although that said, they probably wouldn't believe it anyway.

*But even if Stedman **had** been their parish clerk, so what? **Someone** was their parish clerk then, so what does it matter what the person's name was. Understanding what it really **felt** like to be a parish clerk in the seventeenth century is surely far more important than knowing their name; and as our next correspondent points out, **that** is what's **really** hard ...*

14. Imagining

I've read lots of old newspaper reports and I've looked at lots of old peal boards – and I've seen a good few period dramas on television too – but the truth is I still don't know what it really *felt* like to ring a couple of hundred years ago. Try as I might, I'm missing something vital. How can I find it?

Linda
Staffordshire

How indeed? And that's one of the fundamental problems of getting to grips with history. No matter how hard we try, there's always a vast mismatch between *knowing* the facts and understanding how it felt to actually experience them: how it felt to have been *living* at the time rather than just looking back from our lives and prejudices of today.

Shared Experience

And without trying to get too technical about it all, the central problem is that two people can only communicate effectively with each other if they share a good deal of the same experiences and understanding. And communication is a jolly complicated business anyway. We don't just talk or write to someone when we want to tell them something, we do a whole host of other things too. We smile, frown, shake hands, shrug, turn our noses up, look sympathetic, offer plates of biscuits, kiss, cuddle, and do all sorts of things that convey our feelings every bit as well as words do. They convey *information* too. And even when we *just* use words, we're only able to communicate successfully when both of us – the speaker *and* the listener, or the writer *and* the reader – share a common experience.

So for example, a lady ringer once told me she'd recently written a letter to an African child whose education she was sponsoring. By way of small talk she'd said that it had been pouring with rain all day and she'd got very wet. A few days later the boy had replied, "**We are praising God that he is sending the rains to Tewkesbury**."

Two intelligent people were attempting to communicate with each other but each forgot for a moment that the experience and importance of rain meant something entirely different to the other.

In History

And it's just the same with history. When you and I discuss it, we have the problem that neither of us lived in the period or under the conditions we're talking about. No matter how much we understand about the time, we never understand enough. Worse, for some aspects of the past, *you* understand more, and for others, *I* understand more. It depends on our different life experiences – where we've lived, who we've lived with, what work we've done, who we've worked with, what we've seen, etc.

The way we were taught history in the past affects our understanding too. Popular culture takes small slivers of the past and pastes them on to the present as things that are either eminently desirable or eminently ***un***desirable; and it's very hard to shake those ideas off. So Queen Elizabeth I is commonly portrayed as a woman who enjoyed great wealth, great power and great comfort of a kind that any twenty-first century woman would envy. But in reality she spent her early years in continual fear of execution, and even when she was Queen, she had rotten teeth and an infestation of lice. She was also enormously troubled by having performed the political necessity of executing Mary, Queen of Scots.

So yes, she had power and wealth and, by the standards of the time, comfort, but that comfort was nothing compared to the luxuries and lifestyle of the great bulk of UK people today.

Empathising

Yet even if we know all about her almost never taking a bath; about her having such bad breath that she eventually had to place a scented handkerchief in her mouth when she talked to people; and about her experiencing extreme physical suffering at the end of her life; that *still* doesn't enable us to empathise with her because those were just normal aspects of many people's lives at that time, and a great many people suffered a great deal more.

Of course, we know that those sufferings can't have been pleasant, and we know that the comforts of our own lives far exceed hers, but we cannot know how it *felt* to cope with her problems and to enjoy her advantages because she was adapted to them and we're not. We can only imagine them.

Religion

And the most difficult aspects of all to empathise with, are the *religious* feelings and influences. It's a vastly complex area, but by way of a small example, most people in the UK today are fairly at ease with the idea and influence of God. They're either atheists – in which case they aren't bothered at all – or they see God as essentially supportive and helpful both for the present and the future. He may be demanding but He's not harsh or unsympathetic.

It's an individual matter, of course, but most people don't see God as attending to every aspect of their lives in a day by day and moment by moment fashion. They don't see God as a hands-on micro-manager who helps them in a real, physical and immediate way when they pray hard and act properly, but who punishes them in a real, physical and immediate way when they don't.

Yet for most of the past, God wasn't seen like that at all. People expected to be divinely rewarded or punished – both individually and collectively – for everything they did, and on a pretty immediate basis too. They saw everything that happened to them, no matter how small, as a joint product of their actions and their relationship with God. A boil on the chin was a punishment from God for doing wrong, and a good crop of cabbages was a reward from God for doing right.

And since life was both hard and short, they were much concerned about their immortal souls too; and they saw their conduct in this world as a major influence on their happiness in the next. So although the essential message of Christianity may well have been the same, the interpretation of it certainly wasn't; and it can be very hard for us now to understand many of the individual and group actions which were undertaken as a result of – or in the name of – Christianity. Yet the people at the time saw no problem at all.

Smugness

And that leads us to a point of the most fundamental importance. If we're seriously trying to understand the past, what we really *mustn't* be is smug. We really *mustn't* think we possess greater intellectual understanding and greater sophistication than the people of the past. It's incredibly tempting to think we do but we don't.

Nowadays in the developed world, we have it very soft indeed, and we don't have to cope with the day to day horrors of existence that were the norm in the UK in earlier times and that are still the norm in many countries today. Faced with those horrors, people naturally develop emotional mechanisms and beliefs to cope.

Besides, the people of the past were shaped by massive early influences and conditioning that they simply couldn't shrug off; *and we're no different.* We mainly believe what we were subtly led to believe in our formative years because that's the way natural selection has programmed us. It's a basic survival mechanism and it's a very effective one too. In time we may reject the *details* of our early influences, but the overall direction and prejudices stay with us for ever.

So just as we aren't superior to people from other countries and other walks of life, we aren't superior to our ancestors either. We aren't cleverer, we aren't more sophisticated and we don't have any more common sense. We have a great deal more knowledge in certain areas – albeit a great deal less in others – but *that's it.*

Human Nature

But what *is* really helpful – if disappointing – is knowing that human nature doesn't change. So although the world and culture have changed over time, human nature hasn't, and people in the past almost certainly felt deep down inside themselves much as we feel today. If our current civilisation survives, the people of the future will look back on us now and think they see appalling conditions for some, great luxury for others, and bizarre thoughts and actions by all, but *we'll* still have been simply us.

All the same, the *culture* certainly was very different in times past; and even more important, it was endlessly changing too. There was no *one* culture that existed for many years, and nor was there any one culture for the whole country – let alone for many countries. There were different cultures for different classes, different cultures for different social groupings, and different cultures for different occupations too; *and* they were all changing at different rates.

The Conclusion

So, no, I can't answer your question. But I don't think that matters because it's completely clear from your letter that you've got exactly the right approach anyway. You understand the tremendous difficulties that exist and you're doing your very best to tackle them. And when you get right down to it, none of us can do any more than *that*.

For many years I had the good fortune to be the Ringing Master of an Association with twelve Branches, and so every year I attended a whole batch of Branch AGMs. They were always lots of fun, with great teas to eat and lots of nice people to chat to, and I enjoyed them very much.

The meetings themselves were normally fun too – being short, light-hearted and friendly – but a certain amount of discussion is unavoidable, and one year the Association Management Committee had changed the Striking Competition rules very slightly. The aim was to make the competitions less stressful, and to give everyone the chance to produce their best ringing; so in future, the initial rounds wouldn't be marked unless they exceeded a minute.

Each Branch had one representative on the Management Committee, and each representative faithfully reported the rule change back to their AGM.

Except that they didn't!

In total I heard five different interpretations of the rule change, only one of which was correct. We'd all been at the same meeting and we'd all taken part in the same discussion, but somehow we'd all perceived it a little differently. We'd all seen the reason for the change differently too. We'd taken our individual personalities into the meeting and we'd shaped our recollections accordingly. Everyone was trying to report faithfully but not everyone managed it.

And we can have a very similar problem with history ...

15. Telling Stories

I admit I'm getting on, and I know that things keep changing. But why does history keep changing too? Whatever happened to the past being the *dead* past? It seems every bit as alive as I am!

M.G.
Cambs.

Yes, curious isn't it? Part of it is that historians always build on the work of their predecessors. They uncover new evidence and add it to the evidence that already exists, and so history changes. But they do something else too. They keep looking afresh at the existing evidence and they re-evaluate it in the light of their knowledge of other history. So history changes then as well; and I suspect that *that* is what's troubling you.

And it's certainly troubling when someone challenges the captivating stories we learnt when we were very young. All that *history-for-tiny-tots* stuff is stirring and comforting, but it's often completely false; and even when it isn't, it's normally had its corners well and truly lopped off. So, along with putting aside Father Christmas, we need to put aside some of our early history stories too.

For example, most of us were taught that the last time England was successfully invaded was in 1066. Indeed, many people still believe it. After all, it's comforting, it's repeated over and over again, and it's an essential part of being British. Somehow, patriotism almost *requires* us to believe it. But all the same, it isn't true.

The French invaded in 1216, captured a fair chunk of the country and were in complete control of London for a year. In 1688 William of Orange landed in Devon with a force of twenty thousand soldiers, marched on London, defeated the army of the lawful king in various battles on the way, and having removed all but his own soldiers from the capital, proclaimed himself joint sovereign. True, a great deal of the country were fairly pleased, but it was really only William's clever political spin that caused such a palpable invasion to be referred to ever after as *The Glorious Revolution*.

And even *that* wasn't the last invasion. In 1745 the oddly named *Bonnie Prince Charlie* – an Italian born and bred, albeit with a deposed British king for a grandfather – landed in Scotland and reached as far south as Derby with a force of six thousand men. Indeed, if he hadn't been misled about the British troop dispositions he might well have continued to London and seized the throne. So as invasions go, that wasn't a bad effort.

And for that matter, was all that 1066 business in Hastings an invasion at all? Very likely not. Politics were pretty murky then and Harold's accession was rushed through and doubtful. William of Normandy was arguably the lawful successor to Edward the Confessor anyway, especially as Edward had promised him the throne. And while we're at it, Harold almost certainly *wasn't* killed by an arrow in the eye.

Cultural Corruption

Of course, popular history is full of complete falsehoods because so much of it is created by simple political spin; but more troubling than the inaccurate is the shallow. The dates of kings and queens, for example, were once essential school learning, but they told us almost nothing. Dates of battles didn't tell us much either. We knew who won and who lost – at least approximately – but we were told little about the suffering and human misery of the soldiers – and the destitution of the wives and children left behind, got no mention at all. The impoverishment of the residents of the battle ground got no mention either.

But on top of the false and the shallow, is something far more subtle. Cultural corruption. Society and historians always express history in a way that reflects their personal prejudices and the public mood of the times they're writing in. It's insidious and it's complex but it's always present; and it's *wading through* that corruption that's so hard.

And I completely accept that you'll have to wade through *my* cultural corruption too. For example, I abhor racism, sexism, ageism and just about any other *ism* you can think of. I don't believe anyone should be made to feel inferior through social class, wealth, status, ringing ability or anything whatsoever, and my retelling of history reflects that. I certainly *believe* I'm being entirely accurate, but future generations may not think so at all. When global warming, monetary collapse and war have re-established dictatorships everywhere, people will see the world very differently.

Approaches to History

And cultural corruption isn't so much about facts but about how we look at them; and *that* changes over time. So history was once seen primarily in terms of the activities of leading personalities. *King Someone-or-Other* did this ... or *Admiral Someone-Else* did that ... and the reasons *why* they did whatever they did were only of slight interest. It was the acts themselves and the people who did them that were seen as primary.

So at one time, Henry VIII was seen as a man who arranged for the dissolution of the monasteries and the formation of the Church of England, simply in order to divorce Catherine of Aragon and marry Anne Boleyn. Even his six wives were seen as a quest for personal gratification rather than a series of decisions of state.

His overwhelming need for a wife who would give birth to a male heir – considered essential to protect the stability of the nation – got little mention; and the need for more state revenues and a reduction in the power of the Catholic Church, got no mention at all.

And that's not surprising. A hundred years ago, having six wives seemed both bizarre and unacceptable, and the fragility of national stability wasn't in the forefront of everyone's minds in the way that it had been in the sixteenth century. Twentieth century people simply couldn't understand that sixteenth century people didn't care *who* was king, they just didn't want a civil war resulting from a doubtful succession.

And besides, the dissolution of the monasteries was seen as simply wrong. There were no ifs, buts and perhaps about it; people just thought it shouldn't have happened. The financial problems of the period and the difficulties posed by the power of the Catholic Church, weren't things to be considered at all.

Single Events

And coupled with the *six-wives-how-shocking* approach was the *importance-of-single-events* approach. So the First World War was seen as starting as a direct result of the shooting of the Archduke Franz Ferdinand in Sarajevo. The enormous political tensions in Europe and the other huge pressures leading up to the War, got little mention, and the truly remarkable way it became a *trench* war – simply because the tired retreating Germans dug in when they were about to be overtaken by the French – got no mention at all.

Somehow, it didn't matter that hardly anyone knew who the Archduke was – and that even fewer knew who shot him and why. Still less did anyone know that *six* young men had set out to kill him but – for various reasons – all six had initially failed. Indeed, if the Archduke's chauffeur hadn't taken a wrong turning later – and then stopped to turn round next to where one of the six just happened to be sitting – he'd never have been shot at all. All that detail was regarded as irrelevant. The only thing people were expected to know was that the shooting started the First World War.

The Overwhelming Drift

But although the *single event* view of history is great for producing good stories, the overwhelming drift of the times is as much an influence on events as anything because it *causes* single events to happen. So another approach to history is to view particular people and events as only marginal influences in comparison.

And looked at in that way, the First World War becomes an unavoidable consequence of the times, and the shooting of the Archduke Franz Ferdinand becomes just the spark that lit the inevitable bonfire. The fact that European tensions were perhaps a little less in 1914 than previously – and may even have been slightly decreasing – gets no mention.

Indeed, even the goings-on of Alexander the Great – who essentially started out as a teenager with an attitude problem and then conquered much of the world in a long-extended period of moody adolescence – is seen as merely the inevitable consequence of the times. And of course, when you get right down to it, perhaps it was. You need people to do things, certainly, but you also need the drift of the times to point them in that direction, and you need everyone else to allow it all to happen.

Anthropology

But there's another factor too, and that's that people are simply people. So there's the anthropological – or human nature – approach to history. A sort of *well-they-would-have-done-that-wouldn't-they* approach. And when you get right down to it, that makes a lot of sense too. After all, many decisions are made because of the silent force of unacknowledged instinctive impulses rather than rational thought.

For example, apes have an instinctive respect for silver-backed males, and it seems that human beings have too. So the number of men with grey hair in very senior positions in business and voluntary organisations, far exceeds a due proportion of the age-adjusted population as a whole. And the larger the number of people involved in influencing a decision – through democracy, for example – the more marked the human nature effect will be. So the most brilliant, statesman-like, self-denying and caring politician couldn't possibly become Prime Minister if he was bald, physically ugly and had a squeaky voice. Equally, a truly able and dedicated leader couldn't save his country from disaster if it was instinctively determined not to be saved.

So the First World War can then be seen as the result of the belligerent instincts of a mass of individuals. When it started – and indeed, even *before* it started – virtually the entire male population and much of the female population were in favour of it going ahead. *Some* politicians foresaw something of the consequences – although even *they* never envisaged how utterly appalling it would be in the actuality – but they were powerless to hold back the force of overwhelming public opinion.

Historical History

So with all these – and more – different approaches to history, and the fact that they go through fashions and phases, it's not surprising that history keeps changing. History books and articles reflect the culture and ideas of their time as much as they reflect the past. So reading old history books is like reading old science fiction books. You get two stories at the same time, and nothing will ever change that.

So *dead* past or not, if this book says as much about me as it does about history, I hope you don't mind.

In 1896 the splendidly named H Earle Bulwer – who was Secretary of ***The Central Council of Church Bell Ringers*** *and had a truly prodigious beard – wrote an article on bellringing for the Christmas edition of* ***The Windsor Magazine****. It wasn't exactly a racy read because Earle Bulwer wasn't a racy-read sort of man, but as published it included the sentence,*

> **"The wood is well-seasoned oak, and a good many of the finest frames come from Sussex."**

And although at first sight that sounded OK – albeit of doubtful accuracy – it turned out that Earle Bulwer hadn't written it at all, and the sentence had simply been gratuitously inserted by the editor – presumably because he came from Sussex himself.

Earle Bulwer, though, wasn't interested in the editor's sensibilities. ***The Windsor Magazine*** *was becoming a strong selling national publication – a rival to* ***The Strand*** *– and Bulwer was enraged that those people buying a copy in order to get the pull-out* ***Beautiful Photogravure Portrait of the Queen****, might think him a complete idiot.*

*The sentence, he told everyone, was "***sheer nonsense****," and as well as giving the editor a piece of his mind, he wrote to the short lived ringing magazine,* ***Campanology****, saying the same thing. And to make doubly sure, he vehemently instructed all* ***Campanology*** *readers with a copy of* ***The Windsor Magazine*** *to "...* **cross it out***."*

Sadly, ***Campanology*** *never had many readers anyway, and it folded after a mere six months; and whether any of those very few readers also bought* ***The Windsor Magazine****, is distinctly doubtful. So perhaps no one but Earle Bulwer ever* ***did*** *cross the sentence out.*

But we certainly know that, in other fields, Bulwer wasn't above making up a good few things himself. It was a period when making up new words and definitions was extremely popular, and in 1901 the Central Council published Bulwer's ***A Glossary of Technical Terms****.*

It was definitely a good idea, but Bulwer and his friends had actually invented quite a few of the technical terms and they'd distorted quite a few of the others. It sold pretty well, though, and if you can find a copy today, it's well worth looking through.

Yet the very existence of the book typified the Central Council's pre-occupation with definitions at the expense of practical ringing matters. While they were bothering about things that only a handful of ringers were interested in, the steady influx of women into ringing was ***entirely*** *escaping their notice ...*

The Sight of Gentle Maiden Deftly Handling of a Rope

16. The Very First Woman

There's something I've been wanting to know for ages. Who was the very first woman to ring, and when and where did she do it?

B.Y.
Notts.

What a splendidly interesting question! And like so many of the equally splendid questions in this book, the answer is far more surprising than any of the standard ringing histories would lead us to believe. So forget those late Victorian ladies in long skirts and puff sleeves. *We're* going *way* back.

The Early Middle Ages

And if you're *really* interested in religious history, you can take this moment to read one of those very long and learned books about the nuns and nunneries of the early middle ages. But if you're not, a short summary will have to do, and not surprisingly, the popular ideas – based primarily on blockbuster movies and Robin Hood novels – are well wide of the mark.

Of course, there were plenty of genuinely spiritual and religious nuns a thousand years ago, just as there always have been, but it's human nature that expediency enters into any system, and so for many hundreds of years, the nunneries of Britain and Europe contained far more lay women than full nuns. Some of these were servants, but most were widows and unmarried women who wanted to benefit from the social and physical protection that the nunneries offered at a time when almost nowhere else did.

They brought with them their own money, too, and at this remove it's hard to know to what extent the contemporary unflattering accounts of them were influenced more by religious and political prejudice than accuracy. But it's clear that most lived comfortably, had unfettered social contact with their friends, and were free to come and go as they pleased.

Moreover, many nuns had been forcibly placed in nunneries by their fathers because, for all social classes, the cost of doing that was less than the cost of paying the appropriate dowry. So not only did it offer the father the comfort of knowing his daughter would be getting a lifetime's protection, it saved him money too.

The Religious Side

At the same time, the dedicated nuns of the early Middle Ages saw themselves as having a spiritual role in the wider world and in participating in church services. They weren't supposed to actually *take* services – although in a few places they did – but they certainly did much else.

In those days, many leading churchmen were vehemently opposed to women performing *any* religious duties no matter how trivial; and although looked at from now, the views expressed seem to be based more on male dominance and sexual prejudice than biblical authority, it's impossible to know to what extent they were in tune with the feelings of the time. But what *is* clear is that male clerics made many periodic attempts to reduce women's religious activities, and one of these was at the *Council of Paris* of 829.

The Council of Paris

The ***Council of Paris*** was one of a series of *Councils* that took place from time to time in the early Middle Ages. Various religious issues were discussed by the important church figures of the day, and various decisions and prohibitions were made or confirmed. Indeed, making new prohibitions and reaffirming existing ones was a major part of their work. So for example, usury was confirmed as a sin, and remarriage following divorce as a result of fornication, was confirmed as adultery.

But of special interest to us is that the Council prohibited the traditional female activities of church decoration and housekeeping, accusing women of polluting altar vessels and linen by cleaning them. Most especially, it specifically forbade nuns to light candles and – really hitting home – ***ring bells***. So the simple answer to your question is that the first woman bellringer lived some time in the early ninth century – or probably a good deal earlier still – and was quite likely a nun.

The Effect

"But was that proper ringing?" you ask.

Well, it was as proper as any ringing was at the time. The bells would have been swung chimed, probably to frame height or higher, although whether there was ever any attempt to chime in rounds or some other sequence, we'll probably never know.

But not surprisingly, the pronouncement of the *Council of Paris* no more stopped women's traditional religious activities than it stopped money lending or remarriage after divorce. Mixed sex monasteries, although less approved, continued to exist as they had previously done, but more important, there were also nunneries where no males at all could enter, either as monks or servants, except as male priests to take services. So the bells in those nunneries *must* have been rung by women.

The Cistercians

All the same, it would be nice to have some definite proof of women ringing then. A diary, for example, or an eye witness record. Sadly, I haven't found one – although there's probably one somewhere. But better than that, I *have* unearthed in the British Library a really splendid illuminated manuscript which clearly shows a woman ringing. It's not a photograph, of course, but in many respects it's much better because it wasn't painted to record a one-off event but to portray aspects of the everyday routine.

The whole thing shows religious activities in a Cistercian nunnery and was produced around 1290. The nunnery is shown as though it were on three floors with the viewer looking in through the wall. The women are variously holding devotional books, candles and a cross, and there are two male priests, one of whom holds a bible while the other blesses bread and wine at the altar. Judging by the style of the artist, the nunnery in question was probably in North East France – although it might just possibly have been in Paris – but there would have been little difference between English and French nunneries at the time.

The Ringer

But of most interest to us is the top of the picture. A small bell turret with a little pinnacle above it sticks up from the roof, and in it are two bells swinging vigorously. Below, we see the ringer herself. She has a bell rope in each hand, and she's bending her knees as she hauls away at both of them together. There's no question of a gentle chime here; she's clearly hauling away with considerable effort. Next to her are the abbess and another nun. Possibly they're supervising; but whether they are or not, they're certainly witnessing what they regard as a religious act.

With seven hundred years of hindsight we could do with a rather more detailed close-up than the illustrator of 1290 gives us. But all the same, it's extremely good. The turret shows the bells definitely swinging – rather than just having ropes tied to their clappers or to hammers – and since the ringer is putting in so much effort, the bells must be swinging quite high. No wheels or half-wheels can be seen, so probably there were levers fastened to the headstocks, and there are no sallies either, of course. But there *are* rings – possibly of metal but more likely of wood – on the end of each rope. It certainly appears from the ringer's actions and the positions of the ropes, that the bells are being rung at least frame high.

Sticklers for Accuracy

And just in case you already know a lot about religious life in the early Middle Ages and you're a stickler for historical accuracy, I do indeed realise that, apart from a short period in the thirteenth century, the Cistercians excluded nunneries from their formal Order. Nevertheless, for a very long time, many nunneries claimed to be – or were seen as – Cistercian, so whether this manuscript was of an *official* Cistercian nunnery or an *unofficial* one, we'll never know.

The Sixteenth Century

But although 1290 is good, it would be particularly splendid if we could find a sixteenth century English nunnery where no men other than priests ever entered, yet the bells were hung on half-wheels and definitely rung. Sadly, I haven't found that nunnery myself although it almost certainly existed; and of course, the bells may even have been rung by some of the lay residents for exercise.

But getting at the truth about that isn't easy. Apart from all the other problems, the dissolution of the monasteries and nunneries in the early part of the sixteenth century brought with it its own political spin. The tales of corrupt and dissolute nunneries were a political necessity at the time, and the truth is very hard to know. All the same, it's clear that the nunneries contained significant numbers of influential women of independent means who largely pleased themselves as to what they did. As yet I can find no evidence, but it's certainly *possible* that some of them took occasional exercise by hauling away at the bells.

And Changes?

And here's another thing. Throughout the Middle Ages, nuns were regularly rebuked by the church hierarchy for taking too many liberties with the chants. They developed and embellished them in a way that the monks never did, giving them a depth and vibrancy that the traditionalists severely frowned upon. In short, they enjoyed their singing and were creative.

So what about their ringing? Were they content to chime at random, or were they creative there too? Could they perhaps – before the dissolution of the monasteries and nunneries – have been experimenting with bell control and elementary changes? Perhaps they could. After all, we still don't know how English change ringing actually started.

Perhaps *women* invented it after all!

I'm often asked who the patron saint of bellringers is, but like so many things connected with ringing, it's not entirely clear. Somehow, ringers got missed out in the early stages of patron saint allocation, and the two possible candidates got slotted in late on.

One suggestion is St Dunstan whose main patron saint role is looking after armourers and gunsmiths – although he looks after goldsmiths and locksmiths too. He probably lived from 909 to 988 – which was a pretty good innings in those days – and he turned to a religious life when he mistakenly feared he had leprosy. He became a monk, built himself a small hut next to the Glastonbury Abbey church, and used his metal working skills to make vessels and bells for the church.

Thereafter, he had a meteoric rise through the religious and secular hierarchy. Over time, he became Abbot of Glastonbury, Bishop of Worcester and Archbishop of Canterbury, as well as being a principal advisor to four English kings; and that was a pretty fair achievement for someone who'd started out as a metal worker. Indeed, for a long time after his death he was the most popular English saint, and it wasn't until Thomas à Becket came along that he was supplanted. There's no record of him ever having been a ringer, but his connection to bellringers was presumably through his metal working and bell making.

If you'd like to see a picture of what he supposedly looked like, there's a nineteenth century stained glass window of him in St Dunstan's Church, Cranford. Engagingly, he's holding a book opened at a medieval drawing of himself.

But of more interest to us on the subject of women ringers is the other candidate, St Agatha. Since she was a woman and venerated from at least the sixth century, it would be nice if there were clear records – or at least, clear legends – of her ringing bells at some time. That would then be good evidence of women ringing sixteen hundred years ago.

But unfortunately there aren't. According to legend she

was a member of a wealthy family – possibly in the third century – and she dedicated her life to God, refusing the advances of all men. One of those men – possibly an important Roman called Quintian or Quintinian – attempted to force her to have a relationship with him; and when she repeatedly refused, he arrested her, imprisoned her in a brothel, tortured her, and finally mutilated her in such an appalling fashion, that she subsequently died from her wounds.

So how did she become the patron saint of bellringers?

Well, first she became the patroness of bell founders, and then she moved on from there. It may simply have been that she was adopted by the bell founders of Sicily because she was a popular saint there anyway; or since she was credited with protecting people from the eruptions of Mount Etna, she may have been associated with bells as warnings of fire. But there's a rather more likely reason.

Medieval manuscripts show St Agatha carrying a tray on which two items are placed. They look rather like loaves of bread – and indeed, bread has been traditionally blessed on her feast day – but they might also be two handbells.

Unfortunately, though, that's almost certainly a complete misreading of the image. Medieval illustrators weren't the least bit squeamish about depicting mutilation horrors in the most graphic and realistic detail; and drawings and paintings were made that nowadays would be considered completely unpublishable. So I won't go into detail as this is essentially a family book, but suffice it to say that the items on the tray were most definitely never intended to be handbells.

But all that said, so what? St Agatha was always believed to be a kind and generous person who cared about others, and who was eventually martyred as much for her goodness and honesty as for her faith. She was every bit the sort of person we'd be pleased and proud to have as a ringer, and I for one am entirely happy that she's now seen as our patron saint.

But throughout history it's been one of the great puzzles of religion, that men have been entirely content to adopt female saints as their patronesses, but entirely opposed to having women join them in their craft. So even if ringers had adopted St Agatha as their patron saint four hundred years ago, it would probably have made no difference at all to the way so very few women – and just possibly, none at all – rang in the seventeenth century ...

17. Huntin', Shootin' and Ringin'

I'm told that women didn't start ringing until the end of the nineteenth century. Is that true? And if it is, why is it? Why couldn't women have rung in the seventeenth and eighteenth centuries?

R.W.
Yorkshire

Why indeed? And very conveniently your questions take us from the early sixteenth century – where we finished last time – to the early nineteenth century where we'll be going next.

After the Middle Ages

And just to recap, in the last chapter we established that from at least the early ninth century – that's an astonishing eleven hundred years ago – nuns in nunneries definitely rang bells. We suspect they only chimed randomly – although they *may* have rung some elementary changes – and we suspect the extent to which they rang, tailed off over time; but ring bells they definitely did. By the seventeenth century, though, the dissolution of the nunneries had already taken place and all the ringing took place in parish churches. So what about the women then?

Well, the overwhelming feature of ringing in the seventeenth and eighteenth centuries, was that it had become secular. The bells were certainly *in* churches, but they weren't there solely – or indeed, primarily – for religious use. They had become *public*. Not public in that anyone could ring them, but public in that everyone enjoyed them and expected them to be rung for public occasions and for fun.

The Duke of Stettin-Pomerania

In 1602 when the Duke of Stettin-Pomerania – a part of what's now Germany – toured England, he brought a diary writer with him; and that diary writer found the ringing so remarkable that he recorded it specifically.

> **"On arriving in London we heard a great ringing of bells in almost all the churches going on very late in the evening. ... We were informed that the young people do that for the sake of exercise and amusement, and sometimes they lay considerable sums of money as a wager, who will pull a bell the longest or ring it in the most approved fashion. Parishes spend much money in harmoniously-sounding bells, that one being preferred which has the best bells. The old Queen is said to have been pleased very much by this exercise, considering it as a sign of the health of the people."**

Clearly there was nothing religious about this ringing, nor was it specifically said to be done by men. But what ***is*** clear is that women would not have been excluded from it on religious grounds.

Propriety

So were they excluded from it on grounds of propriety?

Hard to say. You only have to read the writings of the early seventeenth century to see that Victorian sexual prudery wasn't even a twinkle in the average person's eye. But male power and dominance were another matter, and since much of the ringing was apparently done for payment, it would only have been natural for the men to keep women out.

Evidence is thin, but Stow's *Survey of London* published in 1598 reports:

> **"Upon St. James night, certaine men in the lofte next under the Belles, ringing of a Peale, a Tempest of lightning and Thunder did arise, an uglie shapen sight appeared to them, comming in at the south window, and lighted on the North, for feare whereof, they all fell downe, and lay as dead for the time, letting the Belles ring and cease of their owne accord ..."**

In the Country

That certainly only refers to men. But even if it was men-only in London, in rural areas things *may* have been different. In the seventeenth century there were many powerful women who rode, hunted, shot, danced, played skittles and engaged in any sport or pastime they wished to. Indeed, elsewhere in Europe they even armed themselves with spears and took part in wild boar hunts. And certainly, in the seventeenth century *most* ringing was seen as a sport or pastime. Indeed, an Act of Parliament of April 1644 – enacted by the Puritans during the Commonwealth and entitled, *An Ordinance for the better observation of the Lords-day* – makes that entirely clear.

> **"... no person or persons shall hereafter upon the Lords-day, use, exercise, keep,**

maintain, or be present at any wrastlings, Shooting, Bowling, Ringing of Bells for Pleasure or Pastime, Masque, Wake, Church-Ale, Dancing, Games, Sport or Pastime whatsoever ..."

So apart from during that short period, if a powerful woman had wanted to ring a bell, no church authority or secular prejudice would have stopped her.

The Upper Classes

What's more, by the middle of the seventeenth century, class prejudice wouldn't have stopped her either. Groups of well-to-do young men – such as *The College Youths* – were already ringing. To them it was a sport and a challenge – and most probably a way of shocking their elders. They got together, stayed up all night drinking, and did for fun what lower-class men did for money.

In their great houses they also installed dumb bells – lumps of metal and wood on wooden frames, and designed to handle something like real bells. I've put pictures on pages 358 and 359. These dumb bells gave their owners the exercise and pleasure of ringing in their own houses on wet days. It's inconceivable that the young women of the house didn't also try their hand at the dumb bells; and having rung them, *surely* they must have insisted on also trying their hand at the real bells in the estate church. Neither propriety nor lack of access could have stopped them.

Having Fun

And the question of propriety is important. It's easy to assume that in the eighteenth century, girls weren't allowed to do anything but play the harpsichord, embroider samplers and drift demurely around sitting rooms in long dresses. But they also hunted, shot and played games; and to a degree, physical larking about was entirely acceptable too. Here's part of a letter of 1791 written to her younger sister by the 15 year-old Mary Strangways. It's about her visit to Stourhead which was – and still is – one of the really great houses of England. It had been built – and was owned – by the wealthy and influential banking family, the Hoares, so whatever went on there was entirely acceptable anywhere.

> **"The ball at Stourhead ... was very pleasant to *me*. There was only eight ladies that danced, so of course we did not dance much – only six before dinner and six after. Madame Genlis ... would not let her three pupils dance after supper, so we made Lady Digby ... dance instead. We staid there all the next day, and at night Madame Genlis and Mademoiselle d'Orléans played on the harp delightfully. Afterwards we all played blindman's buff till after two. The next day ... we played hopscot all the morning, and hopped up and down (upon one leg) the steps before the hall door."**

It's hard to imagine that playing blind man's buff and hopping up and down the steps before the hall door on one leg, was acceptable, but exercising on the house's dumb bell – and ringing the bells of the estate church when no lower class people were present – wasn't.

A Curious Report

But now that we've got to the eighteenth century we have newspapers to look at. They were no more reliable than today's newspapers, of course, but there's a curious report of six women ringing together in 1760. On 18 February *The Sussex Weekly Advertiser or Lewis Journal* reported:

"London, Feb. 14.
From Gillingham we have received the following Account; That on the 4th Instant was married there Mr. Samuel Warsper, a Perfumer, aged 67, to Mrs. Elizabeth Thompson, a Maiden Lady, aged 75, who was brought to Church on Horseback behind a Farmer's Servant, but without either Pillion or Saddle, whilst the Bridegroom came deliberately after on his Crutches; but at the entrance of the Church several Persons had assembled to carry off the Lady, alledging that she was an Heiress; but after a little Contest, the Bridegroom gained a complete Victory, and the Ceremony was immediately performed.

Six young Maidens went into the Belfry, and rung the Bells, exulting to think, that if they lived to the age of Four-score, they should even then find Admirers; but what is most remarkable, the Bride and Bridegroom both laid aside their Crutches the next Day."

A startling report, certainly, but sadly, it most likely wasn't true. First, there are no similar reports from around that time; and second, it isn't a first hand report but a repeat of something that had apparently appeared in a London paper four days earlier. And four days earlier was *St Valentine's Day*.

Now, back then, St Valentine's Day was a big occasion; and unlike nowadays, it wasn't celebrated by means of absurdly expensive dinners and cards with peculiar poems in. Instead, many old and localised traditions were still being followed, primarily relating to young women's prospects of marriage. So presumably the idea of ***six maidens*** ringing the bells of Gillingham, had overtones to it that meant more in 1760 than they would do today. Quite probably, the bride ***arriving without either pillion or saddle***, had overtones too – as did the groom being a ***perfumer***.

But whatever the facts, the really interesting thing is that the idea of six young women ringing, doesn't appear to have aroused any feelings of shock or disgust in the writer. Instead, he seems to have viewed it light-heartedly and humorously.

Sibsey

And ten years later, there was no shock or disgust in this report in *The Cambridge Chronicle and Journal* of Saturday 29th September 1770.

> **"On Friday last a new peal of bells, cast by Mr. Henry Harrison, of Barrow, was opened at Sibsey in Lincolnshire, on which changes were immediately rung by five ladies."**

Once again this appears to have been taken second hand from another newspaper; and although a ring of five by Harrison was indeed hung in Sibsey in 1770, the previous bells weren't ringable, so it seems unlikely that five local ladies could have rung them at all, let alone to changes. So the five ladies either just chimed them – possibly as a way of giving them added virtue or an extra blessing – or, much less likely, the five lady ringers were brought in from elsewhere.

Peal Records

But what we *can* say for certain is that, unless disguised as a man, no woman ever rang a peal. There were, of course, a number of well documented cases of women of the period passing the whole of their adult lives disguised as men –

apparently for self-protection or increased freedom – so we can't *absolutely* rule out the possibility of a woman ringing a peal in disguise; but it seems extremely unlikely. And the peal records – which are numerous and detailed for the eighteenth century – list only men.

So we conclude that apart, *just possibly*, from six maidens in Gillingham and five ladies in Sibsey, women probably didn't ring at all in the seventeenth and eighteenth centuries as a regular thing. Of course, compulsive peal ringing – like bus spotting and engine number collecting – is much more a boy thing than a girl thing, so women just *may* have rung short touches occasionally. But all in all, it seems most likely that they *didn't*.

Why?

But in your letter you ask, *why* didn't they?

And I can only answer, why indeed? Certainly not because the bells were too difficult for women to handle. That was simply a late Victorian and Edwardian myth that we'll talk about another time. So we're just left with that vague and amorphous reason: it was simply cultural.

Of course, we can point to lots of influences. We can point to the fact that working class women weren't much expected to go out and have fun. We can point to the fact that working men wanted to keep sources of income to themselves. We can point to the likelihood that the laddish atmosphere of the upper class ringing societies was considered undesirable for upper class girls.

We can point to lots of things, many of which stemmed from the very real danger of pregnancy following what was in truth rape – albeit then, a normal part of many women's lives. But the real truth is that cultural forces are hugely complex and only vaguely rational, and they're extremely hard to understand from outside. Pretending to a clear insight into the cultures of the past is a hopeless vanity. Indeed, it's the never ending struggle to untangle the motivations and mind-sets of bygone days, that makes history so perennially interesting. Suffice it to say that in the eighteenth century women didn't ring, and that's that.

Next Time

But in the *nineteenth* century things were definitely going to change. And *that* is what we'll be looking at next time.

Many years ago I spent a ringing weekend in Suffolk. There were splendid bells and splendid countryside, and it was all very interesting and pleasant. But some of the bells were rather heavy, and some of the draughts were very long indeed, and by Sunday evening my right wrist was hurting quite a lot. Indeed, it clicked very painfully when I moved it, so thinking that I might have cracked a bone somehow, I went to the doctor.

"Ah," he said after a cursory inspection, "You've got ***Bellringer's Wrist****." And astonishingly he arrived at that instant diagnosis without even knowing my hobby.*

"Medically we call it tenosynovitis," he expounded, "because your tendons have become inflamed. But it's also known as ***Washerwoman's Wrist*** *because washerwomen used to get it from wringing out washing." And by way of demonstration, he twisted his hands as though limply squeezing the moisture from a small face flannel.*

But the really interesting thing was that he clearly had no idea at all how washerwomen really ***did*** *wring out large items of heavy washing. And nor did he have any idea how much* *strength and energy they put into it. They didn't just* **twist** *their wet washing in the way he showed me, they* **wrenched** *it round in an action of immense energy and power, at the end of which each wrist had turned through an entire 360° and their hands had become almost back to back. What's more they did it over and over again, hour after hour and day after day, often for sixteen hour days, six days a week. So it's not surprising that they got wrist trouble.*

But one thing's certain. It was a sure fire way of building up muscles and stamina in a way that modern olympic athletes could only admire. If these women also got sufficient food, they were far fitter and far stronger than any of the upper or middle class male ringers of the period. Yet bizarrely, they were supposed to be too weak to ring.

Utter nonsense, of course, but it was a myth that lasted well into the twenty-first century, and in many places it will doubtless run for a good while yet. All the same, in the nineteenth century we do at least know of **one** *washerwoman who rang ...*

18. Washerwomen, Sextons and Lunatics

As I'm basically a left-wing *Guardian* reader – not to mention, a child of the Sixties – I've never been happy that so much ringing history deals only with the upper classes. What about the workers? And most especially, what about the *women* workers?

Pat
London

Yes indeed. What ***about*** the women workers? And now that we've reached the beginning of the nineteenth century, they're exactly the people we're going to look at.

Written Records

All the same, one of the great problems of historical research, is that the written records of the past were only written by the people who could write. And the further back you go, the fewer the people who *could* write; and those who could, were generally those with the time and money to be educated.

We often refer to those people as being upper class or middle class, but the term *middle class* isn't a terribly good one because until fairly recently they only constituted a tiny proportion of the population. Naturally, their chief concern was themselves, and equally naturally, their perspective of the world was very different to that of the labouring classes. The result is that written records can give us a very unbalanced view indeed.

Local Bands

But now that we've reached the beginning of the nineteenth century, shouldn't the position of women in ringing be getting clearer?

Well, *possibly*. We now have a few writings and records of local bands and it seems that they were indeed entirely male. What's more, that seems to have been what was expected, and one of the more intriguing evidences of this was the case of the third Earl of Portsmouth.

The third Earl – who, as a curious aside, was educated privately by Jane Austin's father – had serious mental health problems throughout his life. For a while they were kept in check fairly well, but in 1813 after his first wife died, he was forced by Lord Byron and Lord Byron's guardian – a Mr Hanson who was also the Earl's solicitor – to marry one of Hanson's daughters. The marriage took place within 24 hours of Hanson's threat to keep the Earl locked up if he didn't agree, so the Earl was clearly coerced.

Lord Byron gave the Bride away, and saw the marriage as a way of exacting revenge on the Earl for having "**pinched my ear**," over ten years earlier. Indeed, he recorded in his diary that he, "**... tried not to laugh in the face of the supplicants**."

In Court

But once a daughter was born to the union, the Earl's younger brother and family saw their considerable potential inheritance disappearing before their eyes, and so challenged the validity of the marriage. Very long and extremely expensive proceedings followed, but the brother ultimately established in a hearing before *The Lunacy Commissioners* that the Earl had been insane from 1809 and so was incapable of the firm state of mind necessary to be married.

The Judgement

In the final hearing, as recorded in the *All England Law Reports*, the Judge – Sir John Nicholl, who held the post *The Dean of Arches* – found that three main factors established the Earl's insanity. First,

> **"He used to flog his horses unmercifully from a sadistic turn of mind."**

Second – and somewhat bafflingly –

> **"He had a still more decided delusion of his own, relevant to lancets, and tapes, and basins in women's pockets."**

And third, and of most interest to us,

> **"As further proofs of his insanity may be added his propensity for bell-ringing, not – as sometimes young men will do – for exercise, but to share the money. This, too, by a nobleman of 40 at his own parish church, and near his own residence."**

So in this way Sir John created the splendid legal precedent that bellringing is a clear symptom of insanity. But more important to us, he apparently thought that an upper class man could ring for sport – albeit not for money – but that a woman simply didn't.

The Vampire Earl

But the lengthy court case and the very considerable

publicity surrounding it, also gives us evidence about the rest of the band at Hurstbourne Priors Church, and they were all male. Although almost unheard of today, the Earl was probably the most infamous bellringer in the whole of history. He raced dung carts through the village, attacked his servants, and behaved outrageously at the funerals of complete strangers. He became notorious in his own time, and was referred to in the popular press as *The Vampire Earl.*

So it's not surprising that his ringing activities were addressed during the court case, and evidence was given that he had attempted to murder a young male ringer by throwing his rope round the boy's neck as he pulled off at handstroke. Fortunately, the boy got the rope off and survived; but the really interesting thing is that the judge apparently thought that – in a nobleman – ringing with working class men for money was a clearer sign of insanity than attempting to murder a child.

That said, there were a great many stories about the Earl at the time, and a great many witnesses on both sides of the court case had probably been bribed or threatened. Indeed, at least one of the Lunacy Commissioners had received death threats. So it's impossible to know which of the stories were true. All we know for certain is that despite many dreadful deeds, the Earl lived a long and largely unhappy life, and that two years before his death at the age of 85 he was listed in the 1851 Census as "**Earl and Lunatic**."

For Pay

But getting back to the main action, in the nineteenth century not all ringing was done by local bands. Until fairly recent times there was also a good deal of chiming of single bells too, and according to the Book of Common Prayer this had to be done at least twice every day for several minutes.

Sometimes it was performed by a vicar or curate, but frequently it was performed by the church sexton – a paid employee who often had a house in the churchyard.

But chiming a bell for five minutes with the arms alone, is a very tiring business indeed, so sextons used one of two alternatives. They either tied a loop in the end of the rope and chimed with their foot in that loop – as in the picture on page 304 – or they rang the bell halfway up or higher. And although sextons were usually men, they weren't invariably so.

Widows

This was because it was not uncommon for wives to assist their husbands in their tied cottage jobs. Employees such as gate keepers and sextons fell into this category, and later in the century, railway crossing keepers and stationmasters of very small stations, did too. Their wives assisted them, both on a day to day basis and, more especially, when they were ill. So those wives knew exactly what to do. There's an eighteenth century example of this on page 171.

And since the *powers that be* were not always as uncompassionate as we now think, it wasn't uncommon for the widow of such an employee to be allowed to remain in the tied cottage and take over her late husband's job when he died; and in this way there were a number of women in men-only occupations.

The Result

The result was that even at the beginning of the nineteenth century, there were a fair few women sextons who chimed – indeed, even in the *eighteenth* century there were some – and while many of them would have chimed with their foot in the rope, it seems likely that others effectively rung the chiming bell full circle – albeit by themselves –

especially when tolling the tenor after a death or for a funeral. Here's a nineteenth century parishioner from Spalding recalling an incident in the early 1800s.

> **"In the early part of this century the widow of the sexton at Spalding, continuing his duties, used to ring the six o'clock morning bell. She was also a washerwoman. Being engaged in the latter occupation at a clergyman's house with other women, she left the tub to ring the bell.**
>
> **One of her companions putting a white sheet around her, followed her, and in the dark stood on the bench in the south porch, and on the old woman coming out of the church, and while she was locking the door, set up a dreadful moan, thinking to frighten the old lady, but she quickly drew the huge key from the lock and rushed at the figure with the exclamation, 'Be ye live or dead here's a go at yer,' and nearly slew the would-be ghost."**

And also from Lincolnshire, here's a similar recollection of St Mark's Lincoln.

> **"The bell at St Mark's Lincoln ... used to be known by the name of 'Old Kate,' and was rung at six a.m. and seven p.m. all the year round. Old men say that (giving over work at seven in the evening) they used to listen for the welcome tones of 'Old Kate.' It was rung for many years by John Middlebrook, the parish clerk, who lived in a little lean-to tenement attached to the north side of the**

tower. On his death in December 1804, his wife succeeded him as parish clerk (her name was Mary Middlebrook;) ... the old lady consulted her convenience and her duty at once, by bringing the bellrope through the belfry door to her bedside and pulled 'Old Kate' whilst she lay in bed."

Certainly, the story of a lady chiming from her bed doesn't sound very likely, but the detail of the account makes it pretty certain that she chimed somehow.

Joining In

So in the fullness of time, was it then *working class* women who first forced themselves into the male-only world of the change ringing bands?

Regrettably, no. Of course this was partly due to their subservient status, but it wasn't *just* that. In the nineteenth century the great bulk of social innovation sprang from the middle and upper-middle classes because they had the time, the money and the education. But most important of all, they had the freedom.

When you're living on the breadline and dependent for your very survival on the goodwill and charity of your neighbours – who are also on the breadline – you simply can't *afford* to be different. Expressing unconventional views, let alone taking unconventional actions, can put you outside the pale and cut you off from the all-important mutual support. So conformity is essential for survival.

But even though the working classes didn't *instigate* the introduction of women into change ringing, in time they certainly supported it. And the story of how they did *that*, is what we'll be looking at next time.

It's not so long since there was a great deal of chiming. Even on a Sunday, there was normally five minutes chiming before every service, and the bells had to be rung down in time for the chiming to happen. Indeed, the ***five minute bell*** *was a signal to late comers to walk much faster – or even run – in order to arrive at the church on time.*

During the week, a bell was chimed before the vicar said matins and evensong – which he was supposed to say every day whether anyone joined him or not – and there were all sorts of local reasons for chiming too. Even today, a lot of ringers regularly and punctiliously connect a bell to the chiming rope that goes through the ringing chamber floor, notwithstanding that it hasn't been used in years.

So when I'm leading elementary and bell experience courses, I always do a few minutes on chiming; and generally the helpers are as intrigued as the students to have a go at the various options. So in case you've never tried all of them yourself, there are ***four*** *ways to chime a bell.*

The first is the standard tugging with your arms that you do at the end of a lower in peal. It's a great labour and your arms soon get quite tired, so it's best avoided except for very short periods.

The second is to ring the bell until it's halfway up. That's much easier, and you can chime like this for hours on end without trouble. But although it certainly makes a noise, it doesn't sound like proper chiming, so I'm not very keen on that way either.

The third way has always been relatively uncommon but it does produce a very particular effect. You chime the bell with a slightly higher swing than a chime in rounds, but you only give it a jerk on every other swing. When you get it right, you achieve a very slow but regular chime, with silence in between the blows. Of course, if you get it wrong, you produce a lot of random extra blows and part-blows in-between the intended ones, so you really do need to practise in advance.

And the fourth way was the standard way, and by far the easiest. You tie a knot low down in the rope so that you create a loop about twelve inches off the ground. You then put your right foot in the loop while leaving your left foot on the ground. You keep the rope next to your body so that it passes by the inside of your right thigh and right calf.

CHIMING.

The 1891 lady in the picture has it approximately right but not completely so. The artist has drawn the rope unrealistically long instead of putting a loop in just the end of it, and the lady has her foot much too far from her body. She's using her left foot rather than her right too.

But once you get it right, and you get the bell chiming, you keep it going by simply rising up onto your left toes and stamping gently down with your right foot in time with the bell's swing. Of course, it's easier to demonstrate than put into words, so your best bet is to try it out. Make sure, though, that unlike the lady in the picture, you keep the rope close to your body or you'll find your foot shooting out in front of you.

*And in case you'd like a literary reference, Robert Louis Stevenson wrote a rather depressing poem containing the line, "***I know how to chime with my foot in the rope***."*

But if you want, you can go even further. In some towers, one or two ringers used to chime three bells each, especially before evensong. They would stand on one foot and chime one bell with the other foot as well as one in each of their hands. Indeed, some ringers sat on a chair and chimed ***four*** *bells – one with each foot and one with each hand – although I've never seen that done myself.*

Of course, it's essential to make sure the bell is down before you put your foot in the loop, and it's also essential that the knot that makes the loop doesn't come undone. That's why there are ***up knots*** *and* ***down knots****. The* ***up knot*** *will supposedly come undone if you put your foot in the loop by mistake – although it's best not to try it – but the* ***down knot*** *will remain firm.*

And if you're not sure how to tie a down knot, have a look at the two pictures. Note that the down knot is ***not*** *a bowline even though it's rather similar. Indeed, when the two lady sextons in the last chapter were chiming, the bowline knot as we know it today probably hadn't even been invented. The evidence isn't entirely clear but most likely it was*

The Up Knot

A Down Knot

one of the many advances in the mid-nineteenth century.

And of course, there were a great many advances in bell hanging then too. They were very real and very useful but in the long term they did the advancement of women in ringing no favours at all. Instead they simply prepared the ground for **The Great Myth**.

19. The Great Myth

I'm told that women were only able to start ringing at the end of the nineteenth century because of advances in bell hanging. Is that true?

J.H.
Kent

Quite simply, and in one word, no; but you hear and read it so often, I call it, ***The Great Myth***. It was a story invented by enlightened, turn-of-the-century male ringers who needed a peg to hang social progress on; and whilst it was a great idea at the time, it's rather odd that it still appears repeatedly in ringing histories today. So let's look at what *really* happened in the second half of the nineteenth century.

The Weaker Sex?

And first, let's challenge the *basis* of *The Great Myth.* Women, it was said, were physically much weaker than men, so they couldn't ring until the bells became easier to manage. But although *on average* men are indeed a little stronger than women, a great many women are a great deal stronger than a great many men. More important, a great deal of women's work in the nineteenth century was physically very demanding indeed, so most working class women were far stronger than their middle and upper class male counterparts. Indeed, the 1841 census recorded these figures for England alone.

Women working in mining	**6,133**
Women working in metal manufacturing	**1,600**
Women working in agriculture as labourers	**79,256**
Women working as general labourers	**14,615**
Washerwomen	**50,706**
Women in domestic service	**908,471**
Women working as blacksmiths	**512**

It was clearly absurd to suggest that more than a million women could perform these amazingly strenuous jobs for at least 60 hours a week but not ring bells – and the census figures must have been understated anyway. Many husbands didn't want to admit that their wives worked alongside them or as employees elsewhere, so the true number of women in heavy employment probably totalled over *two* million.

Woman's Work

And it wasn't just in traditional heavy industries that women had strenuous jobs. *All* jobs required considerable strength because everything was heavier and huge loads had to be carried by hand. The euphemistically named, *dairy maids*, for example, spent their working lives carrying pairs of heavy, cumbersome buckets full of milk – one in each hand or on a yoke – and they hand-turned great butter churns for hours at a time. Indeed, *all* farm-related work involved heavy physical labour.

In the more traditional women's activities, the strength required was no less. The heavy labour involved in being a washerwoman, for example, was also extraordinary – not just in the carrying but also in the wringing out and lifting. Female domestic servants had to carry endless loads of coal up endless flights of stairs; and in the home, women not only did all the washing and coal carrying for their families, but did much more besides; and *that* was often in addition to their paid work. Of course, working men had very strenuous jobs too, but there really wasn't much difference between *their* work and women's work. A *Punch* cartoon of the period shows a bewigged footman with his nose in the air, carrying a single card on a silver tray up a flight of stairs. Behind him a maid struggles up with a massive coal scuttle full of coal. "**Man's work .... Woman's Work**," reads the caption.

Sports and Pastimes

So if it wasn't improvements in bell hanging that caused women to start ringing, what was it? Well, whatever period of history we look at, *the times, they are a'changing.* It's easy to think of the Victorian era as a period of social and cultural stasis, but that just wasn't so. Women were becoming better educated and more emancipated as the century wore on, and they were gradually entering into the better jobs and professions too – albeit for much less pay. At the same time, they were engaging more and more in the sports and pastimes previously reserved for men.

Bicycling

So by way of an example, in 1894 Constance Everett-Green – soon to become the nation's leading female cycling journalist – wrote,

> **"It is still more or less of an open question in England whether ladies can with propriety ride the bicycle."**

But only the following year at the end of 1895 she wrote,

> **"It would hardly be too much to say that in April 1895 one was considered eccentric for riding a bicycle, whilst by the end of June eccentricity rested with those who did *not* ride."**

Equally in 1895, the first women's cycling magazine was published – *The Lady Cyclist* – and a year later there was also *Wheelwoman and Society Cycling News*. By 1899 women cyclists were regularly appearing in books and stories too; and in ***Hilda Wade: A Woman with Tenacity of Purpose***, Hilda – in order to escape from assegai wielding Matabele – "**... vaulted lightly on to the seat**" of her bicycle and pedalled "**... for dear life**," and *that* was while carrying a rescued baby at the same time.

Ringing

And the very fact that Hilda Wade – whose skirt was "**unobtrusively divided at front and back**" – could *be **A Woman with Tenacity of Purpose***, tells us how things had changed. The last decade of the nineteenth century was known as *The Naughty Nineties* because of the increased social freedom being taken by both sexes, and we can plot the same progress with most pastimes that we can with cycling. So while ringing progressed a little faster than some and a little slower than others, it was essentially just carried along with the flow.

All the modern, enlightened male ringers of the time knew that women should come into ringing, and to their great credit, they welcomed them. Indeed, many men gave women a welcome and support *well ahead* of the ideas of the time. But they needed an argument to use against the backwoodsmen, so talk of the relative strength of the sexes and the advances in bellhanging was as good a fig leaf to shelter behind as any. The real tragedy was that the myth became so damaging to women's progress later on.

The First Steps

But having looked at the myth, when *did* the nineteenth century entry of women into ringing really start?

And unfortunately it's hard to say, not least because the very first women ringers were almost certainly kept fairly secret by the bands they rang with. Probably – but by no means certainly – there were a few women ringing from the 1840s onwards, or even earlier. In 1873 Fred and George Day, bellhangers of Eye in Suffolk, rehung Laxfield bells and encountered an "**old woman**" ringing a bell there. And since she was one of a very large ringing family, she may well have been ringing since she was a girl.

We also know that Christabel and Annot Airy, the daughters of the Astronomer Royal, George Biddell Airy, rang at St Alphage, Greenwich. We don't know the dates, but they were born in 1842 and 1843, so they may well have learnt in the 1850s – although as they continued to live in the parish after their father retired in 1881, it could have been later.

The 1860s

The 1860s, though, give us firmer evidence. The Rev H. T. Ellacombe – inventor of the ***Ellacombe Chimes*** – records giving a talk in Exeter in 1869. By way of an example of change ringing, he arranged for the Trelawney family to ring a course of Grandsire Cinques on handbells, and they stood as follows:

Eleanor Trelawney (aged 12)	**1-2**
Edith Trelawney (aged 13)	**3-4**
Beatrice Trelawney (aged 14)	**5-6**
Mrs Trelawney	**7-8**
Colonel Trelawney	**9-10**
Harry Trelawney (aged 10)	**11-12**

And although there's no evidence, we might reasonably suppose that the four women had at least had a go at tower bells at some time. And certainly at least *one* of the sisters kept her method ringing skills going because the notebook of the Ancient Society of College Youths contains this splendid entry for June 1874.

> **"Plymouth**
>
> **On Tuesday the College Youths were invited to Plympton St. Mary, where they met Colonel Trelawny, the Rev. Mr. Kelly (a College Youth and a ringer), Mr. Woolcombe, and Miss Trelawny, and rang several touches on the bells, with which they were much pleased.**
>
> **Under the porch of this church a circumstance occurred which had not been performed perhaps at any time or place before – a course of Grandsire Cinques was rung in which Miss Trelawny took five-six, and rang them without a mistake, before thirty or forty persons. She appeared to be about eighteen or twenty years of age."**

And women were clearly ringing methods on handbells elsewhere too. The editor of *Bell News* later encouraged it in an *Isn't-the-weather-hot?* editorial.

> **"The recesses of a garden or lawn are particularly applicable for the practice of handbells on a summer evening, and the entertainment – for such it is – is also well worth the notice of the gentler sex."**

The 1880s

But once the 1880s came along, progress accelerated. In 1884 the *Bell News* editor visited Arthur Percival Heywood's estate in Staffordshire. Heywood – later to become *Sir* Arthur

Heywood when he inherited his father's baronetcy – was a very wealthy man and an extremely keen bellringer. In 1891, he was to form *The Central Council of Church Bell Ringers*, and he was also to invent the largely unrung method, *Duffield*, which he mistakenly thought would become as popular as Stedman.

Even more remarkable, one of his hobbies was driving steam locomotives – having learnt to do it by "**... illicit journeyings on the footplate**" – and he even built two miniature steam engines with his own hands, one of which still pulls miniature trains today. So not surprisingly, the Editor was extremely impressed by his visit. But of special interest to us is that he reported particularly on Sir Arthur's women pupils.

> **"After admiring the engineering skill of Mr. Heywood, and the novelty of the work he has wrought on his own estate, we are brought face to face with the fact that not only is he a practical ringer himself, and a bob-caller to boot, but the young lady members of his family are acquainted with the Grandsire method.**
>
> **When the age of the young lady who rang the trebles so well in a course of Grandsire Triples is taken into consideration, it cannot be deemed otherwise than wonderful in one so young. It certainly goes a long way to establish the opinion that Mr. Heywood himself is an enthusiast in the art and that the young ladies are not averse to its practice."**

What was more, the Editor went on to enthuse about women ringers generally – albeit condescendingly.

"We read of a date touch being rung at Huntsham, the seat of Colonel Troyte. This touch was the composition of a lady – Miss E. Cruwys Sharland, who is a lady associate of the Devonshire Guild. The fact of members of the fair sex coming to the front as ringers, is certainly one worth more than ordinary notice. The time may come when we can hear of them in the steeple, taking a light bell and ringing or calling a touch.

This may appear irregular, perhaps, from several points of view. But the presence of a lady in the steeple does not appear to us at all out of place. ... And ringing a light bell in a touch now and then with the village company, would be far preferable to many of those enervating occupations which the female portion of the human family are at the present time, in obedience to the vagaries of fashion, called upon to take part."

Support

But although that's patronising and sexist, and it makes for uncomfortable reading today, it *is* supportive; and the evidence suggests that nearly all the leading ringers of the day were supportive of women ringers too. Indeed, to begin with, there was very little vocal opposition at all. The reaction of most male ringers was not outrage but surprise.

The Colonel Troyte referred to was also a remarkable man who in peculiar circumstances had become squire of Huntsham in Devon. As part of the considerable work he did for the benefit of the area, he rehung the three bells of the parish church and augmented them to six. He then taught himself and his band to ring methods with no help other than occasional letters from J. Taylor, the bellhanger. Later he was to write the big selling learners' book, *Change Ringing,* which was in print for decades; and he also formed the first ever modern ringing Association, *The Guild of Devonshire Ringers*. But at the same time, and of most interest to us here, he taught the unmarried ladies in his household to ring.

And Elsewhere

And it wasn't just wealthy landowners who were bringing women into ringing. It was happening in lots of places. In 1890 a resident of Saffron Walden wrote to *Bell News*:

> **"The band of lady ringers at this town, who are under the tuition of Mr. F. Pitstow, rang upon the tower bells rounds and call-changes in honour of Her Majesty's birthday. We imagine it is the first time in history that a peal of Church bells has been rung by a band of the fair sex."**

And from Middleham in Yorkshire in 1901 we hear:

> **"... a company of lady ringers was established in the parish. ... this band was started 'as an incentive to the stronger sex.' ... The ladies have just accomplished some 6-scores of Bob Doubles and touches of Minor. They were Miss A. Storey, Miss P. Anton, Miss A. Croft, Miss M. Peacock, Miss H. Anton, and Mrs. R. Kerr-Smith."**

And from Ramsey in Huntingdonshire in 1902 we hear:

> **"It is suggested that a band of lady ringers**

shall be formed in connection with the Ramsey bell-ringers association. Throughout the country bands of lady campanologists are now to be met with, and it is stated that several young ladies of Ramsey have expressed their willingness to become members if the suggestion is carried out."

Separation

All of which was definitely progress and very encouraging progress too, but there was still a problem. As the last three reports make clear, these women were certainly ringing, but they weren't ringing *with* the men, they were ringing *separately*. Many women bands were not only *taught* separately, they actually *rang* separately. Their members didn't appear as members of the local band and they weren't elected to the local Association either.

The separation from the local band was probably because they came from a higher social class, and the absence of Association membership was probably because they didn't progress far enough. But it *does* mean that there were probably far more women ringers at the time than records suggest.

All the same, *some* women ringers were fully integrated, and their numbers were increasing. What was more, in 1895 integration was about to be vigorously encouraged by a most unlikely proponent.

And who *that* was, we'll find out next time.

When you're looking at the leading ringers of the past, it's always interesting to find out what they did **apart** *from ringing; and Sir Arthur Heywood, who we met a few pages back, was by far and away the most influential ringer of his time. He was rich, powerful and dictatorial, yet in his non-ringing time he was also an accomplished engineer.*

Indeed, he was **such** *an accomplished engineer that he's better remembered in railway history than in ringing history. He envisaged miniature, 15-inch gauge railways for commercial purposes on the estates of all the landed gentry, and he built one on his own estate, together with tunnels and bridges. Of course, he had labourers to help him, but with his own hands he built small steam locomotives – each about five feet high to the top of their funnels – and he named the first one, "Effie," after his wife.*

Later he made a small, eight-seater dining car to go behind it, and later still, he built a small sleeping car too. The sleeping car was for his children, and in an early form of **sleepover**, *they and their friends spent nights in it as the miniature engine chugged and whistled them round the estate.*

So dictatorial or not, Sir Arthur was kind to his children, and he gave them magical experiences that even Enid Blyton would have thought twice about inventing. But the late Victorian approach to children was curiously ambivalent about them enjoying themselves. Fun, strict discipline and an insistence on duty were mixed in an odd amalgam; and as we'll see in the next chapter, **duty** *was especially important for girls ...*

20. The Girl's Own Paper

Nowadays we're always putting recruiting articles for new ringers in the Parish Magazine and local paper. Didn't they write articles like that 100 years ago, and if they did, what did they look like?

R.S.
Lancashire

On October 5th 1895, as the nights were drawing in, *The Girl's Own Paper* published an article encouraging girls to ring. The magazine was published by *The Religious Tract Society*, and was a sister publication to the well-known *The Boy's Own Paper* and the lesser known *Sunday at Home*. It lasted in one form or another from 1880 to 1956 and was originally intended as an improving journal for girls, mainly of the middle and upper-middle classes. Its rather pretentious aim was,

> **"... to foster and develop that which is highest and noblest in the girlhood and womanhood of England ...**

by

> **... putting the best things first, and banishing the worthless from our pages."**

The Content

And in pursuit of that aim it was a mixture of thrilling stories and useful information. So *ripping yarns* were mixed with articles such as, ***How to Refoot a Stocking***.

From this remove, the early style seems a little stiff and pompous, but for its time it was lively enough; and most importantly, it encouraged girls to advance themselves and aspire to a measure of independence and adventure. Certainly, it assumed its readers to have a far greater intelligence and intellectual sophistication than modern young people's magazines do.

It also assumed its readers to have a remarkable capacity to stick with extremely heavy-going text. One page of our article contains nothing but three columns of densely packed type filled with extremely long sentences, and a single paragraph is actually over a column long.

The Plot

But as was the way of the times, even an article on bellringing had to have a plot – something to lead the reader in and justify female participation in a male dominated activity. So a heroine immediately appears. She has been diagnosed with a serious but unspecified eye complaint, and is absolutely forbidden for two years from engaging in her normal female pursuits of reading, letter writing, needlework and "**... playing music from the printed score**."

Naturally, she's already tried poultry keeping, gardening, regular cross-country walks and tricycling – she's a clergyman's daughter and so unable to propel herself on a mere *two* wheels – but even with these activities, she still needs something else, particularly in the winter and on dark evenings. So she's decided to help her father by chiming every morning before Matins.

Chiming

And as we saw two chapters ago, Matins and Evensong had to be said by the vicar every day whether anyone else was present or not, and as *The Book of Common Payer* said, the vicar "**.... shall cause a bell to be tolled thereunto a convenient time before he begin**." This chiming is what we now call the *five minute bell*, and in those days the normal way was to tie a loop in the end of the rope and then chime with your foot in the loop – as explained on page 304.

The Girl's Own Paper helpfully included a drawing – now also on page 304 – by way of demonstration, and apart from the rope being too long, the loop being too long, and the action being too far from the body, it's pretty accurate.

Full Circle

But although our heroine starts off by simply chiming, temptation soon works its wicked way with her; and the writer tackles this head on.

> **"But bell-ringing has a peculiar fascination of its own, which is well-nigh irresistible, and when a person has once got thoroughly used to the feel of a bell-rope between his fingers, the desire to do more than simply toll or chime very soon follows, and it was so in this case. The presence one day in the belfry of her brother, who had for many years been a 'bell-ringer,' naturally brought out the request, 'Could you not teach me to *ring* a bell? chiming is rather dull, monotonous work.' "**

And of particular note is the archetypal brother figure appearing – as he was wont to do in girls' publications until well after the Second World War. In this story he neither speaks nor acts, and we know nothing of his teaching ability or experience; but he can be safely turned to as a male with whom she can be alone without the slightest suggestion of sexual impropriety. Had she asked the lower class tower captain to teach her, that would have been quite another matter. He might have been young and unmarried – or worse still, married and a potential adulterer – and *The Girl's Own Paper* couldn't leave anything of *that* sort to the imagination.

But regrettably, we hear nothing of her lessons. We're told that she becomes a proper bellringer, "**albeit not a change ringer**;" and although it's not actually stated, we're apparently meant to assume that she can't manage to ring changes because she's a girl and so not sufficiently mathematically minded. She does, though, become a role model encouraging other girls to start ringing with her, but beyond that, we learn nothing more about her and she passes out of our story.

Encouragement

And here the drift of the article changes, because although much of the general public already saw the last decade of the nineteenth century as *The Naughty Nineties*, *The Girl's Own Paper* certainly didn't, and neither did the parents of the middle class girls who read it. So the sensibilities of young women stepping into a previously all-male activity had to be addressed, and some form of justification had to be supplied. So,

> **"Now here is an opportunity for exercise, which in these days, it is agreed on all hands, is so necessary for our girls.**
>
> **When she has mastered the elementary principles of the art, [a girl] may easily hold her own with boys and men."**

Yet not *all* girls could hold their own apparently, but only the bold late nineteenth century girl who read *The Girl's Own Paper* ...

> **"Nor do we mean to say that the dodging about of a rope, as thick and heavy as a bell-rope necessarily is, within a few inches of one's nose, does not require a strength of nerve and a decision of purpose which some girls we have met seem utterly to lack."**

The Moral Dimension

But there had to be a reason for her ringing in addition to simply having fun. For a middle class girl in 1895, having fun could never of itself be a reason for doing anything. She was expected to undertake good works as part of her service to God – sometimes referred to in *The Girl's Own Paper* as, *The Master* – and so the writer neatly shoe-horns ringing into the *good works* category too.

> **"There is genuine work for the Master to be done by our sisters if they will try bell-ringing. The ringers in a country parish are often drawn from quite the rough, happy-go-lucky lads of the village, and not infrequently are a source of great trouble, or at least anxiety, to those responsible for the religious tone of the parish; in many cases they do not think of going to a place of worship, except when they ring the church-bells for Service, and, even then, we have too often seen those who have been engaged in calling the people to worship, themselves troop out of the church just before the service begins."**

And once again we have some archetypal males introduced – this time, the good-hearted but rough and ready country boys who are in danger of going off the rails if someone doesn't save them. But *who* is to save them? *That*, apparently, is the problem.

> **"But further than this, they are very difficult to get hold of; they avoid the clergyman of the parish because they are afraid of him, or uncomfortably shy with him; they have as little to do with religion of any kind as possible, because somehow they think it unmanly. In a word, there is often no influence in a country village which can reach them, since they have given up going to Sunday school; and consequently they loaf about at the street corners on Sundays idle, if not worse."**

Missionary Work

So naturally, this is the opportunity for the girl bellringer to step in. Ringing for a girl will then be both good exercise and valuable missionary work at the same time. Indeed, missionary work that no one else at all can perform. As the writer somewhat unfortunately expresses it,

> **"If once a lady can get hold of them and make them trust her, there is little she cannot do with them"**

What's more,

> **"Her presence in the belfry will tend to humanise and civilise the lads in a way which nothing else can do; it will suppress all coarse words and idle jesting, which are not convenient, and by teaching the lads to**

reverence the lesser, herself to wit, she will gradually lead them to a reverence of the immeasurably greater One, her Maker and theirs."

Pretty heavy stuff in all sorts of ways; and of passing interest is the assumption – almost certainly correct – that most of the male ringers would be young. In 1895, by the time a male reached the age of 18 he was definitely a man and no longer a ***lad***.

Clothes

But having attempted to assuage the sensibilities of outraged parents, the unknown writer gets sharply down to practicalities; and clothing was obviously of considerable importance.

> **"The skirt of the dress should be plain, and of some fairly heavy stuff (e.g., serge), so as not to be in the way of the rope, or to catch it as it moves quickly past; the bodice should be quite loose-fitting, made of flannel or something of the sort, so as to allow a perfectly free movement to the arms. The wrist-bands should be quite easy."**

And head-gear had to be addressed too, because in those days women had to cover their heads in church, and bare-headedness couldn't possibly be sanctioned by *The Girl's Own Paper*.

> **"... a close-fitting outdoor cap will be found most convenient, and this should be secured by an elastic round the back of the head, and not by the long pins that are in general**

use. The discomfort of a straw hat will be very obvious if only tried once, and besides the discomfort, there is some little risk attached to the wearing of any head-gear with a brim."

Nothing here about corsets or other undergarments, of course, because in 1895 the *unmentionables* were still genuinely unmentionable. Jewellery, though, was another matter.

"Rings are also to be avoided, as they have the effect of allowing the rope to slip through the hand, and are efficacious in the manufacture of blisters."

And as if embarrassed by having used such a ridiculous expression as, *efficacious in the manufacture of blisters*, the writer tells us sharply in the shortest sentence of the entire article, **"Bangles are merely a nuisance."**

The Technicalities

So having got the clothes right, we receive a long, complex, and largely impenetrable, description of bell fittings – which I suspect was probably written by a different writer. This is then followed by an even longer and yet more impenetrable description of full circle ringing. Bizarrely, the writer assumes that his readers will not only understand it, but will still be reading at the end of it. What's more, they will actually have mastered the entire theory of full circle ringing and be ready to put it into practice. All the same, since …

"... a not inconsiderable danger attends the timid ringer;"

he wisely suggests an instructor accompany the learner's first attempts. Regrettably, though, neither the teaching nor the advice on bell handling measure up to modern standards, and I doubt they measured up to 1895 standards either. The learner is advised to keep two fingers round the tail end at all times and to catch the sally with the other two fingers only. She is also advised to hold the tail end in the right hand even though all but one of the girls in the ringing room picture on page 329, hold it in the left.

Danger

Health and safety wasn't a big deal then, of course, but a few heavy handed hints about the dangers were still felt warranted.

> **"A heavy thing like a bell is not a plaything for a child, and a mistake might very easily result even in the death of the ringer, the bell-rope in coming down, if it got in any way twisted, might drop round the neck of the ringer, and on its return journey perform the office of hangman."**

But nevertheless,

> **"... with care and guarding against the feeling of presumption, there is no real danger."**

All the same, the editor – though probably not the writer – couldn't miss the opportunity of including a typically over-the-top, Victorian drawing of what *might* happen, labelled rather inadequately, "**An Accident**."

And Then

We then get a paragraph on how to ring in rounds; but raising and lowering is thought best left until later because,

> **"Practice at ringing will develop certain muscles necessary for the work, and these when in working order will materially help her to do that which is harder work than merely ringing,"**

and,

> **"... practice at ringing will teach her to know the bell as a friend, and not to fear her as a possible and dangerous foe. It will give her quickness to catch the rope at the right time; it will give her nerve to overcome the natural discomfort of a rope dancing wildly about."**

Some Final Advice

But all *Girl's Own Paper* articles needed to end with some central pieces of advice, and this article was no exception. Some of these pieces were technical:

> **"Keep your knees firm, and only bend them just a little."**

Some were behavioural:

> **"... so discourage in every way possible talking about outside things, and especially any joking."**

But the last – and clearly most important – was spiritual.

> **"You will have many opportunities of getting to know the characters and tempers of those with whom you may be ringing, and also many opportunities of influencing them for good. Try therefore to use the opportunities gently, firmly, humbly, and**

prayerfully for the Master's glory and the salvation of souls."

A hard task to lay upon anybody, certainly; and particularly while they're still struggling with rounds. But this was the stuff of which girls who read *The Girl's Own Paper* were made. ***Nothing*** was too much for them.

Whenever you write a learner's text on bell handing, pictures are a problem. Photographs are good in a way, but the style of clothes dates so quickly that – for young ringers at least – the book quickly loses its credibility. Fashions changed quickly in 1895 too, so we can be pretty sure that ***The Girl's Own Paper*** *drawings were scrupulously accurate about clothing.*

An Accident

*But that said, as "***An Accident***" clearly shows, they weren't anywhere near so accurate about ringing. Even the most horrendous ringing accident, could never have got the girl into that position.*

The picture on the opposite page, though, is much better; and certainly it's a very clever way of showing the belfry and ringing chamber at the same time. It was obviously drawn from life, and in many ways it's drawn pretty accurately too, but all sorts of inaccuracies have crept in. They were probably due to the artist working up his original rough sketches later, or perhaps because he wanted to make the picture more compelling.

All the same, in case you want to play "Spot the Inaccuracies," I won't list them all; but to get you started, the bell on the right is up wrong, at least two of the ropes are far too long, all the ropes are laid the wrong way round and one girl has her tail end upside down.

And this last mistake was the saddest of all because the 1895 male opponents of women in ringing thought that women ringers – being, indeed, ***women*** *– would* ***always*** *get their tail ends upside down. And worse still, some were quite prepared to say so ...*

21. Resistance!

It's all very well you writing about male support for the early women ringers, but what about the opposition? What about the nay-sayers and the reactionaries? What about *the resistance?*

A.D.
Bucks

What indeed? And that makes this a splendid time to canter through some of those outrageously sexist statements that even the most reactionary, modern-day bigot would think twice about expressing – although that said, there really weren't that many. But before we come to them, let's look at what resistance there was and where it came from.

The Types

And here we have a distinct problem because the greatest resistance probably came from those men who couldn't express themselves well and who didn't write to newspapers and magazines. It seems likely that it was the older, less educated ringers who were the main opposition. They saw the ringing chamber as a male-only area where they could smoke, swear, drink, spit, keep their hats on and tell stories of the sort that would have been considered inappropriate in the presence of a woman. Indeed, we know that drinking, swearing, spitting, smoking and hat wearing were all considered perfectly acceptable ringing room activities at the time.

Those ringers simply took no notice of the suggestion that women might ring. They didn't write about it and they didn't talk about it either. They just declined to teach any girls. This wasn't hard because they didn't teach anyone they didn't want to anyway. They didn't have the *take-anyone-who-shows-the-slightest-interest* approach that we have nowadays. They thought it was a privilege to learn, and it was a privilege they didn't bestow lightly. And since much needed income was involved, it was a privilege they often restricted to family members.

And even those well-educated ringers who *could* write to newspapers with their objections, generally didn't because it wasn't thought acceptable even then. Sexism in all manner of guises was rampant enough, but one of those guises was a belief in elaborate courtesy towards women, and objecting to women ringers without good reason would not have been thought courteous.

The "Good Reasons"

So what *good reasons* did the opponents come up with?

Well, some men saw ringing as *unlady-like,* involving as it did, *sweating.* Of course this was very much double standards since they were content for women to engage in extremely heavy labour in the home – and in all the employments we looked at in Chapter 19 – but they still didn't want them to engage in a little light exercise for fun.

In a similar vein, some men saw the ringing chamber as an inappropriate place for women because men kept their hats *on* and took their jackets and detachable shirt collars *off.* At times, they even rolled up their sleeves and lowered their braces too – with the occasional result that their trousers fell down – and *that* wasn't thought suitable in the presence of a woman either.

A more puzzling – to us – reason was that men could supposedly enjoy themselves better when women weren't present, so they had the right to keep women out. The proponents of this view – which was to be occasionally voiced in *The Ringing World* until well after the Second World War – apparently genuinely believed they had a greater right to enjoy themselves than women did.

Then there were those who saw – or who thought they saw – the religious objections that we'll look at next time. And lastly, there were those who simply knew deep within themselves that ringing was a man-thing, and even though they couldn't sensibly explain it, that was reason enough for them.

And to be fair, like all of us, they had imbibed prejudices from their families and communities at a very early age, and those prejudices had been continuously strengthened and reinforced throughout their lives. The wonder is not that those men had those prejudices in the first place, but that so many of them were able to put them aside.

A Woman's Place

And there's another piece of historical context here that's very easy to miss. In the late nineteenth and early twentieth centuries many of the opponents of women ringers didn't think they were *opposing* women, they thought they were *supporting* them.

As we've already seen, social emancipation was taking place in a great many ways, and a great many people supported it. Indeed, to a greater or lesser extent *most* people supported it. But they were genuinely troubled as to how far it should go, not just because of its effect on men, but because of its effect on women; and they were troubled about its affect on society too.

Even among the doubters there was a genuine desire to give women a *place* – to give them a specific but respected role in the home and in society; but many people – women as well as men – felt that venturing into male occupations and preserves – such as voting – lessened and diminished women. And at a time when few unmarried adult women could decently support themselves by working, they worried that engaging in male pastimes would decrease a girl's marriageability.

They worried about society itself too. A strong but compassionate female home builder who could hold a family together and educate her children and husband in proper moral behaviour, was seen as essential to a strong and healthy society. She was seen as essential to the proper running of the British Empire too, and that was also a matter of public concern. And indeed, the British Empire apart, many people feel much the same way today; and certainly, many cultures throughout the World hold the matriarchal ideal in considerable reverence.

In Politics

And on top of all that, in the rarefied circles of top politics, a *woman's place* was also thought to include advising men and moderating their behaviour and decision making. So in the *Establishment* there were many women who exercised considerable political influence; and it was believed they could do that precisely *because* they had no outright power. They were seen as outside the overt political process, and that enabled them to provide a different perspective. And losing that perspective was seen as worrying.

So although a great deal of the opposition to women's freedom came from men's desire to protect their positions of privilege, much of it wasn't anywhere near that simple.

"The First Blast of the Trumpet"

But getting down to the truly outrageous statements, the published ones were certainly a very long time in coming. As we saw in the last chapter, by 1895 even *The Girl's Own Paper* was recommending that girls should start ringing, but we have to wait until the 1910s before there was anything like a serious written objection. Here's a good one though. It consists of a letter signed, "Grandsire," and it was published in *The Hants and Berks Gazette* in February 1913.

> **"What can possibly have induced ladies to take up this strenuous and essentially men's work in the belfry? ... ... although it is a very healthful exercise and a splendid body developer, ... it does require a good deal of stamina to be a successful bell-ringer. ... I honestly say I view this intrusion with not a little concern. In fact, I am quite unable to understand why ladies should prefer to leave their many womanly pursuits and pastimes and to range themselves with a number of men in a belfry to manipulate a huge bell of so many hundredweight. We of the sterner sex rightly take a pride in doing some big, strong and manly work ... but I trust the day is far distant when any great number of ladies will unnecessarily seek to imitate us in that respect. ... I believe the fact is that when a lady has been anxious to learn to ring ... it has been regarded by the ringers as merely a freak.**
>
> **Well, all I can urge now, and I do so most earnestly, is that if the ladies must form a guild and desire to advance the art of**

> **change-ringing ... let them procure some sets of handbells and pursue their practice in a comfortable room or shady nook ... and so avoid the belfry, which for all time, by the nature of the occupation, has properly been regarded as a special sanctum for men."**

Of passing note is that a letter about ringing appeared in *The Hants and Berks Gazette* at all. But suffragette *outrages* were big news at the time, so there was general debate about what women should and shouldn't do. And looked at in that light we can see that – outrageous though the letter is even by the standards of the time – the writer is a person who is genuinely troubled by social changes he simply can't keep up with.

The Replies

But by 1913 there were plenty of first class women ringers, many of whom had ringing skills of the very highest standard no matter who you compared them with. Edith Parker, for example, who had just formed *The Ladies Guild*, had already conducted over thirty peals, many of them of London Major, and that was a remarkable achievement for *any* ringer at that time. Nevertheless, all those women had the good sense to ignore what they probably saw as a ridiculous and unrepresentative rant.

Some men, though, *did* reply, generally trying to use rather more logic than *Grandsire* had done. So H. Sharp wrote,

> **"He asks: 'What can possibly have induced them to take up such a strenuous and essentially men's work in the belfry?'**

> **I would ask 'What could possibly have first induced men to take it up?' When he has answered one question he has answered both."**

B. Keeble, although opposing *Grandsire,* did so in a more sexist vein, first expressing his predilection for women cyclists.

> **"It is said that cycling is a healthy recreation: so is ringing. Who is there that would debar the ladies from the use of the cycle? What would be said of the man who did such an injustice to the fair sex, in which there are so many graceful riders?"**

And he then gets down to his main theme.

> **"There is, however, another point my experience teaches me. That is that the presence of ladies, or even one lady, it matters not where among a body of men, raises the whole tone of the surroundings, be it in the tower or otherwise."**

But most of *Grandsire's* opponents wanted to make simple and heart-felt statements of their views. So the splendidly Victorian-named ***Thos. Best, Junr.*** wrote,

> **"I sincerely hope that lady ringers will take little notice of the remarks made by 'Grandsire' as I am sure from my experience with the North Bucks Branch that they do not express the feelings of ringers generally; on the contrary lady ringers are very welcome in the tower."**

And ***"Treble Bob"*** wrote,

> **"No one seems to have realised any serious objection to the presence of ladies in the belfry, and I can only suppose this to be because there is none to raise."**

And Albert Jagger of Halifax appeared to sum up most people's feelings in the simple but splendidly expressed statement:

> **"Any young woman who is a ringer may have a cordial invitation to Lightcliffe, and I assure you all our band will welcome her."**

Wives and Sisters

But in the Edwardian era the real test of appropriateness was, "Would you allow your wife or sister to do it?" – a question which implicitly assumed male dominance in the husband-wife and brother-sister relationship. So several men addressed this too.

> **"We pride ourselves that our belfries are NOT AS THEY WERE. I can remember the time when, in my own district, I would not have introduced my sisters and wife to some of the companies, but the situation is now changed, and the companies in those same towers are always welcome at my home."**

And,

> **"Not so very long ago there were happenings in our belfries to which we dare not introduce our lady friends, which even kept many men out; but these are things of the past, and will never return."**

Another Attack

No letters signed, "*Grandsire*," were ever written to *Bell News* but several appeared signed "*Plain Bob*" – who may well have been *Grandsire* under another pseudonym. In one letter he stated baldly,

> **"Ringers, as a body, do not welcome the advent of lady ringers. They would much rather they stayed away. There are several reasons, and all are sufficient."**

But as a number of replies pointed out, at no time did he state what any of those reasons were. "*Maximus*," though, who may or may not have been *Grandsire* and *Plain Bob*, saw social collapse as the necessary consequence of women in the belfry.

> **"Why does woman seek to push herself in wherever man is to be found? It can only be their love of notoriety. But the novelty will soon wear off, and then exit the Ladies Guild. The place of a woman is in the home, not gallivanting about the country seeking notoriety at the end of a bell-rope. Women, young, middle-aged, or otherwise, require some recreation, but not of the sort we get in the belfry. It bodes ill for the coming generations that the women of the present day are setting themselves out to vie with men in almost everything, What will the homes of England be like when a generation or two of pleasure-seeking notoriety-loving women have had the bringing-up of her children. Will it make for a better England? I trow not."**

Next Time

A rant indeed! And not surprisingly, those women accused of ***gallivanting about the country seeking notoriety at the end of a bell rope***, sensibly ignored it. But vicars' objections were much harder to ignore; and *those* are what we'll be looking at *next time.*

We've just been looking at a letter in ***The Hants & Berks Gazette****, so to put it in its 1913 context, although subtitled,* ***& Middlesex & Surrey Journal****, the newspaper was primarily a Basingstoke local broadsheet. Even so, it was a complex mixture of local, national and international news, with reports of the annual tea of* The Girls' Friendly Society *rubbing shoulders with local suicides, executions at Reading Prison, and the health of the Pope. There was even a* London Correspondent.

And although their leading advertiser was ***The Native Guano Company*** *– "... the only supplier of genuine native guano," – the* ***Corn Exchange*** *also regularly advertised their roller skating rink. Indeed, roller skating was such a craze in the years leading up to the First World War, that when* ***The Ringing World*** *started in 1911, a number of ringers who ordered a copy from their newsagent, received the considerably more popular – though far shorter lived –* ***The Rinking World*** *instead.*

THE SPORT OF THE SEASON.
EVERY BODY'S DOING IT!
ROLLER SKATING.
CORN EXCHANGE, BASINGSTOKE
THREE SESSIONS DAILY.
10.30 to 12.30, 2.30 to 5, 6.30 to 10.30 p.m.
ADMISSION, 6d to each Session. Admission to view only, 3d. Hire Ball-bearing Skates, 6d.
Free Tuition to Beginners.
MUSIC AT EACH SESSION.
On Wednesdays the Rink is closed for the morning and afternoon sessions.
PRIVATE LESSONS CAN BE ARRANGED.

But getting back to women ringers, in the south porch of Gloucester Cathedral is a stained glass window featuring two ringing angels. Both angels appear twice – once very large, and once in miniature – but in exactly the same poses. The one angel is clearly male and is striking a bell vigorously with a long-handled mallet; but the other is clearly female, and she's ringing ***her*** *bell in the normal way with a rope and wheel – or at least, within the scope of artistic licence she is. Yet the really interesting thing is that the window was installed in 1871, well before the late Victorian wave of women ringers started.*

Of course, there's no biblical authority at all for female angels, and the way angels became generally female in the public mind is a fascinating subject in its own right. But leaving that aside, in 1871 no one would have been surprised to find a picture of a female angel. What ***would*** *have surprised them, though, would have been a picture of a woman ringing, so how did the window come into existence?*

And unfortunately, we simply don't know. 1871 is not so long back and we know that the window was made and installed by one of the leading stained glass firms of the time, ***Heaton, Butler and Bayne****. But all the correspondence relating to the design of the window has been lost.*

We do know, though, that it was donated by a local man, William Nicks, and that ought to give us a clue. He'd started a timber company at a time when Gloucester was becoming such a major port for timber and grain that in 1890 more timber was imported through Gloucester than either London or Liverpool.

So Nicks was forward-looking and well-to-do; and since Nicks and Co are still in business and have trading records going back over a hundred years, they might well have had some papers filed away somewhere. But regrettably, they haven't. What they **do** *have, though, is a photograph of William Nicks, and that shows conclusively that – unlike many donors of stained glass windows – he didn't arrange for the male figure to be modelled on himself.*

So who were the angels modelled on? The male one has an exceedingly prominent nose, so it was presumably modelled on an actual person, and the female one is very pretty but not particularly angelic. So maybe they were modelled on his daughter and son-in-law.

But whatever the background, what **is** *clear is that the Cathedral's Dean and Chapter had no problem with the idea of a female ringing a bell.*

Whereas the vicar of Dagenham ...

22. Curates, Vicars and Deans

Two things I'd like to know. First, what did the nineteenth century Church say about women starting to ring? And second, why did *The College Youths* keep women out when all the other Ringing Associations let them in?

J.U.
Bedfordshire

Two very intriguing questions, and starting with the first, the simple answer is that the Church, as a body, said nothing at all. In typical and extremely wise *Church of England* fashion, it left individual church members and individual vicars to sort things out for themselves. And not surprisingly, they generally did.

Ecclesiastical Objections

All the same, that didn't stop a number of church members being worried that biblical authority didn't support women ringing; and G. F. Margetson of Chigwell wrote to *Bell News* to express his theological worries.

> **"St. Paul, in his Epistle to the Corinthians, warns us that women are to observe silence in the Churches, and commanded to be**

under obedience to the men. In the belfry we have already allowed them to take charge of the peal, and I can quite understand why some men feel their inferiority and resentment."

And – rather presciently – he added for good measure,

"We may in the future, find them in the pulpit!"

Interestingly, no one at all tried to answer his question, partly because most ringers steered well clear of making theological pronouncements, but mainly, perhaps, because they saw nothing worth discussing. B. Mitchell of Derby, though, reported vicar problems.

"I am voicing the opinion of the majority of change-ringers in Derby when I complain of the new rules recently issued by the authorities at St. Peters. The rules, taken *en bloc,* are a little far fetched, but the last clause in Rule 1 states that no ladies are to be allowed in the belfry."

And lest prejudiced Londoners should put this down to a general laxity of moral standards in the Midlands, he helpfully added,

"I can safely say that no town in England can beat Derby as regards belfry etiquette and also behaviour."

Not surprisingly, nobody attempted to contradict his views about the standard of belfry behaviour in Derby, but *Treble Bob* tackled the essential point that women already did the bulk of the work in churches anyway.

> **"I know no reason whatever why our wives, our sisters, and our sweethearts should not take a string with us, any more than they should be excluded from the other organisations in a parish. We are quite willing to allow ladies to take the lion's share of the drudgery."**

An Objecting Curate

Two years earlier, though, a ringer from Dagenham in Essex had written the same letter to both the *Bell News* and the recently started *Ringing World.*

> **"Our Vicar has been seriously ill for some time and a deputy has taken his place. He expressed a wish to meet the ringers so as to make their acquaintance and accordingly paid a visit to the belfry and found we have in our band a young lady, who, I may say, has made good progress in the art of change-ringing. Shortly after, he asked to see our Captain, and informed him he most absolutely forbade the young lady in question from entering the belfry under any circumstances whatever, and on being pressed, gave as his reason –**
>
> **'The belfry is not a fit and proper place for any female, as it might lead to questionable actions taking place.' "**

The general response to this letter was absolute outrage, not so much because of the overt sexism but because of the suggestion of sexual impropriety. Not only were the reputations of the girl and the other ringers being impugned in a general way, but since the girl's father and brother were in the band, there was an implicit accusation of incest. So the *Bell News* Editor led the counter attack.

> **"We can scarcely trust ourselves to speak calmly to such a person. It is the deadliest insult ever offered to a ringer of either sex."**

And Alfred Barnes wrote,

> **"Such a statement, and above all emanating from such a source, is truly an outrage on the ringing fraternity; an insult to their integrity, manners and intelligence."**

And W. S. thought that an early example of *naming and shaming* should take place.

> **"... but I certainly think the Ringing Exercise should be given the name of this deputy clergyman, so as the ringers (if any) wherever he goes, might be warned."**

And interestingly enough, he was indeed named and shamed, and apparently other official complaints were made against him too, although we don't know the outcome.

Hitching a Ride

J. R. Jerram, though, while fully agreeing that the curate was completely beyond the pale, still felt moved to oppose women ringers generally.

> **"At the same time this latest craze for female ringers seems to me to be a mistake. I know that in the present day women engage in all kinds of men's work, which is a very wrong principle altogether. I blame the men quite as much as the women, for**

encouraging this sort of thing, and am persuaded that any man with a true respect for women would not do so. Women would be far more honoured in keeping to their own sphere than in trying to compete with men in men's work. If this sort of thing goes on we shall have women working at all sorts of men's trades, while the men stay at home and do the cooking and housework. Certainly the belfry is no place for women, and it is a false notion of chivalry on the men's part to encourage them there. It may seem rather hard lines for those few ladies who have learnt to ring to abandon their pastime; nevertheless I think they would do well to do so, and take up some other kind of amusement more suitable for them."

And it was this sort of vague and illogical sexism that was to dog women ringers for decades. J. R. Jerram made no arguments that could be refuted or opposed; he was simply sexist as a matter of faith. But, of course, the great majority of people of his time were sexist as a matter of faith too.

Vicars' Wives and Daughters

But whatever was thought in Derby and Dagenham, vicars' daughters were certainly ringing elsewhere; and as *The Evening Standard* of 1913 reported, so were vicars' wives.

"The ringing of church bells has been found to be a health-giving exercise for women, and at Twineham, Haywards Heath, Sussex, the Rector's wife, Mrs. E. Creswell Gee, and the schoolmistress, Mrs. Comber-Taylor,

take their places in the belfry regularly. 'I think Mrs. Creswell Gee is the only Rector's wife in England who takes her place with the ringers,' the Rev. E. Creswell Gee writes, 'and I am given to understand by many experienced ringers that if the bell is light and easily handled there is no grander exercise for chest development.' "

There was no follow up report as to exactly how well developed Mrs Creswell Gee's chest had become, but Evelyn Steel, a president of both *The Ladies Guild* and *The Bedfordshire Association* recalled that the vicar of St Paul's, Bedford once told her that he …

"… didn't think it nice for ladies to ring because men rang *without their coats*."

And Later

And just in case these examples from Edwardian times suggest that strange clerical attitudes existed only in the long past, regrettably they didn't. Even in 1952, two first class women ringers from Leicester – Phyllis Poole and Jill Staniforth – were banned by the Dean of Liverpool Cathedral from ringing at the dedication of the Cathedral bells solely because they were women. What was more, they were then excluded from the ringers' lunch afterwards because they hadn't rung!

Sadly, when it comes to the Church, it's not just the ways of God that are strange.

In the early 1990s, largely by mistake, I got sucked into a dizzy – well, fairly dizzy – round of television and radio programmes about ringing. It was all rather fun – albeit quite hard work – but one thing led to another, and I regularly got phoned up by national newspaper reporters and television researchers who wanted ringing information.

Or at least, they ***sort of*** *wanted ringing information.*

More accurately, they wanted information if it fitted in with what they wanted to write but they weren't so keen if it didn't. Essentially, they didn't want to ***inform*** *their readers, they wanted to* ***entertain*** *them; so they needed me to confirm or supply 'facts' that would engage, amuse, shock, titillate or enrage their readers rather than simply bore the pants off them.*

So ***my*** *role was to turn all the good things we know and love about ringing: the inclusiveness, the camaraderie, the mutual support, the fundraising and the hands-on maintenance – not to mention how physically and mentally skilful it is – into exciting and newsworthy items that newspapers would want to publish.*

Overall, I think I did rather well and I found they were quite happy to print the truth – or ***more or less*** *the truth – as long as I could make it human and entertaining enough. But my biggest problem was when they asked about women.*

"You don't allow women to ring, do you?" They'd say.

"Oh yes we do," I'd reply, "About half of all our ringers are women."

"But isn't your leading society called ***The Old Schoolboys*** *or something, and don't* ***they*** *keep women out?"*

So I'd explain that there was indeed a ringing society called ***The Ancient Society of College Youths*** *but having been in existence since 1637, it still had an old rule as a quaint but minor anachronism, totally out of sync with ringing as a whole. And then I'd explain that all the College*

Youths were perfectly nice ordinary people who welcomed and rang with women all the time and who weren't the least bit sexist in any way at all. And then I'd swiftly move the conversation on to something else.

But although when asked about The College Youths I always told reporters the truth, I never told them the ***whole*** *truth; and the whole truth was that the women exclusion rule – now repealed, of course –* ***didn't*** *date from 1637 as I'd implied, but only from 1919.*

So as J.U. from Bedfordshire asked at the beginning of the chapter, ***Why ever did they introduce it?***

23. On the Sixth Day of Christmas

There's nothing I like more than history articles. I can't explain it but it's something to do with endlessly puzzling out how things happened as they did. So I've read lots of *ringing* history articles too, and *The College Youths* have always featured strongly. So why don't they feature so strongly in yours?

Tom
Oxfordshire

The Ancient Society of College Youths – known generally as simply *The College Youths* – certainly do feature strongly in lots of ringing histories. And that's not surprising because they began in 1637 and have been going ever since; and any organisation that's been in continuous active existence for over 350 years, is bound to grab the imagination.

Then again, at various times over those more than 350 years they've had a considerable – and extremely beneficial – influence on ringing generally, often in quite subtle ways. And third – and most important of all – from their very beginning they've had members who could read and write; and since most histories are based on written records, the very existence of so much written material puts them in pole position.

And besides, lots of ringing histories have concentrated on peals – not least because they're a very easy source of material – so since over the centuries The College Youths have rung a large number of peals – many of them ground breaking – they've naturally featured quite a lot.

Quality-Approved

But there's something extra too. The College Youths – with a good deal of justification – have always seen themselves as an elite organisation. Their standards are high and they want to keep them that way, and they don't just welcome anybody and everybody in the way that our territorial ringing associations do. So human nature being what it is, the society has become in the eyes of some of its members, a pat-yourself-on-the-back club. Those members see their membership as a *quality-approved* seal on their wrapper, and they naturally want to show it off. Indeed, until fairly recent times *The Ringing World* assisted them by listing every single member of the several hundred who attended their annual dinner.

So since most ringing history writers of the past were members – and since we all feel very attached to our own societies – The College Youths may have received rather more emphasis than complete objectivity warranted.

The Vote

All the same, they've definitely been historically important in all sorts of ways, and they appear in a good many places in this book. But the issue we're concerned with here is that on 30 December 1919, by 27 votes to 6, they passed a motion that women would no longer be admitted as members. They didn't ban women from membership – so those women who were already members *remained* members – but they stopped any more women *becoming* members.

And since no other ringing society ever did that – and since The College Youths held the leading position we've just been talking about – why did this happen?

And at this remove it's not at all easy to understand. All the other ringing societies were very supportive of women ringers, and no doubt the great majority of College Youths were supportive too. Indeed, they already had nine women members, and the proposer of the motion was Albert Hughes of the *Whitechapel Bell Foundry*, where lunch had been provided for the entire band of the first ladies peal in 1912.

The Minutes

Unfortunately, many of the records for the period were destroyed during the Second World War, but it was recorded in the minutes that the reason for the motion was,

> **"…there may be a large number of ladies seeking membership to the Society, which … would be breaking away from old traditions …"**

And the minutes also recorded an extra reason in that Mr Beams …

> **"… pointed out that the title 'Youths' suggested the male sex ..."**

But in retrospect neither of these reasons makes any sense. Certainly, sexism was an old tradition, but then so were slavery, wife-beating and child prostitution, but no doubt the College Youths wouldn't have voted in favour of any of *those*. And in the same way, the second reason made no sense either. *Youths* also implies being young, and in 1919 the great bulk of College Youths certainly weren't that.

Additionally, there's an oral tradition which appears to date all the way back to 1919 that an unstated reason was that the Society wanted to prevent one particular woman from becoming a member. But even if that were true, it's hard to believe they would exclude half the human race simply to keep out one person – especially as they could have declined to elect her anyway.

The Great War

But decisions of this sort are never made in a vacuum, and whatever the superficial reasons may have been, there would have been much stronger influences under the surface. And the event of truly cataclysmic proportions that had taken place shortly before the vote, was the First World War.

Of course, the influence of the War on ringing – as on absolutely everything – was massive. Foremost, a huge swathe of the ringing population – the great bulk of them young and male – had been killed in the fighting. A significant number more had died from wounds during the year after; and the 1919 influenza pandemic – which killed a much greater proportion of younger people than older people – removed a very great many more. And if all that weren't bad enough, a large number of those young male ringers who survived, gave up ringing due to their blindness, physical disability or mental disability, so by the end of 1919, the *old guard* of The College Youths was numerically far stronger.

Yet perhaps even more important than the War itself, was the very difficult year of peace that followed. There were now almost two million more women in the population than men, and during the War, many of these women had filled the jobs previously held by men. Most of those women were summarily ejected from their posts in 1919, but even so, there was still a serious national problem in that large numbers of returning soldiers couldn't get employment.

There were many reasons for this, not least of which was that a significant proportion of those returning soldiers had serious disabilities. But all the same, there was a widespread perception that women were taking men's jobs, and a strong anti-women sentiment had quickly grown up. And since many women had started ringing during the War too – and had taken men's positions there as well – the anti-women feeling would certainly have been in The College Youths' minds.

And to be fair, the older ringers who hadn't been at the front and who knew very little of the realities of it, probably felt more deeply for their unemployed sons and grandsons than the former soldiers felt for themselves.

Christmas

Yet I doubt if either or both of these things would have been sufficient if the vote hadn't been taken between Christmas and the New Year. Although the Armistice had been signed in November 1918, demobilisation did not take place until 1919, so for most men under the age of forty, the 1919 Christmas was their first normal Christmas for six years; and almost certainly, the great bulk of them would have been with their families.

We can't be certain since the loss of the records means we have no details of the numbers or names attending; but I suspect that a group of unrepresentative and mainly older members took the chance to force through the change at a time when most ordinary members – of all ages – were trying to get back to peace-time normality. The date of the vote would have been a most extraordinary one if the real view of the entire membership was being genuinely sought, and besides, the advance notification of the meeting was wholly – and presumably deliberately – inadequate.

But however it happened, we can at least smile at the fact that the men present saw nothing two-faced in being completely anti-women yet acting like gentlemen at the same time. So the minutes recorded:

> **"Mrs. Hairs stated that she did not think there would be a large number of ladies seeking membership and expressed disappointment at the result of the voting. She was assured by Messrs. A. A. Hughes, W. D. Smith and the Master that she and other existing lady members would receive a hearty welcome to the meetings, and this feeling was expressed by all the company assembled."**

And Afterwards

But what's particularly intriguing is the literary silence that followed. By now *Bell News* had folded, and *The Ringing World* was the only ringing journal left. John Goldsmith, the Editor, was a very strong supporter of women ringers and had chaired the inaugural meeting of the *Ladies Guild.* Indeed, he was to remain a strong supporter all his life, yet he made no editorial mention of the decision at all, and there were no letters published either for or against. Only one vehemently anti-women piece by a non-member appeared.

So was this editorial censorship or did the bulk of ringers simply think that a decision by the College Youths was irrelevant? We'll never know, but I suspect the former. The College Youths have always been a little sensitive about being discussed, and the no-women rule was of particular sensitivity. Probably, most of them were quite embarrassed about it, and so taking an *it's-nobody-else's-business-but-ours* stance was probably as good a buffer as any.

Next Time

But fortunately, despite this little setback, women ringers continued to progress and to become more numerous. Indeed, back in 1912 they'd done something which their male colleagues had found truly startling. And what *that* was, we'll be finding out *next time.*

And in case you're feeling that that one dark moment in the College Youths' history has blackened their reputation for all time, do remember that it was only a small group of them anyway, and that among their many other achievements, they helped make ringing socially acceptable for all classes. Before the mid-seventeenth century, ringing had been an occupation solely of the labouring classes, and the well-to-do young men who took it up probably did so precisely ***because*** *they were doing something below their class – like dying their hair purple or putting studs in their tongues. But whatever their motives, we owe them a great debt. They led the way in making ringing an acceptable pastime for all.*

And precisely ***because*** *many of them were aristocratic and rich, they were also able to invent the* ***dumb bell*** *that we came across in Chapter 17. And if you've ever wondered what one looked like, on the next page is a drawing of the dumb bell in Knole House in Kent. It consists of a wooden cylinder with iron bars fastened through it, and each iron bar is tipped with a lump of lead. It sat in an attic, and a rope went round the middle of the cylinder and down through a hole in the floor to the Leicester Gallery below.*

Essentially, you pulled the rope so that it unwound from the cylinder, causing the wood and metal to spin round. The rope then wound itself up again the other way, like a huge upside down yo-yo.

But unlike with a yo-yo – or, indeed, a bell – the kinetic energy created by your pulling wasn't turned back into potential energy again a few moments later. Instead it could only be dissipated by your arm muscles and weight at the other "stroke." A bit technical if you're not into physics, but essentially, there was no conversion of potential energy into kinetic energy and back again as there is with a bell.

And all that meant that it was very strenuous work to get it turning in the first place, and it was equally strenuous work to stop it turning and heave it back again. And the more effort you put into one stroke, the more effort you had to put into the next, so it gave its users a very good work-out on wet days.

And quite clearly, that was its primary purpose. It was an early exercise machine that was especially useful at a time when winter mud made walking difficult. But at the same time it must have been quite similar to ringing a real bell – except, of course, that there was no handstroke as both strokes were backstrokes. Besides, real bells were very like exercise machines then anyway as they were much harder to ring than now.

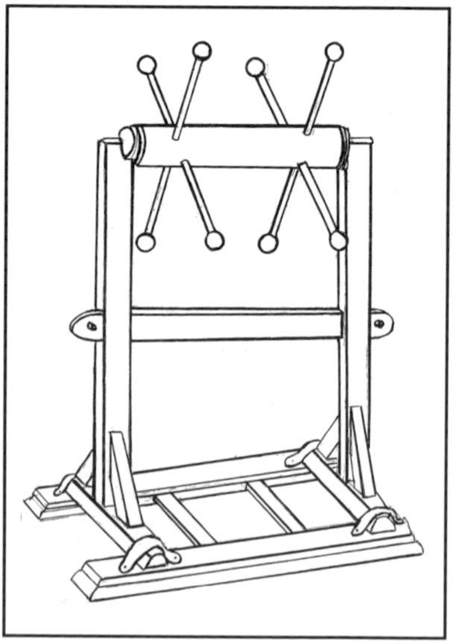

And most likely it was the exercise aspect that attracted well-to-do young men to ringing in the first place. Indeed, until not so long back, posh ringers used to call ringing, ***The Exercise****, especially when they wanted to make clear what* ***posh*** *ringers they really were.*

*Unfortunately, we don't know how many dumb bells there were, but there must have been a good many because there are references to them in sermons, plays and essays – so the writers must have expected their listeners to know what they were talking about. "***A dumb Believer is like a dumb Bell***," wrote one cleric, "***All Lumber and no Melody***."*

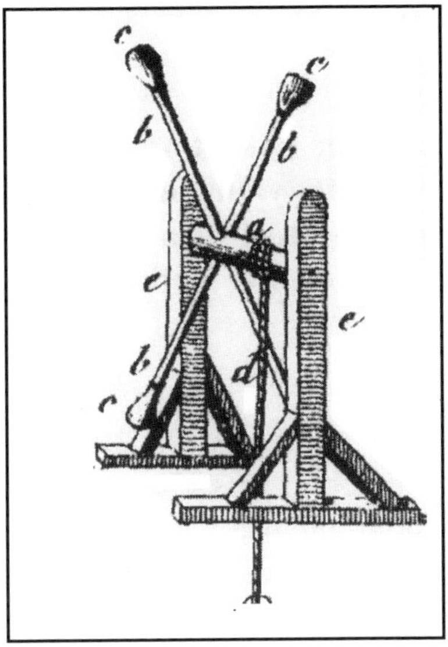

*A century or so after the Knole one had been installed, **The Gentleman's Magazine** of September 1746 included this drawing. You can see that it's very like the Knole dumb bell but it only has one pair of bars instead of two. There are letters on the picture because the writer goes into some detail about its construction. But engagingly, he also tells us:*

> **"This contrivance ... affords the exercise called RINGING ... and was practised by an eminent physician who was very fat."**

*But of course, when it comes to being described as **fat**, the average body mass index was far lower in 1746 than now, so in modern terms the doctor may not have been so very fat after all. All the same, in 1912 it wasn't considered right to use the word **fat** when speaking of a young lady, so Eva Belcher, a heroine in our next chapter, had to be described in another way completely ...*

24. Cubitt Town

Can I say how glad I am you almost never mention peals in your history articles and talks. Most ringing history stuff seems to be nothing *but* peals, and they bore the pants off me!

W.D.
Powys

Well, thank you. But grateful as I am for your kind words, I'm afraid this chapter is *only* about peals. Or at least, it's about *one* peal – and a very special peal at that. It's about the first peal ever rung by a band consisting only of women.

The Background

Of course, individual women had rung peals before. Indeed, quite a lot of them had; and the very first girl to ring a tower bell peal was Alice White, the daughter of the tower captain of St Michael's, Basingstoke. On 12 February 1896 at the age of 15, she rang the treble to a 5040 of Grandsire Triples.

In truth, there were many girls of the same standard at that time, so there was nothing really remarkable about her achievement except symbolically. But symbolically it certainly *was* remarkable, and the Editor of *Bell News* eulogised about it in his customary sycophantic but distressingly sexist style.

"This is the first time on record in which one of the gentler sex has taken part in a peal upon church bells, and the young lady herself, as well as her father and friends, are to be heartily congratulated upon its successful achievement. By our touch reports, we find that Miss Alice White had previously rung the treble in a quarter-peal of the same method. When we read so much foolishness about what is termed the 'new woman' and her athletic (?) pursuits, it is more than refreshing to read of a daughter of the Exercise like Alice White, who by her ingenuity and application to a scientific and health-giving practice, has put to shame and rebuke those females who, being on what is considered as the wrong side of middle life, have the effrontery to advocate occupations and pastimes for their sex which are repulsive to all true womanly feeling. The name of Alice White will long be remembered and treasured by the Exercise. If other young ladies can be induced to enter into the practice under similar conditions, it will be a good thing for them."

Alice soon went on to ring more peals, and other girls began ringing peals too – and *Bell News* continued to express its enthusiastic if condescending support; but exactly where the idea of a women-only peal came from isn't clear. It had probably been bubbling under for some time when on 17th December 1898 the *Bell News* Editor became the first person to suggest it in writing.

> **"We think this performance is another proof that the practice of change-ringing, under suitable conditions, is eminently fitted for the gentler sex. We shall doubtless see before long more of them taking a part among the ropes, perhaps on a light ring we may hear of a peal being rung solely by ladies."**

The Build Up

But in those days, a women-only peal, even on a ***light ring***, was no easy thing to arrange. The number of women ringers was still low, and the number of women *peal* ringers was lower still. Transport was difficult, not just because of the need for lengthy train journeys, but also because in the Edwardian era a young woman – and most of the women ringers were indeed young – needed to be accompanied by a suitable adult.

Additionally, even when they got the chance to ring, very few young women got the chance to conduct – indeed, very few young *men* got the chance to conduct – so the conductor would have found herself taking the lead role in a grand and expensively organised occasion for which she was – by force of circumstance – ill prepared.

So it's not surprising that the first attempt didn't take place until 1st July 1911; and it's not surprising either that it was unsuccessful. Nellie Gillingham from Portishead called it but had to change bells at the last minute because of technical problems with the seventh, and after a while she missed a bob.

Or at least, the contemporary reports and accepted tradition say she missed a bob. In fact, a detailed analysis of the composition in the light of the end result, makes this unlikely. Much more likely is that the little bells got crossed, but Nellie – like all the very best conductors – thought it better to take the blame herself rather than damage the confidence and cohesion of the band by pointing the finger at anyone. But whatever, all the listeners – and there were plenty of them – stoutly declared that the ringing was excellent, and another attempt was confidently anticipated.

Another Attempt

But although the will and the talent were definitely there, organisational problems got in the way again, and it wasn't until 20th July 1912 that a band once again met at Cubitt Town on the Isle of Dogs in London. It wasn't the same band because two substitutes came in, one of whom replaced Alice White who, despite ringing a number of peals, never really recovered from being barged by a bullock that got loose in Basingstoke. Indeed, she suffered all her – very long – life from a bad back. The conductor changed too, and Edith Parker who had rung the seventh in the earlier attempt, took over.

And despite Nellie Gillingham's clear abilities, this was undoubtedly a very good move. Edith was a person of enormous intelligence, common sense and determination, and she had already rung forty-nine peals, twelve of which were of London Major and thirteen of Superlative Major. If anyone was going to be able to cope with the pressure of the occasion, it was she.

The Reports

And cope she did. But even with Edith in charge, the peal was by no means plain sailing, and we know this from three contemporary, first-hand reports, all written in very different styles. The founding editor of *Bell News* had now died, but the new man maintained his predecessor's pompous style.

"On another page will be found the record of a peal rung entirely by girls. Such a peal ought to make the Exercise throughout the kingdom feel prouder. To think that a band could be got together from all parts and to successfully accomplish that which we men practice regularly together seems almost incredible. But one by one the lady ringers have made their presence felt in various Associations, and if in some Societies they have not been acknowledged – well, more's the pity for the men. …

We went down to Cubitt Town and heard over two hours of the peal, including the finish, and it goes without saying that those who remained gave the girls an ovation. We may say that altogether the ladies were in the tower about five hours, and had any of them at the back end been compelled by fatigue or dry-running of the bells to give up before the finish, no one could have blamed them; but they did not. Although fatigue was there – occasional trips showed that – the desire for success prevailed to the end, and the result is that the Ladies' Guild can hand on to posterity something to be proud of.

To Miss Parker came the *double* honour. This was her 50th peal, a record no girl has hitherto achieved. Those who doubted the wisdom of girls ringing with the opposite sex need doubt no more. Just as Ringing Associations raised ringing from its squalid

environment, so the presence of a girl or woman in the belfry to-day brings with it a purer atmosphere – where it is necessary. Those of us who mix regularly with them have no doubt at all – we *know*. The consummation of this peal was, in the words of Hamlet, 'devoutly to be wished,' and having seen it, or rather heard it done, we lift our glass, as in the olden time, to the toast and say – 'The Ladies: God bless 'em.' "

The Ringing World

But by 1912 *Bell News* had acquired a rival – and a very successful rival – *The Ringing World.* It had a far lighter touch and a far lighter tone than *Bell News*, and the Editor, John Goldsmith, was also at Cubitt Town that afternoon. Unfortunately, he arrived late, but nonetheless rose to the occasion with a splendidly lively account.

"The band met at the various Metropolitan railways by appointment and were invited by the courtesy of Mr. A. Hughes of Messrs. Mears and Stainbank to the Bell Foundry in Whitechapel where luncheon was served. Ultimately ... the start was made but alas trip after trip came along, and stand was called. The day grew warmer and the belfry atmosphere denser, with the result that the girls could not settle down, and after about two hours Mrs. Whittington suggested tea. About this time your scribe arrived, and felt very despondent upon hearing no bells.

However, the girls returned refreshed and

determined on a final attempt. A re-arrangement of the band was made, and they ultimately 'got away' at 5.50 p.m. ... Would they get through? After all, however courageous a woman may be, she has not a man's stamina, and with a view of preventing an accident, Mr. John Thomas kindly volunteered to sit in the tower, in case of emergency. Johnny was a good boy, and went to sleep in a corner, to awake only in the last half hour, when one or two of the back bells began to clip one another, which told us outside plainly enough that either the oil had gone or the girls' arms and hands were beginning to tell their tale.

The last part was rung distinctly slower, and exactly at six minutes to nine the last single was made, and the bells were round. We mere men then went up the tower, and, after a touch of Stedman, rang the bells down in peal."

William Willson

And if that excellent account were not enough, we have yet another. The ringer of the third was Lilian Willson from Leicester, and her father, William Willson was a regular ringing writer as well as a ringer of very considerable skill. He wrote for *Bell News, The Ringing World* and the short lived *The Bellringer,* and he came up trumps for the first ladies peal with a superbly written and very entertaining poem – although curiously, he had to write it twice as the first time he got the band in the wrong order. He began it in fine Edwardian style:

Like a breath of Summer laden,
like a cheery ray of Hope,
Is the sight of gentle maiden
deftly handling of a rope;

Welcome girlhood to our Science,
sunshine o'er our pathway cross,
You can win, by the alliance,
all the silver from our dross.

You have heard of Boadicea,
you have read of Joan of Arc,
You have known both Sage and Seer
who have tried to make their mark;

But I sing the Art of Ringing
to my harp, ah! hand it down,
Tribute paid is to the ladies
for their peal at Cubitt Town.

But having splendidly rhymed "ladies" with "paid is," the poem wanders off a bit, before having a tilt at sexism.

Aye, would ring it all together
as their brother-ringers stood,
Show the world outside them whether
***theirs* was test of womanhood.**

Of real interest, though, is the verse mentioning clothing.

Bared were arms and bared to shoulder
ready for the Captain's call,
Hoping as the day grew older
for the welcome "This is All."

And since Willson was intimately acquainted with one of the band, we know that the girls here – and no doubt women ringers generally – *didn't* ring in puffed, long sleeves as all the standard ringing histories lead us to suppose. The photograph taken afterwards shows them in proper Edwardian dress, but that tells us nothing. The photographs of male ringers of the same period, show them in bowler hats and jackets, but we know that *those* items weren't worn while ringing either.

The Band

But getting back to the poem, since his daughter and her friends were ringing, Willson obviously felt he had to name them individually. My favourite verses are those in which we learn that Eva Belcher was *a bonnie girl of sturdy build* – although she doesn't look remotely sturdy in the photograph – and that *Leicester* rhymes with *Sou'-Wester.*

Sarah Pigott took the treble,
representing Worcester's Guild;
Eva Belcher on the 2nd,
bonnie girl of sturdy build;

Lilian Willson came from Leicester;
rang the 3rd and struck it true;
Mary Jukes – a true "Sou'-Wester" –
rang as good Bristolians do.

From the place where once the author
of "Pilgrim's Progress" scorned a peal,
Came to ring the 5th in honour –
Bedford's delegate – Eva Steel.

Next stood Portishead's fair daughter,
Nellie Gillingham her name,
Sweet bell music sought and caught her
and it brought her into fame;

Edith Parker, aye, "The Peerless,"
at the 7th she took her stand,
History will tell how fearless
a conductress led the band.

Through the ripples of their Triples,
on its consummation bent,
With Clara Beasley ringing easily
at the tenor, on they went.

And we end with a rousing finale.

Tell it out and tell it ever
how the ladies brought renown
To our Art by their endeavours
in the peal at Cubitt Town.

And then there's a repetition of the first verse. And in case you haven't already realised, that's where the title of this series of chapters comes from.

Like a breath of Summer laden,
like a cheery ray of Hope,
Is the sight of gentle maiden
deftly handling of a rope.

Next Time

But significant achievement though the peal was, Edith Parker didn't intend to let women's ringing rest there, and she immediately set out to create *The Ladies Guild.* And how she did *that* is what we'll be looking at next time.

One of the perils of writing history articles is the lurking presence of sticklers for accuracy among the readers. They're ever alert for the slightest slip, and their pens are ever poised to write indignantly at the least opportunity. And to be fair, I have a lot of sympathy with them as I find mistakes in history books extremely distressing myself.

So I try to ensure that everything I write is as absolutely correct as available evidence allows – or if it isn't, I try to explain the doubts. But since I can never go into everything in the minutest detail, some statements have to appear without a full justification, and I just have to hope that people will trust me.

But not surprisingly, they sometimes don't, and a case in point was when I said a few chapters ago that the Duke of Stettin-Pomerania came from what is now Germany. Nothing depended on that, I just thought people would like to know, and I really didn't think anyone would be interested in challenging it. But someone was, and he wrote indignantly to The Ringing World *saying so.*

> **"SIR, – I do not know exactly what subdivision of Pomerania the Duke of Stettin-Pomerania in 1602 drew his title from, but Stettin itself and all Pomerania eastwards is nowadays in Poland. Only 'Vorpommern', the western part, remains in Germany."**

So to save people thinking I'd misled them, I had to reply. And of course, since the political history of the area is so endlessly fascinating, I couldn't resist replying fairly fulsomely.

> **"SIR, – Golly! I never expected to stir up a modern day Pomeranian controversy, so just to clarify, the Duke of Stettin-Pomerania did indeed come from what is now Germany. Rather bizarrely, his effective dukedom included neither Stettin**

nor most of Pomerania but only a part of Vorpommern – which is now in Germany. He lived in modern-day Germany too – in Wolgast on the West bank of the River Peenestrom.

Curiously, there was actually *another* Duke who *did* live in Stettin, but he controlled what was then called *Farther Pomerania* in what is now Poland.

Needless to say, centuries of political turmoil and power changes had caused this. But of interest to us is that our own Duke, Philipp Julius – who on state occasions rejoiced in the full title of *Duke of Stettin, Pomerania, the Kashubians and the Wends, Prince of Rügen, Count of Gützkow, Lord of the Lauenburg and Bütow Land* – was neither a nice man nor a good ruler, and his reign resulted in the destitution and death of great numbers of his peasants. Nevertheless, he spent considerable sums on travelling, and since the camera was yet to be invented, he took his own diary writer with him.

I quoted the diary in the article, but quite by chance, it also gives us an insight into the timings of early seventeenth century ringing. In the extract in question it's 1602, and *'His Princely Grace,'* having just arrived in London – and moored his ship at '*Leimhaus*' – hears the bells being rung *'in almost all the churches'* until *'very late in the evening.'* But just as we're wondering what he regards as *very late*, we're told that the

> **same thing also happens *'on the following days until seven or eight o'clock.'***
>
> **So no 9.00 p.m. finishes in 1602, but simply a confirmation that the normal working day invariably started much earlier."**

But if getting the past right is hard, getting the future right is impossible. Between 1602 and 1912 the political map of Europe changed out of all recognition. The nation of Germany not only came into existence but was about to launch the most horrific war that the world had ever seen. Yet although in 1912 many expected a war, no one in their wildest dreams anticipated the full horror of what was actually to come.

So although Edwardian England had its fair share of troubles and stresses, for many, 1912 seemed a year of prosperity, stability and peace – and the ideal time to launch a ringing association solely for women ...

25. Ladies and Women

You've been saying that male ringers were largely supportive of female ringers 100 years ago. But if that's right, why did *The Ladies Guild* need to be formed in the first place?

J.S.
Surrey

At the end of the last chapter we reached July 1912, and the first all ladies peal had just been rung. And yes, the overwhelming reaction from male ringers appears to have been complete approval. Within a short while, there was a snowstorm of congratulations, and motions of support were passed by many of the territorial Associations.

That was certainly good, but did it mean that everything on the sexual equality front was fine? Unfortunately, it didn't. And to understand why, we need to look at what Edwardian sexism was all about in the first place – and we need to look at what Edwardian female emancipation was all about too.

Sexism

Nowadays, of course, most ringers see women as entirely equal to men. They see them as equally intelligent, equally able and equally entitled to the same ringing opportunities. Regrettably, they don't actually *get* the same opportunities for all sorts of reasons that we'll look at next time, but except in a tiny minority of cases, that isn't due to male ringers having intentionally sexist views.

But in 1912 things weren't like that at all. There was a small proportion of men who believed as most men believe today, but the great majority didn't. Indeed, the great majority of *women* didn't either. That didn't mean that men were opposed to women leading decent lives and – to a limited extent – having decent opportunities, it just meant that they thought the bulk of women were inferior to men in intelligence, common sense and inherent ringing ability.

Racism and Class

It was the same with racism. The Edwardians thought slavery was wrong and that black people were entitled – to a limited extent – to lead decent lives, but they nonetheless thought they were less intelligent and had less ability than white people.

They saw *class* in the same way too, The upper classes genuinely believed that an upper class person was more intelligent than a working class person. They were largely in favour of decent living conditions for the working class – although they rarely understood how bad things really were for the poor – but that didn't mean they thought all classes were equally able. Indeed, if asked, they would have ranked the world in order of intelligence, with white upper class men at the top and black, working class women at the bottom.

Indeed, in many ways the majority of Edwardian men thought of women in the way most people today think of animals. We're opposed to animal cruelty and we think that they should be able to lead reasonably decent lives – until we eat them – but we certainly don't see them as intelligent or having the right to vote.

And less we're inclined to feel smug about our current social sophistication, it's important to remember that the entire population then was bombarded throughout their lives with sexist, racist and classist indoctrination, not least from the pulpit, and it was very hard indeed to resist.

So since most tower captains knew for a certainty that girls had inherently inferior ringing ability, they naturally give them fewer opportunities. They gave them fewer opportunities to ring, they gave them fewer opportunities to progress and they gave them absolutely no opportunities at all to conduct. The women who *did* get decent opportunities, generally only got them because their ringing fathers and husbands gave them to them. So *The Ladies Guild* was formed to compensate for that.

The Very Beginning

And it's often said that the idea sprang into life out of the euphoria surrounding the success of the Cubitt Town peal. And maybe it did. Maybe the girls who rang in the peal, and the many supporters who were with them, simply said, "Let's start a Ladies' Guild," and the idea was so obvious that it went on from there.

But myself, I'm not so sure. The driving force from the start was Edith Parker – the conductor of the peal – and she was not only highly intelligent but also extremely politically astute. I suspect she'd been planning the Guild for some time but realised she needed the Cubitt Town peal as a launching pad; and certainly, that would have been entirely in character. But whatever the inspiration, on 2nd August 1912 this advert appeared in *The Ringing World.*

PROPOSED LADIES' GUILD

Will all Lady Ringers (tower or handbells)

wishing to join the above Society, kindly communicate with Miss E. K. Parker, 97, Edenbridge Road, Bush Hill Park, Enfield, who will send full particulars.

And to put that date in context, the peal had taken place on 20 July and was reported in *The Ringing World* and *Bell News* in the issues of 26 July. So the advert appeared only one week later, exactly thirteen days after the peal. John Goldsmith, the *Ringing World* Editor, had been present at the peal and was a strong supporter of women ringers; and it seems likely Edith had arranged the advert with him immediately afterwards. The *Bell News* didn't carry a notice but it did carry a very supportive editorial.

"The effort to form a National Ladies' Guild is only a natural sequence, and is bound to succeed, because it is in the right hands. Those who could gather from the four quarters of the country as it were, and without practice ring a peal of Grandsire Triples without previously practising together, are just the folk who would make a good job of organising and running a Guild.

We note that Miss E. K. Parker is doing the organising, and will be pleased to hear from any ladies who wish to become members. She will furnish full particulars to any such."

The First Meeting

And since Edith was not a woman to let the grass grow under her feet, she arranged the first meeting for 26th October. She had a set of Rules ready, and extremely politically astute Rules they were too. Nowadays most ringers aren't too much bothered by Association Rules, but that certainly wasn't the case then, and Edith knew that hers would be pored over by those male ringers who opposed her as well as those who supported her. So Rule 7 read:

> **"That the Guild shall in no wise consider itself antagonistic to existing societies, but at all times an ally, as set out in Rule 3; its members look to their brother ringers for the courtesy and opportunity necessary to attain their legitimate aspirations."**

Indeed, she made it clear from the outset that *The Ladies Guild* was intended to be a mainstream organisation that would *add* to the work of the other Associations rather than oppose them.

Women and The Vote

But The Ladies Guild faced an even bigger problem because it was coming into existence at a time when the women's suffrage movement – the campaign for women to have the vote – was at its most active. And to understand what a major problem this was, we need to take a detour into general history because, as with many of history's captivating stories, the modern retelling of the women's suffrage movement often contains as much myth as accuracy.

So to put things into context, it simply *wasn't* the case that before the First World War men could vote but women couldn't. Indeed, until 1832 very few people of *either* sex could vote, and elections were subject to massive bribery and corruption. Some Members of Parliament represented boroughs with only a tiny handful of voters – in some instances, fewer than ten – and those voters were normally paid or coerced to vote a particular way.

The Reform Acts

But there was considerable public pressure for change, and that came with a piece of legislation called, *The Representation of the People Act, 1832* – although it's generally known as *The First Reform Act*. But it wasn't *great* change. The figures aren't completely certain, but the number of people who could vote probably went up from about 400,000 to about 650,000 – which was still only 5% of the population and excluded virtually the entire working class. Women were now specifically excluded too although previously they hadn't been.

The 1832 Act didn't do away with the bribing of voters, though, it just made it more expensive; and much more important, in most people's eyes it didn't extend voting rights anywhere near far enough. The appetite for increased suffrage was not only strong, it gathered momentum over the next 35 years; and a really massive public rally in Hyde Park that the police and army weren't able to control – together with some rather odd politicking between the Whigs and the Tories – resulted in 1867 in what's now known as *The Second Reform Act*.

Progress

And once again this was progress, but once again it was limited. The number of eligible voters went up from about one million to about two million, but this was still only 20% of the adult male population and it still excluded all the adult *female* population. What was more, votes for women had now become an issue – at least for some – so in 1884 there was – yes, you've guessed it – *The Third Reform Act*.

And yet again, this was more – but still limited – progress. The number of eligible voters went up to about five and a half million – vastly more than in 1832 – but that still left 40% of adult men – primarily working class – *without* the vote. So by the time the women's suffrage movement was in full swing, it wasn't just women who were disenfranchised, it was nearly half of all men too.

The 1918 Act

So when people glibly repeat that women didn't get the vote until 1918, they're only telling a small part of the story. Indeed, even the change in 1918 wasn't primarily about women. The essential issue was that the great bulk of soldiers returning from the First World War wouldn't have been able to vote in the General Election that immediately followed, so *The Fourth Reform Act* was passed giving virtually all adult men the right to vote. At the same time, *most* – but by no means *all* – women over the age of thirty were given the right to vote too.

But even *that* right was limited. As well as having to be over thirty, a woman could only vote if she was married to a voter or had a property qualification; so many single women were excluded; and it wasn't until 1928 that women got the same voting rights as men. All the same, in 1918 the electorate went up to well over twenty-one million, more than fifty times what it had been ninety years earlier.

The Suffragettes

So the whole question of electoral reform had been a recurring and major issue for a century by the time the *Suffragettes* came along. The women's suffrage movement had been going for a good while too – although until then it had been both entirely peaceful and entirely unsuccessful. But when Emmeline Pankhurst started the Suffragettes, it wasn't the vote itself that primarily concerned her. Instead, she was outraged by the plight of working class women, and she believed that nothing would be done about that until women gained political clout through the ballot box. So in 1903 she formed *The Women's Social and Political Union.*

And of course, everyone now knows about at least *some* of the tactics of civil disobedience which they increasingly employed; and most of us either sympathise or actively approve. Chaining yourself to the railings of Buckingham Palace seems mild enough to us now, so it's hard to appreciate how seriously it was viewed at the time. Indeed, we see it as so blindingly obvious that women should have the vote, that we think a campaign to that effect was entirely reasonable.

But in 1912 it wasn't seen like that at all. The Suffragettes were thought by many to be undermining the very fabric of society – indeed, to be fermenting revolution – and some of their *outrages* did indeed have the taint of what we would now call terrorism. What was more, marching in protest was thought so very unlady-like, it was seen as massively subversive in its own right, and the Suffragettes were therefore viewed as revolutionaries of the worst kind.

Ladies versus Women

So with all that going on in the background, Edith Parker had to be extremely careful. Her new Guild had to advance the cause of women yet completely distance itself from the Suffragettes, and that made the choice of a name decidedly tricky. The word, *lady*, then had very strong class connotations, and many – indeed, probably *most* – of the potential members didn't see themselves as *ladies* at all. They didn't want to be tainted by the snobbishness associated with the word, but additionally, they saw themselves as *women* because that was the modern thing to be. And since they were all young, forward-looking and energetic, they were probably tacit supporters of the Suffragettes too.

But the slogan of the Suffragettes was ***Votes for Women***, and the real name of the Suffragettes was *The Women's Social and Political Union*, so calling the new organisation, *The Women's Guild* would have been fraught with the real danger of it being seen as an association of ringing Suffragette sympathisers – something that would have immediately put it beyond the pale. All the same, principles are principles, and even at the very first meeting there was strong support for exactly that name. Indeed, the point would be raised several times in the future, and even the Guild minutes for 1933 – five years after all adult women got the vote – record:

> **"Proposed: That the title of the Guild be changed from The Ladies' Guild of Change Ringers to The Women's Guild of Change Ringers because the members felt that the original title was out of date and they considered the word women to be a much nobler title and in every way more comprehensive. The resolution met with no support."**

And although there was more support in 1912, Edith Parker's view prevailed and *The Ladies Guild* was what it became. But even Edith had to agree there could be a problem with the joining Rule. To restrict membership to *ladies* would have been open to confusion on class grounds, while to restrict it to *women* would have opened up the Suffragette problem. So very cleverly, she wrote as Rule 2:

> **"That the Society consist of members of the feminine sex who are able to ring either upon church bells or handbells."**

The Rules required the election of officers too, and with John Goldsmith, the Ringing World Editor, in the chair, Alice

White – the first woman to ring a tower bell peal – was elected President. She wasn't present, though, due to her health problems following the Basingstoke bullock incident, so Edith Parker stood in for her. More important, Edith became Secretary and Treasurer, and immediately set out to give the Guild a national position and voice by getting it affiliated to the Central Council of Church Bell Ringers.

The Central Council

This was itself a far-sighted thing to do. In 1912 the Central Council was just 22 years old and was viewed with a fair amount of scepticism. All the same, having the Guild affiliated would give it national recognition, and Edith was determined to arrange it. Sir Arthur Heywood – who we met with his miniature trains in Chapter 19 – was still the bizarrely autocratic president, so Edith went to him first.

Essentially – and very astutely – she'd decided on a softening up approach, and she arranged for Heywood to raise the issue at the 1913 Annual Meeting even though the Guild didn't yet have the necessary 75 members. The Council was then packed with clergymen, and one of them, G. F. Coleridge – later to be Master of The Oxford Guild – tackled the *tainted-by-Suffragettes* problem head on.

> **"We live in moving times. We could scarcely take up a paper without reading of a firing of a building here, the discovery of a bomb there, or the tampering with a letter-box somewhere else by women for whom no sane man or woman could have any conceivable affection or regard, but there are others who uphold the law and order as good citizens, and the question arises:**

should ladies not only be allowed to vote, but to be represented by their sex in the councils of the Church. I think they have every right to be represented on this Council."

Needless to say, not everyone was in favour, but since no vote could be taken, the supporters were naturally more voluble. So only the outspoken and outrageously reactionary George Burton of the Norwich Diocesan Association seriously opposed.

"I'm sorry if I appear ungallant in endeavouring to keep the ladies out of the belfry. We were threatened with ladies in *my* belfry, but we arranged to get over the difficulty."

And in 1914

Sadly, he left everyone wondering *how* he'd *got over the difficulty*, and he didn't reveal that the following year either. But he certainly made his views felt because by then the Guild had achieved the required 75 members and a vote could be taken. It's not easy to tell from the minutes what doubts members had and what pre-meeting discussions had taken place; so the best evidence comes from this splendid note made by J. Armiger Trollope.

"The feeling in favour was evidently more marked than at Newcastle, and those who spoke, including C. E. Matthews, C. W. O. Jenkyn and A. T. King generally supported the ladies. Not so Mr. Burton ... Fortified by the opinion of the committee of his association, he entered his protest against the admission of the Ladies' Guild to the

Council. So far as he was aware they had not yet rung a peal, and he asked if they were suitable creatures to come and sit with men. The day before they had burnt down a church.

Paradoxically this speech clinched the whole matter and turned a certain victory for the ladies into an overwhelming triumph. The members who had been sitting on the fence slid down quietly on the women's side, and those who had been trying to screw up their courage to oppose, when they heard their side of the case put so nakedly and so brutally, stole over to the enemy. A solid mass of hands was held up when the question was put to the vote, with Mr. Burton as the solitary dissident. I looked round curiously to see what had become of those who the night before had pledged themselves to opposition. One and all they voted for the ladies."

Of course, the reference to burning down a church related to the Suffragettes rather than *The Ladies Guild*, but the important thing was that even in those times – and even in a Central Council with a fair preponderance of what was seen as *stuffy old men* – only one person opposed. It was a striking example of how socially advanced and sensible most ringers have always been.

Head-Gear

But there was one sex-based issue which it seemed no one wanted to address. In those days, women were expected to cover their heads in church, and since the ringing room was part of the church, many wondered if their heads should be covered there too. Indeed, in Chapter 20 we saw how *The Girl's Own Paper* recommended the sort of cap girls should wear while ringing.

Evidence of the discussions is thin, but it seems that even in 1890, most ringers thought it daft, and the rule was almost universally honoured in the breach rather than the observance. All the same, the Ladies Guild found themselves faced with it from time to time, so in the Guild minute book for 1916 we read:

> **"Mrs. Reeves brought before the meeting a resolution which was passed by the Committee of the Oxford Guild to the effect that the rule of the church should be observed by women in the belfry and that they should wear a covering for the head. She spoke on behalf of the Oxford Guild and thought that The Ladies Guild might devise some form of headgear to be worn so that no further discussion need arise. The idea was strongly opposed by several members and after a considerable discussion the matter was deferred 'til the next meeting."**

In fact it wasn't raised at the next meeting at all – probably because Mrs Reeves was well and truly sat on – but in 1923 the minute book records:

> **"A question had arisen in the Western District regarding the wearing of headgear in the belfry. A specimen of a cap worn by some of the members was shown, but after considerable discussion it was decided that**

> **no rule should be made by the Guild but that members should use their own discretion."**

Sadly, we have no record of what the cap looked like, and I haven't been able to trace any lady's ringing cap still in existence. Probably no one would recognise it for what it was even if they found one.

And Onward

But by 1923 the Guild was well set and going from strength to strength. Indeed, at one point the membership rose to around 400. Nevertheless, from time to time over the subsequent decades it was suggested that the Guild had fulfilled its purpose and should be wound up. The reason given was always that, by then – whenever *then* was – women and men ringers were being treated equally.

But that simply wasn't true, for all the genuine courtesy and consideration they received, women ringers *weren't* at any time being treated equally with men. And very curiously, they still aren't being treated equally now. And *that* is what we'll be looking at next time.

From time I'm invited to be the guest speaker at a Ringing Association annual dinner, and unless I'm already booked, I say, yes. I get to chat to lots of ringers from lots of places, and the food's normally pretty good too. And although there are far fewer annual dinners now than there used to be, there's still something pleasantly traditional about them.

But after the food, I have to speak; and after dinner speakers are supposed to be gently amusing by telling a few tastefully funny stories. So afterwards, someone usually asks,

"Were those stories true?" And while most of them are, some of them aren't; but the ones that aren't, are meant to be so clearly spoofs, that no one will be the least bit confused. All the same, one or two people always ***are*** *confused, and if someone reports those stories dead-pan in* ***The Ringing World****, they end up looking a lot more real and serious than they were ever intended to be.*

John Goldsmith had exactly that problem shortly before the Second World War. As the Proprietor and Editor of ***The Ringing World*** *from its launch in 1911 to his death in 1942, he spoke at a lot of annual dinners, and in 1937 he was at the Ladies Guild's. He was certainly a very amusing man, and in order to be appropriately entertaining, he read out a spoof extract from "***The Unpublished Diaries of Samuel Pepys***." In it, Pepys supposedly recorded witnessing six ladies ringing the bells of St Olaves and, "***... entertaining me afterwards to dinner***."*

It went down well, so he repeated it in his ***Ringing World*** *report of the dinner, and somehow it looked less of a spoof on the page than it had sounded at the end of a convivial evening. Besides, as a Pepys take-off it was very realistic, and the result has been its faithful citing in several history books as evidence of women ringing in the seventeenth century. I'm afraid it isn't, though, and sadly, Pepys' diaries are pretty silent about ringing.*

But that said, if you want to listen to something ***really*** *funny, you don't need to go to ringing dinners. Vicars' sermons at Ladies Guild meetings can do just as well ...*

26. Keeping their Seeds in the Packet

I have read all your articles on conducting, I have studied hard, I have done all the homework and I have mentioned diffidently to my tower captain and District Master that I would like to call some call changes or touches if at all possible. Yet I almost never get the opportunity. It's always the men and boys who get asked. Indeed, I kept a personal record over three months and found that 95% of the calling was done by men and only 5% by women. Don't you think this is unfair?

Sarah
Home Counties

Yes, I do think it's unfair. I think it's grossly unfair. And what's more it's a huge waste of potential conducting and ringing ability. But the really intriguing thing is, how on earth has it happened? Given all the support being given to women ringers a hundred years ago, what went wrong in the middle.

Unrecognised Sexism

And very disappointingly, the truth is that *nothing* went wrong. Over the period since the First World War, the nation's attitude towards women has moved on, and the ringers' attitude towards women has moved with it – indeed, it's moved a little ahead of it. But stop the clock at any time over the last hundred years, and most people wouldn't have thought women ringers were being treated unequally at all. Indeed, if you stopped the clock right now, most ringers would say exactly the same thing. It's only ever in retrospect that things look odd.

So in 1914 people said, "*Of course* women are being treated equally, the Bedford District has a woman vice-president." They simply couldn't see that one woman vice-president as against well over a hundred men presidents and vice-presidents, wasn't equal treatment at all. And in 1928 when the largest ever ringing tea took place in Croydon, people thought it another demonstration of modern sexual equality that there were seventy-one women present out of a gathering of two thousand four hundred.

Attitudes

Indeed, until recently it was entirely acceptable to be sexist as long as you dressed it up as something else and pretended you weren't sexist at all. So in 1935 Harold Warboys wrote to *The Ringing World,*

> **"I do not think women realise that men at least sometimes wish to be together. Now there are many ways in which men do get together, and I think the most honourable is the brotherhood of bellringers. There is something wonderful in the fact that six, eight, ten or twelve men each depend on one another and have a personal feeling for one another as brothers. (Unusual in present times.) This personal contact with others seems to be the very essence of living. Exactly the same thing applies with homes,**

wives and lady friends, or it should do, and each particular connection seems to be worth living for, and so it is in the belfry amongst men.

When a lady steps into a belfry permanently amidst such a company of men as described, things will start to go wrong. The men do not feel the brotherliness that used to be, and the belfry is not so comfortable a place as before. It is not the ladies' fault, but they do not understand what is happening. I do not object to ladies ringing at all, but I do think that they could leave men to do just one thing in harmony together in this world."

And I doubt that he himself thought it illogical to say he didn't object to ladies ringing, he just didn't want them to be allowed to ring.

The Clergy

The clergy, too, could often be relied upon to be thoroughly sexist even when they were trying to be supportive. Here's an extract from the sermon at the 1968 Ladies Guild AGM.

"Among the great gifts and possibilities with which you were born, one you have developed is that you have learned to ring. You have learned to work in a team and play an important part in the work of the Church which is a team of teams. Women have to be tactful and understanding, and often can bring into a tower something of those qualities. But it must not stop there. If

you have learned something from your tower – self control, discipline, tact – and if you leave it upstairs it will be a great loss to the Church, the nation and the world. You have seeds which can bear much fruit. It will be a pity if you keep them in the packet."

Of course, it was the time of *Flower Power*, but even so, suggesting that the ladies shouldn't ***keep their seeds in the packet,*** must surely have given them a few belly laughs. More seriously, though, the vicar apparently had the bizarre idea that the women had only acquired self control, discipline and tact from ringing.

More Recent

But rather than look at similar examples from all eras, what about more recent times? Well, it's always hard to decide what counts as recent because the present is continuously turning itself into history, but the very detailed and comprehensive ringing survey carried out in 1988 found that while women ringers were 44% of all ringers, women tower captains were only 13% of all tower captains. Indeed, 10% of tower captains were men over the age of 80.

Ten years later in 1998, of all the peals rung, only 1.75% were called by women, and the leading woman peal conductor was only 175th in the leading conductors list. In 2002 at a leading national ringing course, over half the students were women, over half the helpers were women, but *all* of the tutors were men.

The Reasons

Come right up to date and look back at this year at the end of December, and you'll probably see improvements – perhaps even considerable ones. But they'll be patchy. You'll see them very much more in some towers than in others, and you'll see them very much more in some *Branches* than in others. You'll see some bands with complete equality but you'll see others with almost no equality at all. But however hard you look, you'll still find that in the majority of places women aren't encouraged to ring big bells and they aren't encouraged to conduct. They're *allowed* to – albeit sometimes grudgingly – but they aren't *encouraged* to. Men and boys are encouraged to but women and girls aren't.

They aren't taught to either. If a twelve year old boy and a twelve year old girl both ask to try ringing a moderately heavy tenor, the boy will often be allowed to but the girl won't. If they're *both* allowed to – often with some condescending smiling from the band – they will both, quite naturally, make a poor job of it. And that's fine because it's a skill they both need to develop, and they're only having their first go. But while the boy will be told it was *good experience* for him, the girl will be told, "*I'm afraid it's just too big for you.*" It's out and out sexism, of course, but it happens entirely innocently without those involved having the remotest idea they're being unfair.

The Legacy

So why in our extremely enlightened and inclusive hobby does it still happen?

Well, the underlying and unspoken cultural sexism of Society plays its part. But more important, we still labour under the historical legacy left to us by those forward thinking men of the late nineteenth century. As we saw in Chapter 19, they invented – as an excuse for why women could then start ringing – the idea that recent improvements in bell hanging meant women could at last ring light bells when they hadn't been able to before. All nonsense, of course, and they knew it, but it was a convincing argument to the doubters, and a good enough fig leaf for the faint hearted.

So the *women-round-the-front-and-men-round-the-back* idea caught hold, and regrettably, it's been with us ever since. And it still holds in most places no matter what the size of the back bells. And since the back bell ringers have traditionally been the people asked to conduct, conducting has traditionally stayed with the men; and in most places it's still with them.

Sad to say it, but the progress of sexual equality in ringing still has a long way to go.

We've looked at women quite a lot in the last few chapters, but equally interesting are the men behind them. By Edwardian times, the women had plenty of male supporters but in the early 1890s it was very different. The men who led the way then were genuinely brave in their challenge of the accepted ways, and they must have faced considerable opposition and unpleasantness from some quarters. So what do we know of Henry White – the man who taught his daughter to ring in 1891 and then arranged for her to be the first woman to ring a tower bell peal five years later?

And fortunately, Derek Jackson of the Winchester & Portsmouth Guild has researched him in detail, and he's established that whatever opposition Henry White may have faced from **some** *people, in general he was widely respected. He was a born and bred Basingstoke man and he lived there all his life. His father was a labourer before him and he himself became a carpenter – so he wasn't in any sense middle class – but he was clearly intelligent and educated,* *and in 1885 at the age of only 28, he was elected tower captain of St Michael's, Basingstoke. He was apparently a first-rate ringer and conductor too, and – perhaps fortunately – he was a close friend of George Williams.*

We met George in Chapter 9 – along with "Harry," as Henry was known to his friends – riding penny farthing bicycles on ringing trips. But George wasn't just an outstandingly talented ringer and conductor, he was also a ringing teacher way ahead of his time; and his wife, Martha, had been the first woman to ring a handbell peal in 1892.

So George probably encouraged Henry to teach his daughters – or he at least supported him in doing so – and Henry started teaching Alice in 1891 when she was just ten. Later he taught two of his other three daughters, Dora and Delia, and they became life-long ringers too. He also taught his son, Harold; but although Henry was a good teacher of ringing, he seems not to have been a good namer of children. Alice, Dora and Delia all took their ***middle*** *names rather than their first names, Rosetta, Ellen and Ethel.*

As well as his tower and church duties, Henry held posts in ***The Winchester Diocesan Guild****, – which in those days claimed to cover a vast area right up into London. In 1902 – by which time, according to the 1901 census, he had progressed from carpenter to commercial clerk – he was asked to be Guild Secretary. Indeed, he was offered £20 a year to do the duties – and since at that time many working men maintained a family on around £50 a year, £20 was a considerable sum.*

But he turned it down, apparently on a point of principle, because he thought a vicar should do the job. Later, though, he became the Guild Auditor.

But sadly, although he was the patriarch of what was to be later called the ***well-known family of Basingstoke***

***bellringers**, Henry only lived to 61. He was then still tower captain of St Michael's after forty-three years – and parish sexton as well – and he was much missed by all.* The Winchester Guild *sent wreaths to his family, and on the west wall of the belfry there is still this plaque.*

TO THE
GLORY OF
GOD
AND IN
GRATEFUL MEMORY
OF
HENRY WHITE
SEXTON AND CAPTAIN
OF BELLRINGERS IN
ST MICHAEL'S TOWER
1885 – 1918
WHO LABOURED WITH
UNTIRING ZEAL FOR THE
IMPROVEMENT OF
BELLRINGING AND THE
CULTIVATION OF THE ART
OF CHANGERINGING
DIED SEPT 27th 1918
AGED 61 YEARS

*But what about the most famous ringing member of the **well-known family** – how did Alice White end her days?*

As we saw earlier, although a strong Ladies Guild supporter all her life, she had to give up most of her ringing due to the bullock accident. Worse, Charles Russell, whom she intended to marry, died on his way home from the Boer War in 1900.

*Or at least, he was **reported** to have died then, but since neither Alice nor Charles's family ever found out where and when he died, he may well have died earlier. One of the really appalling statistics of the Boer War, is that of the 22,000 British soldiers who died there, at least 14,300 died from* *disease, mainly typhoid, most without ever being involved in any fighting at all. But eventually, in 1920, even though by then she was nearly 40, Alice married someone else; and later she and her husband moved to Canada where she died in 1979 at the age of 99.*

And splendidly, her gravestone reads:

ROSETTA A. WHITE
1880 – 1979
WIFE OF J. C. SULLIVAN
FIRST LADY TO RING A TOWER
BELL PEAL IN ENGLAND

Going Way Back

27. On Special Occasions

I wrote to you before about us being a completely new band and about how we all learnt together after getting our bells rehung. Ringing-wise everything's going fine, but the non-ringing villagers now want us to reinstate an ancient ringing tradition. They don't know *what* ancient ringing tradition and they don't really mind, they just want us to discover one. It's the sort of thing our village does – especially as it helps the tourism – and since they raised so much money for us, we don't want to disappoint them. We already ring the New Year in – after reading your chapter in *The Bellringer's Bedside Companion* – so what other ancient special occasion ringing traditions can we choose from?

L.B.
The South

A tricky question, this, especially as it all depends on what your villagers feel is *ancient*. Most supposedly ancient traditions date back to Victorian times at best – or they were re-invented then – and a great many others are even *more* recent. The *traditional* Christmas turkey, for example, only became traditional after 1840, and even then, it was only traditional for the middle and upper classes. Most working class families couldn't afford one until well after the Second World War, yet many people still think that a turkey at Christmas is an ancient tradition.

The Truly Ancient

So if your villagers want a tradition that's *truly* ancient, that's not easy at all. Certainly, in medieval times there were a great many church bells and a great many traditional reasons for ringing them; and among other things, they notified the curfew, warned people of fires, gave notice of attack and signalled all sorts of routine events. But although ringing for those things might be ancient and traditional, I don't suppose your villagers want you to re-introduce a primitive communication system.

I don't suppose they'll want you to re-introduce the ancient religious uses either. In medieval times a bell was rung at various points during the Mass – such as at the Elevation of the Host – but if your church doesn't do that already, they're not likely to want to start. And although it wasn't a tradition for long, the Puritans rang a single bell when the sermon started so that parishioners could pop in for that bit of the service and not bother with the rest; but no one's likely to want you to do that either.

Rejoicing

So ruling out a communication system, and assuming what your villagers *really* want is all the bells rung in a festive way, you'll need a tradition that dates from around 1600 or later; and as I've mentioned before, the truly great ringing tradition in that period was anarchy. The local ringers went into their tower exactly *when* they liked and rang exactly *what* they liked, without asking anyone's permission at all. What's more, that tradition lasted well into the nineteenth century.

But I don't suppose *that* tradition will do for your village either, partly because they'll need to know why the ringing is happening, and partly because random and uncontrolled ringing isn't likely to please them at all. And *that* means you'll have to link your ringing to some form of public rejoicing.

Mind you, if you're trying to be *truly* traditional, that won't be easy either. Back in the seventeenth century, the rejoicing ringing was itself strongly linked to the ringers' ability to ring without permission. A certain amount of rejoicing ringing certainly *was* pre-arranged – and we'll come to that in a moment – but a great deal more wasn't. It was just a spontaneous expression of public joy.

Put simply, when the public mood was for the bells to be rung, they *were* rung. As we saw in Chapter 17, the overwhelming feature of ringing in the seventeenth and eighteenth centuries, was that it had become secular. The bells were certainly *in* churches, but they weren't there solely – or indeed, primarily – for religious use. They had become *public*. Not public in that anyone could ring them, but public in that everyone enjoyed them and expected them to be rung for public rejoicing.

The Restoration of the Monarchy

For example, in February 1660 there was a general belief that the monarchy would be restored and that that would be a good thing. But people weren't at all sure it would happen, and even if it would, they feared massive upheaval or even war. And since a greater percentage of the population had died in the recent Civil Wars than were to die in both World Wars combined, their fears were very soundly based.

So when General Monk marched from Scotland to London with no one knowing what his intentions were, the citizens of London were very apprehensive. So when he eventually arrived in Whitehall and showed by his actions that he was clearly for peace, spontaneous rejoicing broke out and ringing took place everywhere. As John Evelyn wrote in his diary:

> **"[General Monk] marches to Whitehall, ... and convenes the old Parliament, the Rump Parliament ... being dissolved; and for joy whereof were many thousands of rumps roasted publicly in the streets at the bonfires this night, with ringing of bells, and universal jubilee."**

Presumably the bonfires were spontaneous too, and as we'll see later, special occasion bonfires and special occasion ringing have traditionally gone hand in hand. So since your village is likely to be even keener on bonfires than on ringing, adding at least *one* bonfire to your reinstated tradition would definitely be a good idea.

And certainly, when Charles II was eventually crowned in April 1661, bonfires went with the ringing then too. Indeed, there was such a very grand procession on the previous day that John Evelyn recorded it in considerable detail before adding:

> **"This magnificent train on horseback, as rich as embroidery, velvet, cloth of gold and silver, and jewels, could make them and their prancing horses, proceeded through the streets strewed with flowers, houses hung with rich tapestry, windows and balconies full of ladies; the London militia lining the ways, and the several companies, with their banners and loud music, ranked**

in their orders; the fountains running with wine, bells ringing .... Thence, with joyful acclamations, his Majesty passed to Whitehall. Bonfires at night."

Who actually arranged the bonfires isn't clear, but the ringing this time was almost certainly organised in advance by the Court, and probably paid for.

Battles

But although ringing on the anniversary of the Restitution certainly took place for many years, that probably won't do for your village either. Most people aren't much interested in Charles II now, and in some years his coronation day coincides with Good Friday – which would be tricky. Besides, the good times expected in 1661 didn't last. The truly dreadful war with the Dutch soon followed, and the plague and *The Fire of London* joined in; and although the plague was at its worst in 1665, it dragged on until after the Great Fire in 1666, so there was no sudden end to celebrate. And certainly the end of the Great Fire itself wasn't celebrated because the devastation had been so appalling.

Nevertheless, victory in battle was a traditional reason for ringing, and that was just as true in 1666 during the Dutch War as it was after the battle of El Alamein in 1942. But in 1666, communication difficulties meant the outcomes of battles at sea weren't immediately clear, and the Duke of Albermarle's retreat in June was initially – but mistakenly – thought to be a British victory. And by the time the truth came through, the order for ringing had already been given and couldn't be stopped. As Evelyn recorded it:

"There were, however, orders given for bonfires and bells; but, God knows, it was rather a deliverance than a triumph."

And that makes it quite clear that the bonfires were arranged and paid for just as the bells were – although once again, exactly *how* they were arranged, isn't clear.

Being Paid

But whatever the arrangements for ringing in London were, in the rest of the country things were different. Victory ringing took place, certainly, but while some of it was arranged in advance, a good deal more was spontaneous. Either way, local worthies often paid for it out of patriotism or expectation. But duplicity could nonetheless occur, as this 1793 letter in *The Northampton Mercury* makes clear.

> **"TO THE PRINTERS. – We cannot refrain from communicating to the public, with contempt, the erroneous paragraph which made its way into the Buckinghamshire Herald on the 10th of August instant, under the signature of 'A Constant Reader' ... wherein it sets forth that a Mr. Botham, banker, in this town, on receiving the news of the surrender of Valenciennes to the British arms, ordered the bells to be rung, and gave a very handsome present for that purpose. We, whose names are hereunto subscribed, the ringers in and of the said parish, do declare to a man, we know no such person as Mr. Botham, and upon the strictest enquiry cannot learn who he is. And we also declare, and wish it to be made publicly known through the channel of your paper, that on every occasion that does honour to our King and Country, we come forward as Britons, without any solicitation whatever, and the gentlemen in our own**

parish, without the assistance of any other person or persons, cheerfully second our endeavours, and give us every gratification we wish for. Witness our hands this 8th of August, 1793."

And this letter shows clearly that the ringers normally got paid by ***the gentlemen of their own parish*** only *after* they'd rung, and without any guarantee beforehand. It was like a waiter receiving a tip; the ringers rang spontaneously and were then given money afterwards for their trouble.

But thoroughly traditional though ringing for battle victories may be, these days it wouldn't be thought in good taste; and ringing for anniversaries of battles that we probably shouldn't have been involved in anyway, would be even worse. So for your village, we'll need to look elsewhere.

Local Matters

And perhaps something truly local would be a good bet. Famously, the ringers of Ottery St Mary in Devon are captured every year by children dressed up as pixies. It's a festival that dates back a long time apparently, and it's based on a legend involving, monks, bells and pixies who didn't like bells. Of course, the ringers can't actually *ring* while they're being captured – so something similar wouldn't really do for you – but it's certainly good for tourism.

You could try finding an ancient legend in your own parish and then re-creating it – but that might be hard – or since tourism is involved, you could make one up. Lots of villages do, and as long as it includes plenty of colour and dressing up, everyone's happy. Alternatively you could find a local noteworthy event from the past, and then ring for its anniversary.

But local noteworthy events from the past don't normally carry forward very well, mainly because they weren't very special to start with. For example, Parson Woodforde records special ringing when the Squire's wife went into labour in 1781.

> **"... Weston Bells rung yesterday and again to-day, on Mrs. Custance being brought to bed in the New House."**

And since Mrs Custance had eight children, even in 1781 that wasn't particularly special. Besides, as the Squire's wife, she got the benefit of a good deal of special ringing – presumably because the Squire always tipped the ringers generously afterwards. Here's Parson Woodforde's diary for 30th May 1792.

> **"... Great Rejoicings at Weston House &c. Bells ringing, Guns-firing &c. on Account of Mrs. Custance coming down Stairs for the first time for the last 5 Months. I gave my People on the Occasion a bottle of Gin to drink this Evening in Kitchen. I am most heartily glad that Mrs. Custance is so much recovered. Dinner to Day boiled Chicken and Oyster Sauce, a Pigs Face, cold Loin of Veal rosted &c."**

Beer and Cider

One ancient tradition *you* might like to re-introduce – even if the villagers aren't so keen – is being paid in beer or cider whenever you *do* ring. That's certainly a genuine tradition, albeit not such a good one if you're all teetotallers. There used to be a good deal of nonsense written about ringers regularly taking copious quantities of drink into the ringing chamber and getting drunk there, but as a regular thing that just wasn't true. Most ringers were very poor men and they could rarely afford to get drunk *anywhere*, let alone in the ringing chamber. But what's certainly true is that paying ringers in drink suited everybody. The ringers liked it because they got a payment they couldn't possibly share with their wives and children; the payers liked it because they got a discount for bulk from the publican; and the publican liked it because he made a profit selling drink that the ringers couldn't afford to buy themselves. Here's Parson Woodforde again, this time writing in January 1764 – *Cream* is the name of his horse.

> **"After Breakfast I went upon Cream to my Curacy at Babcary, where I read Prayers and Preached, read prayers in the morning and preached in the afternoon. This is the first Sunday I ever officiated at Babcary Church; and I like it very well. ... I was rung into the Parish by Mr. John Bower's order, who gave the ringers a pail of Cyder on purpose to ring me into the Parish. They gave me another ring this afternoon after Service, and for which I gave them 2. 6."**

So Woodforde was clearly a good deal more generous than Mr Bower – although to be fair, he could afford to be. Certainly, if you don't do it already, you'll want to start a tradition of ringing all new vicars, curates, lay readers and such, into the parish – and that's whether or not anyone gives you a *pail of Cyder* for your trouble.

Ringers' Jugs

But even if no one *ever* pays you in drink, you can still get your very own *ringers' jug* – sometimes called a *gotch* – just in case. That would be splendidly traditional as well as adding considerably to the look of your ringing chamber; and when you've got it, you can invite the whole village in to see it. And if you've never seen one yourself, a ringers' jug was a large vessel – indeed, sometimes a *very* large vessel – which the ringers handed to people who wanted to pay them in liquor.

A local potter can make one for you, and you can put it on its own special shelf. You can even use it to supply all the congregation with a cup of punch after the annual carol service. A verse under the glaze on the jug's side will be especially good – and thoroughly traditional too – and to give you inspiration, here's the verse on the nineteenth century Beccles jug.

When I am fill'd with Liquor strong
Each Man drink once & then ding dong.
Drink not to much to Cloud your Knobbs
Least you forget to make the Bobbs.

That has the merits of rhythm, rhyming and humour, as does the verse on the Hadleigh ringers' jug – although with this one you have to slur the last two words of the first line. *Small* means weak beer.

If you love me due not lend me,
Euse me ofton and keep me clenly,
Fill me full, or not at all
If it be stroung and not with small.

Round the Village

The verse from the Hinderclay ringers' jug, on the other hand, falls well short of the ideal. It suffers both in the rhyming and the scanning, and the extra line on the end only makes it worse. The jug is eighteenth century and you can see it in the Moyse's Hall Museum in Bury St Edmunds.

From London I was Sent
As plainly doth appear
It was with this Intent
To be filled with strong Beer
Pray remember the Pitcher when empty

The Ixworth ringers' jug was said to have been carried round the village each year for the parishioners to pour their offerings into. From our perspective that doesn't sound very nice, but if you used your jug for charitable collections, you might find it very effective. The original 1716 jug is now in the British Museum and an 1816 replica – with updated spelling – is in the ringing chamber. Here's the original verse – *hanst* means honest, and *baly* means belly.

Here you may see what
I reqvst of Hanst Gentlemen
My Baly filled of the Bast
I com Bvt now And Then.

And less you're in doubt about the genre, do make sure that your verse has no pretensions to poetry as that would miss the point completely. Aim for something well-crafted, well-rhymed and funny. And if you can give it a contemporary slant, so much the better. This verse from the Swansea jug – now in the Swansea Museum – doesn't *quite* get there.

Come fill me full with liquor sweet
For that is good When friends do meet
When I am full then drink about
I ne'er will fail till all is out

Royal Visits

Of course, whether and *how*ever you're paid, a special occasion for all villages is a visit by the Queen – although for your own village that's probably *so* special it will never happen. All the same, if it ever *does* happen, everyone will want you to ring for it, and that's very traditional too. Or at least, it's *fairly* traditional. Back in 1529 in Henry VIII's time the ringers of St Laurence, Reading *didn't* ring when the Queen visited the town, and the churchwardens accounts record them being fined in consequence.

> **"It. to the queen's armersmt for that the bells were not rong at her comyng into the town, viij^{d}"**

"It" in churchwardens' accounts means "Item" so every entry starts that way; and if eight pence doesn't seem much, sometimes the fine was greater. For example, the accounts for Bray in Berkshire for 1601–02 show:

> **"It. payd for not ringing when the Queen dyned at Folly John, iii^{s}. iiii^{d}."**

That's three shillings and fourpence. And at St Mary, Lambeth in the accounts of 1517–18 the fine was two shillings and fourpence:

> **"Itm. paid to yem a amyner for defawtts off the ryngginge off the bells at the kynge's comynge, ij^{s}. iiij^{d}."**

No one gets fined nowadays, of course, but when the Queen went to Gloucester Cathedral in 2003 to hand out the Maundy Money, the ringers had to get special Royal permission to ring during Holy Week.

Other Royals

Of course, the visit of *any* member of the Royal Family, no matter how minor, would be an occasion for ringing now, and in times past that applied whether or not the Royal personage was legitimate. The philosophical and religious basis of *The Divine Right of Kings* is a fascinating subject in its own right, and we haven't got space for it here, but it did mean that men who were then called *Royal bastards* – with no overtones of shame whatever – were accorded considerable respect.

Indeed, sometimes they were accorded *too much* respect, and the king became worried that rebellion was in prospect. So when Charles II's illegitimate son, the Duke of Monmouth, came back unexpectedly from Holland in 1679, there was a real concern that another civil war was in the offing. And it was a justifiable concern too, as the Duke did indeed attempt to seize the throne from James II six years later. All the same, the Duke – being a professed protestant – was very popular with the masses, and on 28 November 1679 John Evelyn wrote:

> **"Came over the Duke of Monmouth from Holland unexpectedly to his Majesty; while the Duke of York was on his journey to Scotland, wither the King sent him to reside and govern. The bells and bonfires of the city at this arrival of the Duke of Monmouth publishing their joy, to the no small regret of some at Court. This Duke, whom for distinction they called the Protestant Duke (though the son of an abandoned woman), the people made their idol."**

Guy Fawkes Night

But in the absence of any Royal visitors – legitimate or otherwise – there's one genuinely ancient ringing tradition that all your villagers will most definitely welcome. It's not only ancient but it fits into the modern world superbly – largely because the original meaning and feeling behind it is long forgotten. It's ringing on Guy Fawkes Night.

Nowadays, Guy Fawkes Night – or Bonfire Night, or 5th November, or whatever you like to call it – is an occasion for fireworks, a good bonfire and a roast pork sandwich. It's a family orientated celebration at which adults and children of all ages are welcome; and in many villages it's now a truly communal get-together. If you ring for half an hour beforehand while people are making their way to the bonfire, you'll please everyone.

But to put it in context, for several centuries Guy Fawkes Night wasn't just a pleasant social event at all. The attempt to blow up the King and Parliament in 1605 was seen by the bulk of the population as a papist coup of the worst possible kind, and it was especially frightening as it so very nearly succeeded. What was more, the fear was well grounded as the terrible atrocities committed in the name of Catholicism by Queen Mary were still within living memory. So the foiling of the plot was a matter for great public rejoicing.

Bonfires

And as we've seen, public rejoicing required both ringing and bonfires, with the bonfires being every bit as important as the ringing. It isn't particularly clear why, but rejoicing bonfires have featured throughout Europe and beyond for well over a thousand years and probably for *several* thousand years. In many countries, bonfires are connected with religious festivals too, but their origin – like the origin of most Christian festivals – is probably pre-Christian. Besides, bonfires are simply fun.

But fun or not, how big *were* those seventeenth century London bonfires, and how were they organised so quickly?

London was a big city with a lot of people packed tightly together, and the wood had to be brought in from a long way outside by cart or boat. Yet when the people felt it was an occasion for bonfires – or the King ordered them to be lit – there they were. It's certainly curious.

On the Anniversary

But getting back to ringing, the anniversary of the foiling of the Gunpowder Plot continued to be a matter for genuine rejoicing for over 200 years. Essentially, the British saw themselves as a protestant nation, and the thought of being effectively ruled by the Pope and his overseas allies was completely abhorrent to them.

And as time went on, the opposition to Catholics became not only religious but secular as well. There was a fear that the loyalty of Catholics was primarily to the Pope and the Catholic Church rather than to the state, and until 1829, Catholics could neither vote nor take a seat in parliament. And when those impediments were finally removed, the bulk of the population massively disapproved.

So with feelings continuing to run high, ringing and bonfires went on being the appropriate form of annual rejoicing; and a hundred and fifty years after the Plot, here's Parson Woodforde on 5th November 1763:

> **"The Ringers desired me to give them something to drink, it being customary, therefore I sent them, it being a custom, 0. 1. 0."**

And in the nineteenth century there was *still* ringing on bonfire night; and as late as 1896 the Rev G. G. Tyack tells us that not only were people ringing then but they were firing the bells and calling it, *shooting old Guy.*

So that's my suggestion. I dare say most of your villagers aren't worried about a papist plot any more, and I don't suppose they're the least bit anti-catholic either; but since they'll still enjoy a bonfire, a pork sandwich and a few fireworks, why not give them some nice ringing to go with it.

Good luck!

As you've probably noticed, all the quotes in this book are exactly as they were originally written. I haven't changed any words – even when they're archaic – and I haven't changed any spellings apart from a very few simple misprints. The real words are important because they convey the writer's particular way of looking at things, and the real spellings are important because they help bring out the feeling of the particular period.

But original spellings can make some of the quotes difficult to understand, and the extract from the 1518 Lambeth churchwardens' accounts on page 412 is a case in point. It seems almost to be in a foreign language, and even by the standards of the time the spelling was eccentric.

Using "y"s instead of "i"s in words like "ringing" and "coming" was certainly common practice, and even William Caxton – whose printing did much to standardise spelling – spelt "finished" in at least five different ways by variously putting "y"s instead of either or both "i"s – and even instead of the "e".

But once the eighteenth century got going, spelling became pretty standard – and spelling pedantry became pretty standard too. Pompous old men and pompous old school teachers were as pedantic then as they are now, and in 1750 Lord Chesterfield – in one of his splendid letters to his son – strongly advised him to get his spelling better by providing a chilling example of failure.

> **"I know a man of quality, who never recovered the ridicule of having spelled wholesome without the 'w'."**

*But by then even greater standardisation was already in preparation, and in 1755 Samuel Johnson's great dictionary was completed. It was the very first comprehensive English dictionary, and it was completed more quickly and with far fewer assistants than the ground-breaking French dictionary which preceded it. Samuel Johnson became immediately famous as a result, and even Lord Chesterfield was bowled over; although this time he wrote to **The World**.*

> **"I hereby declare that I make a total surrender of all my rights and privileges in the English language, as a freeborn British Subject, to the said Mr. Johnson, during the term of his dictatorship."**

But amongst Dr Johnson's many and remarkable abilities, his most important were a clear understanding of the world and a sound common sense. So although he'd just compiled the authoritative work on word usage as at 1755, he never believed he was setting English usage in stone. He fully realised that word usage and word meanings would adapt and change as time went on, and he welcomed that.

Of course, he was a writer and poet himself – as well as having a deep and knowledgeable appreciation of other writers and poets – and he knew there were some thoughts and feelings that simply couldn't be satisfactorily expressed without stepping outside the accepted words of the time Subsequent dictionary compilers have understood that too, but a fair chunk of the population haven't.

So when new words have been added into new editions, dictionary compilers have invariably been accused of such horrendous crimes as, "**... surrendering to the permissive school ...**", *being* **bolshevik** *and,* "**... failing to defend the purity of the English language**." *All very sad, especially when* the purity of the English language *is already packed with literally thousands of richly expressive words that we've purloined from all over the World.*

But the one thing we apparently ***didn't*** *purloin from elsewhere was full circle change ringing. It certainly seems to have been an entirely British invention; but as Paul from Berkshire asks in the next chapter,* ***when*** *did we invent it?*

28. What Queen Elizabeth I Heard

We were in the pub after the practice, and some of the locals started asking about ringing, and we tried to explain; and we *sort of* did, and we sort of didn't because they seemed completely baffled – and not so much about *what* we did but about why we did it. And we decided perhaps they had a point, so we said, "It's traditional," and they said, "Well, how long's it *been* traditional then?" and we didn't know. So please help us out. When did it all start?

Paul
Berkshire

If you're not a ringing history buff – and most ringers aren't – there's no reason at all why you should know that the evidence of when change ringing started is distinctly thin. There are a few sets of changes scratched on old walls – and a few more jotted down on the backs of old manuscripts – but although some of these are thought to date from the first half of the seventeenth century, specific dating isn't possible. So it's not surprising that ringing historians have always been keen to quote the one piece of written evidence there is.

It's a paragraph from a book published in 1668 and it was written by a chap called Richard Duckworth. As far as we know, this was the first ever ringing book – snappily titled *Tintinnalogia* – and although it's mainly about practical ringing, Duckworth also included a brief historical piece.

> **"For within these Fifty or Sixty years last past, *Changes* were not known, or thought possible to be Rang: Then were invented the *Sixes*, being the very ground of a *Six score*: Then the *Twenty*, and *Twenty-four*, with several other *Changes*. But *Cambridge Forty-eight*, for many years, was the greatest peal that was Rang or invented."**

What He Meant

Not a great piece of writing, that, and when he referred to the *Twenty,* the *Twenty-four* and the *Cambridge Forty-eight*, he wasn't talking about methods as we know them, but about something akin to call change sequences. But it was change ringing nonetheless, so for the last three and half centuries historians have clung to his words as the best dating evidence they were ever likely to get. The general view was that Duckworth was probably sufficiently close to the start of change ringing, to have been more or less right.

But even so, most of them knew that that was a bit optimistic. Duckworth wasn't trying to write a history, and in the complete absence of written records, he only had hearsay to go on. He was only in his mid thirties in 1668, and he was an educated man of the upper classes, so the men he rang with were also young, educated and upper class, and he likely didn't know many ordinary – or indeed, old – ringers.

So why should his understanding of the past have been correct? Few young ringers today could accurately say what the bulk of ordinary ringers were ringing sixty years ago, and without going back to published material, they'd be hard put to find out. Lives were generally much shorter then too, so reliable hearsay – even if diligently sought – would have been hard to come by.

That said, in support of the assumption that change ringing was *at least* 50 years old when *Tintinnalogia* was published, a sermon helps. A preacher called Thomas Adams published one in 1614 and it contained the phrase, "**Some ring the Changes of opinion**."

Of course, he may not have been referring to change ringing, but he probably was, and if so, he must have supposed that at least some of his listeners and readers would have understood him. And that means that in 1614, change ringing of some kind was taking place; and until recently, that was essentially that. What's more, after so much searching by so many historians for so long, evidence earlier than 1614 seemed most unlikely ever to surface.

First Steps

But nonetheless, it did. From time to time I give ringing history talks which are intended to be bright, entertaining and fun – albeit scrupulously accurate – and while giving a talk about the history of women in ringing, Pam Donovan, a ringer from London, was by great good fortune, in the audience.

I quoted the piece written by the diary writer of the Duke of Stettin-Pomerania – which you can find on page 287 – concerning the Duke's visit to London in 1602. He tells us of hearing a considerable amount of church bell ringing – apparently being undertaken for fun and exercise – although he doesn't say whether it was random ringing, rounds or change ringing. Pam, though, had recently been listening to a recording of the musical work, *The Bells* – composed by the sixteenth and seventeenth century composer William

Byrd – and she immediately realised that the piece was expressing exactly what the Duke's diary writer had heard. So she kindly sent me a rendition of it on the harpsichord.

Historical Evidence

And at this point, I'm going to digress a bit, because historical evidence is quite a complicated business, and the evidence here is more complicated still. Put simply, there's a great deal of fiction in fact, and great deal of fact in fiction.

For example, just because someone wrote something as being true, that doesn't at all mean that it was. They may have been mistaken, they may have been lying or they may have been expressing themselves badly. They may even have been doing all those things and more. So whether or not they were *trying* to be accurate, they simply may not have been.

Historians know this, so if a statement comes to light, they ask themselves, "Is it corroborated?" "Is it consistent with other evidence?" "Is the source inherently reliable?" and so on. And they keep on re-evaluating *old* evidence as *new* evidence comes along. We looked at this in more detail in Chapter 13.

Fact in Fiction

But equally, even when someone's telling us a fictional story, they're normally also telling us a great deal of truth. That's because most people set their stories in settings they know a lot about, so much of the background detail is entirely correct.

For example, if in 500 years time, historians came across a 1990 *Mills and Boon* love story in which two people met on a train, they could reasonably assume that in 1990 there were trains. They might get a lot of other evidence about 1990 too because – wildly improbable as the plot might be –

the background world would be largely right. So evidence in art is in no way different to any other evidence. Indeed, in some ways it's *more* reliable because the artist isn't trying to put a favourable gloss on facts. But in other ways it's *less* reliable because an artist can always change facts under the principle of *artistic licence*. As with any evidence, you need to evaluate it carefully.

Evidence in Music

So when it comes to evidence in music, what are we looking for?

Well, the title is a good start. Huge numbers of composers have written bell inspired music. If we didn't know, we could reasonably conclude from Ketèlbey's *Bells across the Meadows*, that in Ketèlbey's day, bells were loud enough to be heard across meadows. We could also reasonably conclude from *The Bells of London Town* that when it was composed, there were bells in London.

The music itself tells us things too. The tune of *Bells across the Meadows* suggests that you could hear rounds on eight. The great body of *French* bell inspired music – Debussy's *La Cathédrale Engloutie*, for example – tells us that rings of bells in France are generally tuned to the pentatonic and rung randomly.

The point is that when a composer calls a work, *The Bells*, he's expressing in music something that has stirred within him as a result of hearing bells. He's not trying to *reproduce* what he's heard, but he *is* trying to base his work on what he's heard. So the test here is, could William Byrd have composed *The Bells* if the only ringing he'd ever heard was random ringing? Alternatively, could he only have composed it if he'd heard some form of early change ringing?

The Music

And obviously I'd now like to play it to you. But since this is a book, I can't. So if you want to listen to the piece you'll either have to buy a CD or download a version from the web – where there are plenty to choose from. Otherwise you'll just have to take my word for what it sounds like.

Essentially, *The Bells* is a pleasant little piece, written for a keyboard instrument called a virginal – which was an early and small kind of harpsichord. When you've heard it several times, it definitely grows on you, and amongst those who are into that sort of thing, it's one of Byrd's most famous works. It's certainly very popular with "early music" fans, and many different artists and instrumental groups have performed and recorded it. It's even been arranged for brass ensembles and jazz bands.

What it Shows

It clearly sets out to have a solid basis in real ringing because near the end, a set of bells are unmistakably rung down in peal. Indeed, it's such an extremely accurate effect of bells in the final stage of a lower that no one at all doubts that that's what it is. The rest of the piece appears to be based on several rings – of different numbers and in different keys – all being heard at the same time – something that would have been very common in London at that time. And most importantly, some of those rings of bells are ringing rounds, others are ringing reverse rounds and others are ringing a non-diatonic form of queens. There appear to be other changes too.

It's not method ringing of course, but it appears to be change ringing in which a particular change is rung for a number of whole pulls before a different change takes over. That's something akin to what in the seventeenth century they called *walked changes*, albeit it also includes *jump changes*. Some of the changes are on six, some are on five, some are on four, some are on three and a few may be on eight.

In Doubt

If you're still in doubt once you've listened to it, ask yourself whether the composer can possibly have written it and called it, *The Bells*, if he'd only ever heard rounds and random ringing. If you're a natural sceptic – as I am – you could only suggest *that* if you also supposed that Byrd called his work, *The Bells*, and then accurately represented, not what he actually heard, but what he would – unknown to him at the time – be able to hear twenty years in the future. And surely that's too improbable for anybody.

It would be like listening to *On Hearing the First Cuckoo in Spring* and supposing that Delius had never heard a cuckoo but had put the cuckoo sound in entirely by chance because he thought it was pretty.

And splendidly, *The Bells* first appeared in print in a collection of music published in 1612.

Going further

So how about that? After three and a half centuries, evidence had finally come to light that put back the earliest known date of change ringing by two years. And lest you're now heaving an *oh dear* sort of sigh, I stress that, for myself, I found it immensely satisfying. But could we go further? *The Bells* was certainly published in 1612 but that didn't mean it was composed then. Could we find evidence of when it *was* composed?

And at this point things got tricky. I was encouraged by the fact that even if it had been composed *much* earlier, it wouldn't have been *published* earlier because no keyboard music was published in England before 1612. So the 1612 compilation certainly included pieces that Byrd had written decades before. I hunted for evidence that Byrd – who was born sometime between 1539 and 1543 – had played the piece on some particular occasion or had composed it for some particular person; but if that evidence exists, I couldn't find it. Of course, something may yet come to light, but in its absence I researched Byrd's life.

Byrd's Life

Now, I don't suppose you want to hear about Byrd's life in detail – fascinating though it is – so suffice it to say that Byrd was a lifelong Catholic, living and working in a Protestant era. Even under Elizabeth I, religious tolerance only went so far, but Byrd survived and prospered because of his enormous talents and his Court connections.

From 1590 he devoted almost his entire energies to composing music for Catholic masses, and in 1593 he left London completely. On that basis, the chances of him composing *The Bells* later than 1593 seem extraordinary slim. *The Bells* would have been completely out of character as well as out of the style of all his later works. And that gives us a very high probability that we can date change ringing back to the 16th century. But since certainty is another matter, I tried the Byrd experts.

The Byrd Experts

I settled on three internationally renowned ones. The top man is Joseph Kerman, Professor Emeritus of Musicology at the University of California and the person who contributed the Byrd entry in the latest edition of *The New Grove Dictionary of Music and Musicians*. And in case you're not into music, I should explain that *Grove* is the definitive musical reference work and consists of 29 beautifully produced, but vastly expensive, volumes – essentially, a kind of musical *Encyclopaedia Britannica.*

So since I am myself the *Grove* contributor on *Change Ringing*, I wrote to Professor Kerman as one *Grove* contributor to another. Unfortunately, despite several reminders I got absolutely no reply, either because he was already too elderly or because – quite rightly – he saw the *Change Ringing* contributor as being by several steps his musical inferior.

Neighbour and Moroney

But the other two experts, Oliver Neighbour – who has written the definitive scholarly book on Byrd's keyboard music – and Davitt Moroney – who has recorded the whole of Byrd's keyboard works – are decidedly of the view that *The Bells* was written in the sixteenth century. Moroney is in no doubt that it was written before 1600, while Neighbour considers it was most likely written in the 1590s but that Byrd was most probably imitating something with which he and his audience were very familiar from long before 1600. Their view is based on the style of the piece, but to avoid boring non-musical readers, I won't go into the technical details.

Thomas Robinson

All of which was very satisfactory but just a little bit vague to be considered hard evidence. Fortunately, though, further musical evidence came along. Ruth Darton – another ringer from London – is not only a ringer but also a music archivist. She kindly researched other music of the period and brought to my attention *Twenty Waies upon the Bels* by the lutenist, Thomas Robinson.

This was published in 1603, and my immediate thought

was that Robinson was basing his composition on *The Twenty* call change sequence referred to by Richard Duckworth in *Tintinnalogia*. It's just possible that he was, but on reflection, I don't think so. Thomas Robinson was not only a lute player and composer, he was also a lute and music teacher to the aristocracy. His 1603 publication was called *Schoole of Musicke* and his *Twenty Waies upon the Bels* was one of the first two pieces. But at that time, the word, *waies*, had a technical meaning, and since I'm sure you'd like to know, it was the title given to:

> **"a series of short contrapuntal compositions in two or three parts – often in canon – on a cantus firmus."**

Or put more simply, *Twenty Waies* was a practice piece made up of variations on Byrd's *The Bells*. And indeed, you only have to listen to it to realise that. So in 1603, *The Bells* was already sufficiently well known that Robinson was composing variations on it. That doesn't take us back to 1590 but it *does* take us back well before 1612.

From Here

So that, I think, does it. It shows pretty conclusively that Queen Elizabeth I – who died in 1603 and as regards ringing was said by the Duke of Stettin-Pomerania's diary writer to have been,

> **"... very much pleased by this exercise considering it as a sign of the health of the people,"**

was actually listening to an early form of change ringing. More, it opens up an avenue for further research for anyone who cares to follow. And perhaps one of the most interesting things about Byrd's composition is that, as it's a piece of music which can be, and is, performed, it gives us a direct impression of what sixteenth century ringing actually *sounded* like in a way that written descriptions never can. So if *you're* interested, and you come across anything relating to William Byrd that seems to help – or any other piece of sixteenth century music that seems to be based on bell ringing – please drop me an email and we can have a chat about it.

Who knows? Maybe even Queen *Mary* was listening to change ringing.

And that, I'm afraid is the end of the book. I hope you enjoyed reading it as much as I enjoyed writing it, and I hope you're now fired with enthusiasm for ringing history too. And if there's a ringing history story we haven't talked about but which you wish we had, don't despair. Perhaps it will be in The **Second** Ringing in History Companion.

Sources and Thanks

In case you'd like to know where you can find some of the background papers to this book – and who was kind enough to help – here goes:

The Wartime Government papers can be found in the National Archives and are Crown copyright. The quotes appear by virtue of the Open Government Licence v1.0. The quotes from the House of Commons and the House of Lords can be found in "Hansard."

The snippets from the newspapers are all referenced in the text, and the names of the newspapers can be found in the index. If you want to read a large but extremely readable compendium of ringing-related newspaper extracts from the 1700s, John Eisel's really excellent book, "Order and Disorder in the Eighteenth Century" is exactly what you're looking for

Equally, I'm extremely grateful to John Eisel – first rate ringing historian that he is – for his assistance on a number of points of detail.

I'm also extremely grateful to *The Ladies Guild* – an organisation for which I have the greatest respect – for kindly giving me access to their entire archive. If you're looking for more information on the Guild, Janet Stevenson's "A History of The Ladies Guild of Change Ringers" is what you want.

Derek Jackson of the *Winchester and Portsmouth* Guild kindly allowed me to quote from his detailed researches on George Williams and the White family of Basingstoke.

Diane Stillwell kindly gave me permission to reproduce Peter Devenish's poem, "The Tower Grabber."

Sue Reilly kindly gave me permission to quote extracts from Pauline Fairall's – her mother's – record of ringing and other activities in Godstone.

The BBC kindly gave me permission to reproduce their internal memo.

DVDs of the early copies of *The Ringing World*, *Bell News*, *The Bellringer* and *Campanology* can be obtained from the Librarian of *The Central Council of Church Bell Ringers*. The Central Council library also has an extensive collection of books and papers, as well as a transcription of The Laughton Manuscript.

The kindness and hard work of all those ringers who were prepared to tell their personal recollections of the Second World War for the benefit of posterity, is inexpressible. I'm overwhelmingly grateful, and I've attributed every one of those recollections individually in the text.

I'm also extremely grateful to Pam Donovan and Ruth Darton for their very considerable assistance as regards sixteenth and seventeenth century music.

And I'm grateful to Mary Stanwell, too, for kindly bringing *The Girl's Own Paper* article on bell ringing to my attention.

Equally, Chris Ridley – formerly the Librarian of *The Ancient Society of College Youths* – kindly supplied extracts from the minutes of their December 1919 meeting.

Dan Willis, Monica Hardy, Anita Morgan and the Moyse's Hall Museum kindly supplied information on their ringers' jugs.

And lastly, many thanks to all those ringers who sent me letters, or who were just happy to chat, about ringing history.

Index

The Bellringer's Bedside Companion

by Steve Coleman

This beautifully bound and printed, 440 page hardback book, contains 52 chapters of advice, information and help all written in Steve's easy-to-read, enjoyable and exceptionally clear style.

It covers

* Ropesight	* Method Learning	* Up & Down in Peal
* Ringing Safety	* Call Changes	* Leading Up & Down
* Ringing Teas	* Ringing half-muffled	* Ringing Etiquette
* Slipping Wheel	* Striking Competitions	* Tower Captaincy
* Firing	* Arranging Outings	* Ringing Left-handed
* Tower Visiting	* Ringing Panic	* Full Circle Tunes
* Standing Behind	* and much else besides.	

Outstandingly informative and thoroughly entertaining as well. Now in its sixth edition and believed to be the biggest selling ringing hardback of all time.

The Method Ringer's Companion

by Steve Coleman

This beautifully bound and printed, 440 page hardback book is the ordinary ringer's easy-to-read guide on how to ring all the widely rung methods on all numbers from Bob Doubles upwards.

It covers

* Plain Bob	* Grandsire	* Stedman
* The Other Doubles	* The Plain Minor	* Doubles Variations
* Kent and Oxford	* The Classic Triples	* The Basic Major
* Surprise Minor	* Surprise Major	* Listening
* Striking	* Method Naming	* The Fun Methods
* On the Wild Side	* and much else besides.	

Packed with clear and simple explanations, learning tips, ringing hints, diagrams, stepping stone methods, and fascinating historical background.